Habermas, Religion and Public Life: Religious and Secular Worldviews in European and Iranian Thought

Masoumeh Bahram

London Academy of
Iranian Studies, 2012

- **Habermas, Religion and Public Life: Religious and Secular Worldviews in European and Iranian Thought**
- Masoumeh Bahram
- Page and Cover Design: Mohamad A. alavi
- ISBN: 978-0-9552298-1-7
- London Academy of Iranian Studies

This book is dedicated to the Great Prophet Muhammad and my dear husband, Dr Hadi Ehteshami

Acknowledgements

My thanks must go to Dr Seyed G Safavi for his patience during the preparation of this manuscript for publication. I have furthermore benefited from interviews with a number of Iranian and European scholars, in particular Professor Ahad Faramarz Qaramaleki and Professor Ruhollah Alemi.

My greatest debt, however, is to my husband Dr Hadi Ehteshami, my daughter Dr Zahra, and my son Ali, for their love and support, upon which I have been able to rely in difficult times.

Abstract

Although many scholars view Habermas as the most important philosopher and social theorist since Weber, his account of religion has been relatively neglected. This may partly be a reflection of the fact that he appears to offer quite distinct views of religion, although it may also reflect the strong secularist assumptions of his early work. In this book, Habermas's early and later views of religion are outlined, and the change in his understanding of religion from one of the sources of modernity's inner problems to a principal source of the passions and motivations underpinning cultural life today is mapped. I argue that the relative neglect of Habermas's work on religion is unfortunate, as it offers a creative and important attempt to move beyond the secular assumptions that have characterised much modern study of religion, providing it with a central role in the mediation of the costs and benefits of modernity.

In exploring the nature of and changes in Habermas's thought on religion, which, I suggest, are still developing, I draw upon the writings of the Iranian sociologist and political activist Ali Shariati to help illuminate the value and the limitations of Habermas's work. The introduction of an Iranian intellectual perspective on the encounter between tradition and modernity is of particular value because it broadens debates about religion and modernity beyond a Eurocentric focus on secularisation as a phenomenon of Christian history, and because it necessarily locates these debates within a global context – one wherein the resurgence of Islam is of immense importance.

Alongside this global context, however, I also emphasise throughout this book that, in order to understand Habermas's ideas on religion, it is necessary to understand broader fundamental elements of his thought. Consequently, after an introduction that clarifies the nature and scope of Habermas's work and how I plan to interrogate it, I examine several key themes that cut across his work as a whole, before examining the relationship between religiosity and rationality in the key intellectual influences that shaped his ideas, and then outline how he moved beyond these with his notion of communicative action. In subsequently mapping in more detail his evolving views of religion, however, I note a significant movement away from an inherently secularist position to one where religion is central to his engagement with notions of democracy, citizenship and intra- and inter-cultural dialogue. While, as I note at several points, Habermas has himself sought to participate in such dialogue with Iranian scholars, the final substantive chapter of this book pushes this inter-cultural dialogue further: after outlining influential trends within Iranian views on the encounter of traditions and modernity, I examine religion and public life in Shariati's work, utilising it to cast fresh light on the nature and value of Habermas's thought. In the concluding chapter, I emphasise that it is through Habermas's focus on the importance of religion within what he calls the 'lifeworld' that he seeks to draw an image of a better society with peace, unity and human happiness as its bases.

Masoumeh Bahram,
University of Leeds,
30th January 2012

Table of Contents

List of Tables

Chapter 1: Introduction

Many modern philosophers, social scientists and cultural analysts have taken it for granted that religion has lost much of its significance in the public arena, particularly in terms of running and managing communities. Specifically, it has been assumed that religion has retreated as a consequence of the processes of rationalisation. In the dialectical analysis of history, for example, religion was construed as an obsolete phenomenon which had come to its end as a result of the growth of rationality. Today, however, this marginalisation of religion is no longer viable. Religion has regained an important role in the political sphere of some countries, and religious motivations are increasingly evident in a range of social and cultural contexts. As a consequence, scholars are now forced to return to long-established questions about why religion has remained such an important aspect of human life and culture despite all the cultural changes that have occurred over time, and why humanity in the modern and post-modern ages has not been able to release itself from this preoccupation. Contemporary scholars and philosophers from various cultural backgrounds and intellectual disciplines try to define the nature of religious beliefs and the ways in which they are configured, and attempt to answer questions about why these beliefs play such significant roles in shaping and determining the course of our social life.

The restoration of religion to the public sphere has had a more lively and luminous manifestation in non-western countries than in western ones, particularly in Islamic countries such as the Islamic Republic of Iran. Indeed, religion and its rites manifest themselves forcefully and energetically in all public and private sectors, as well as in social and governmental spheres. In this context and beyond, studies and research on religion can no longer be perceived as focusing on an ancient and obsolete phenomenon, or on a declining dogma, but need to engage with a lively, objective and effective phenomenon, that is, if anything, becoming progressively more influential in human communities.

Alongside this restoration of religion to the public sphere, however, the final decades of the twentieth century also saw the development of a new form of globalisation that left its indelible mark on all aspects of social, occupational, familial and cultural lives. Geographical boundaries faded and the free flow of information heightened, bringing to light the conflict of economic interests that were, in the past, always defined in terms of religion and values. Along with the project of the enlightenment, with its Cartesian outlook, this new development also assumed an expansionist role that had ambiguous implications for religion: while this process of globalisation served to establish religion as a 'global category' (Robertson, 1992: 42-43), it also offered a direct challenge to key assumptions about economics, solidarity and human freedom in major religious traditions. In this regard, religion presents a challenge to many elements of the economic and technological dimensions of globalisation as an all-encompassing system. A Persian proverb says, 'Ten commoners can sleep on a rug, but no two kings can abide in a realm', implying that it is inevitable that the relation between these two issues will be one of either subjugation or opposition.

What seems certain is that religious practices have brought bifurcations and factions that have fanned the flames of conflict, and debates about social policies.

Jurgen Habermas – a philosopher and sociologist – is one of the major participants in the international debate over the proper positioning of these conflicting systems. He has examined the issue in all its objective and subjective dimensions, and not only considers the role of religion in present Western communities, but also challenges it philosophically and culturally. The translation and publication of his various works (in particular those on communicative action among Western societies) have been well received by both religious and secular intelligentsia in Iran. His presence in Iran for one week during 2002, during which he delivered speeches on secularism and the role of religion in the public sphere, had a long-lasting influence on discussion in the press as it resulted in disputes between Habermas's supporters and his opponents. His positions are also widely respected in scientific and academic circles.

The Habermas effect is felt in every major discipline of the human and social sciences. Habermas towers over the contemporary fields of communication, ethics, hermeneutics, law, linguistics, philosophy, political theory, sociology, and critical social theory (Matustik, 2001: 237).

It is important to bear in mind that Iranian Muslim reformists such as Ali Shariati have offered accounts of religion and modernity, in recent decades, in an attempt to reform Iran. In this book, my main aim is to critically examine Habermas's account of the role of religion in public sphere and critically assess his views in the light of an alternative account provided by Shariati. Hence, the questions raised and addressed by this book are:

1. Has Habermas's view on the role of religion in public life evolved or remained the same over time?

2. How does Shariati's thought help to assess the value and limitations of Habermas's work?

The hypotheses of this book are:

1. Habermas has fundamentally changed his viewpoint on the role of religion in public life, and it is still in the process of development.

2. By utilising Islamic doctrine, Shariati illuminates the value and the limitations of Habermas's work.

I shall shortly explain and engage with these questions and hypotheses in more detail, but first it is necessary to introduce the key themes that are required for understanding Habermas's writings. The key themes of this book are highlighted in greater detail in the following chapter, but, by way of introduction, they can be summarised as follows.

The first key theme is the *public sphere*. According to Habermas, the public sphere serves as a network where information and different perspectives can be exchanged. It is an arena in which political life is discussed openly by a reasoning public, and in which people from churches, universities, professional groups and voluntary associations gather together to 'confer in an unrestricted fashion – that is, with the guarantee of freedom of assembly and association and the freedom of express and publish their opinions – about matters of general interest' (Held, 1990: 260). Habermas holds that the public sphere loses its autonomy and distinctive character through the intervention of the state into private affairs, and the penetration of society into the state. In order for truth and democracy to be attained, a country's citizens must take a critical approach to the policy directions of their state. Any attempt to curtail such critical meditation by the state will ruin the fundamental structures of democratic institutions.

The second key theme is *globalisation*. In his vision of the globalisation process, Habermas strives to bring any principle into consideration universally, and searches for supranational solutions to problems. He refuses to accept the state as an axis in his political theory, because he believes that governments have increasingly lost their capacity for solving problems. He believes that economic growth provides an opportunity for nations to flourish, whereas realisation of a democracy seems difficult in the process of globalisation. According to Habermas, religious traditions and communities have recently been granted with a new and unexpected political importance.

The third key theme is *modernity*. Modernism seems to imply the cultural revolt against conventions and beliefs. According to Habermas, this erosion of traditions and creeds has resulted from an incursion of instrumental rationality into the cultural sphere. Habermas expresses this incursion in the *Theory of Communicative Action* in terms of the 'colonisation of the lifeworld' by the imperatives of the system. He (1987: 356) contends that:

According to our hypothesis, a "colonialization of the lifeworld" can come about only when traditional forms of life are so far dismantled that the structural components of the lifeworld (culture, society, and personality) have been differentiated to great extent.

Thus, although modernity has provoked much progress in cultural, political and economic areas as a result of technological developments, it has also led human beings into a vacuum in meaning and identity by removing moral elements from their lives. Habermas considers modernity to be an 'unfinished project' that has been deviated from its path by purposive or goal-directed rationality. His solution to this is his critical theory, which utilises a model of psychoanalysis (which will be described in chapter 3).

The fourth key theme is *democracy*. Habermas proposes a typical deliberative democracy, where citizens are emphatically advised to participate in a free and unlimited process of dialogue that is void of any forces, in order to reach an intersubjectivity of mutual understanding and consensus. Habermas terms such discussion as 'the communicative action', with language as its centre. In fact, he raises the idea of deliberative democracy vis-à-vis the theory of liberal democracy. Minority interests are weighed down in the process of liberal democracy and the values of the majority command those of minorities. However, deliberative democracy focuses on the provision of community interests, religious or non-religious, for any decision-making level.

The fifth key theme is *positivism*. Positivism contends that all human cognitions are based on experience and observation. This knowledge is neutral with respect to ethical values. Thus, religious and metaphysical concepts are deemed as false because they are unverifiable. According to Habermas, positivism is converted into an instrument that allows its technicians to impose their power upon others and hold the opinion that they are the only persons who possess valid social knowledge.

The sixth key theme is *hermeneutics*. Hermeneutics seeks to reveal original and latent meaning in texts, whether they derive from religious or secular traditions. Up until the nineteenth century, hermeneutics had been associated with the interpretation of the Bible. Habermas sides with Gadamer, and against Schleiermacher and Dilthey, in holding that the task of interpretation does not require approaching the experience of the original author. Rather, he holds that the meaning of a text always exceeds that of the original author, because meanings frequently emerge and change in the course of tradition.

In this book, I shall seek to analyse and criticise Habermas's conception of religion in the public sphere in relation to these key themes, but I shall also seek to reassess it utilising Shariati's social thought. There are two main reasons for focusing on Shariati's work in this context. First, Shariati, as a hero of the Iranian reformists and a religious intellectual who is widely respected in the contemporary Islamic world, has an intellectual stature that makes him an appropriate partner in dialogue for Habermas. Indeed, he is not merely a respected social thinker, but also one who has laid the intellectual foundations for Iranian religious reform. Iranian reformist thinkers have developed their ideas by re-building Shariati's thought in the social arena over the latter half of the 20th century and the start of the 21st. Second, despite the fact that Shariati and Habermas share certain ideas and assumptions, they also differ significantly about some important issues, and looking at these similarities and differences helps to clarify the value as well as the limitations of Habermas's thought. It is worth noting that not only is the subject of this book novel and innovative, but its achievements could also be effective and useful in enriching and expanding the existing literature.

1.1. Limitations and Advantages of the Research

A researcher who studies Habermas's work for the first time can be daunted by his obscure language, intricate abstract knowledge, and his other difficult philosophical, social, political and technical discourses. As Adams (2006: 28) explains, Habermas uses 'a highly suggestive language which contains a number of vaguenesses and ambiguities'. Therefore, it is necessary for us to approach his work with caution. Another problem is that his published work includes hundreds of articles, interviews, essays, notes and books, which reflect a network of interrelated ideas that have gradually evolved to form his current views. It is, thus, rather difficult to extract individual issues from the bulk of his writings and interviews without paying attention to the context in which they have been discussed. Furthermore, as most of Habermas's works are written and published in German, this researcher has had no option but to rely on the English translations of his works. On the other hand, this researcher knows the Persian language, culture, and history that form the backdrop to Shariati's ideas, which can be counted as an advantage in this research.

While Habermas can be quite difficult to understand, such a study can be quite rewarding and enjoyable. In the introduction of *Legitimation Crisis* (Habermas, 1976: vii), McCarthy states that:

To have brought Kant, Fichte, and Hegel into contact with Wittgenstein, Popper, and Peirce, to have fashioned a language in which Marx, Dilthey, and Freud as well as Dewey, Mead, and Parsons can all have their say, is grounds enough for a claim to intellectual distinction.

In fact, Habermas's works are attractive because his wide range of knowledge allows any researcher to become familiar with various authors of social sciences and humanities from disciplines including philosophy, sociology, theology, politics, ethics, psychology and linguistics. In other words,

Habermas has used all his brilliance and scholarship to take his readers beyond his own views and into carefully established new points of reference within classical texts that he has brought to life in so many strikingly new perspectives (Pusey, 1987: 121).

While Habermas's work includes the academic, abstract and ambiguous discussions covering various fields of knowledge, he seeks to establish a rational connection between these branches of sciences:

Habermas has always affirmed the need for serious intellectual engagement, not only with the philosophical tradition of Kant, Hegel, and Marx, and its development into later social and political theory, but also with the principal theoretical movements in the human and social sciences (Outhwaite, 1996: 4).

Likewise, Habermas is always engaged in revising and improving his thought in order to solve the problems of modern society and to help transform it for the better. He has, for example, as I shall consider later in this book, changed some of his own ideas as a result of recent international incidents. In the introduction of *Religion and Rationality: Essay on Reason,*

God, and Modernity (Habermas, 2002b: 24), Mendieta says that:

After almost half a century of public intellectual and scientific work, Habermas' contribution is both impressive and humbling. Habermas has remained vital, creative, engaged, and most importantly attuned to the *zeitgeist*, without sacrificing intellectual honesty and rigor. There is no field that he has left untouched, and this includes religion, even if in this his reception has been mixed and skewed.

Habermas's works contain important topics, such as how religious and non-religious people can interact with each other, the nature of modernity, the public sphere and the revival of religion.

His work on the exchange of views and the intersubjectivity of mutual understanding between secular and religious sects, as well as on dialogues between religions and civilizations in the modern world, aims to help to establish peace and tolerance, and to prevent violence and war. Indeed, Habermas holds that religious people must be able to translate their ideas in such a way that it becomes intelligible to secularists.

In his effort to save modernity from the captivity of instrumental rationality, Habermas came to hold that the project of modernity had deviated from its course through the intermediation of new science and reason. The result of this has been the development of 'rationalisation as reification' through the media of money and power. His solution to this is *The Theory of Communicative Action.*

According to Habermas's analysis, the public sphere is the most appropriate place to recognise social problems and gain access to the truth of everything, even religion. People in the public sphere can involve themselves in free and unbounded dialogue in order to reach an intersubjective mutual understanding and consensus. While Heelas, Lash and Morris (1996: 2) state that 'with the development of modern societies, tradition gradually declines in significance and eventually ceases to play a meaningful role in the lives of most individuals', Habermas holds that religion is reasserting itself in the public sphere.

This book has been organised into six chapters. Chapter 1 provides background information on the topic, research questions and hypotheses. This chapter also draws out the limitations and advantages in Habermas's social, political and philosophical arguments.

Chapter 2 provides a literature review surrounding the concepts of the public sphere, modernity, democracy, positivism and hermeneutics. It also focuses on globalisation as Habermas has been among the most influential advocates for an unashamed universalism in the political and moral arenas.

Chapter 3 gives an account of different theories on religion, and provides historical background on Christianity and Islam and the critical theory of the Frankfurt School. Habermas's philosophical defence of universal pragmatics and the ideal speech situation has remained as it was prior to the publication of the theory of communicative action. Accordingly, this chapter will concentrate on instrumental rationality and the theory of communicative action, which is the process whereby people reach mutual understanding with one another. This chapter then examines what Islam means by *Shura* (consultation), and look at Habermas's theoretical distinction between society conceived as a lifeworld, and society conceived as a system. This main role of this chapter is to supply the basis for the second half of this book, since these conceptual cores structure all of the other aspects of Habermas's work.

Chapter 4 explains the role of religion in Habermas's early work, and contrasts it with how he has come to understand it as a result of incidents. In his earlier work, Habermas held that religion was one of the sources of modernity's inner problems. However, in his more recent work, religion is viewed as a principal source of the good life.

Chapter 5 then presents the critical intention, as well as the sociological and philosophical foundations of the Iranian intellectuals' work. This chapter is chiefly concerned with the debates in which Shariati has engaged, and provides a detailed account of Shariati's thought in order to compare his arguments to those of Habermas. It will also explore what I believe to be the central strengths and deficiencies of Habermas's ideas. I intend to present Shariati's ideas in the form of a dialogue and challenge to those of Habermas. Despite the fact that Habermas's works are abstract, obscure, difficult, and, as I shall argue, too optimistic about the inherent potentialities of modernity as an unfinished project, his great theoretical achievements cannot be ignored. Consequently, although I will challenge some of Habermas's ideas, I will also argue in support of a number of his positions, such as his focus on democracy, and his assault on some of the most challenging central issues facing people in modern society. This will allow me to offer a new, critical understanding of Habermas's contribution to debates about the nature and role of religion in the public sphere, and thereby contribute to the further development of studies of Habermas, given that his work on religion has been relatively neglected by other scholars.

Finally, Chapter 6 will summarise all the key conclusions to be drawn from my book.

Chapter 2: Theoretical Definitions of the Key Themes in Habermas's Thought

As Habermas's engagement with religion is inextricably intertwined with the broader philosophical, social and cultural dimensions of his work, it is important to introduce Habermas's key themes (such as the public sphere, globalisation, modernity, democracy, positivism, and hermeneutics) in order to assess his work on religion. These main themes are utilised throughout the whole book.

2.1. The Public Sphere

The place of the public debate was the first issue that Habermas tackled after his PhD thesis. He achieved fame through the publication of his work *The Structural Transformation of the Public Sphere* (1962). As Matustik (2001: 35) suggests, 'This book soon becomes the core working text of the increasingly radicalized progressive students'.

Using Hegelian and French conceptions of civil community, Habermas presents his conception of the public sphere as follows:

The public sphere cannot be conceived as an institution and certainly not as an organization. It can best be described as a network for communicating information and points of view (1996: 360).

Bernstein (1995: 38) claims that what Habermas means by a public sphere is an arena of our social life, in which we are able to develop distinctively public opinions. When citizens consult with one another, or freely and unconditionally exchange their views about issues of common concern and public benefits (that is, under conditions of ensured freedom of assembly and the freedom to express and publish their opinions), they act as a public body. As McCarthy (1994: 50) notes, Habermas states that the nervous system of the political public sphere is established by churches, universities, professional groups and voluntary associations in civil community, that is, 'largely with the unofficial networks of private people communicating about public matters'.

According to Habermas, modernism and development not only failed to bring rationality and emancipation at the start of the 20th century, but also in fact brought about profound irrationality. Corporations directed public participation in order to stabilize and realise the interests of the dominant class through the mass media, particularly through television. Indeed, Habermas 'calls a manipulated public sphere in which states and corporations use publicity in the modern sense to secure for themselves a kind of plebiscitary acclamation' (Outhwaite, 1994: 10). Therefore:

The collapse [of the public sphere] occurs because of the intervention of the state into private affairs and the penetration of society into the state. Since the rise of the public sphere depended on a clear separation between the private realm and public power, their mutual interpenetration inevitably destroys it ... Party politics and the manipulation-of the mass media lead to what Habermas calls a 'refeudalization' of the public sphere, where representation and appearances outweigh rational debate (Holub, 1991: 6).

Accordingly, the public sphere serves overwhelmingly hidden policies and plans of interested groups. Habermas holds that the objective of freedom of speech still leaves much to be desired within the political sphere of capitalist communities, and the functional domain of the public sphere has been gradually restricted due to intensified state commitments to stabilise the economy.

In his article 'New Social Movements' (1981b: 33-37), Habermas points to contradictions in advanced Western communities. He believes that these new disagreements have arisen in the areas of cultural reproduction, social integration, and socialisation. Thus, these contradictions can never be settled by using instruments such as money and political power, because no major insufficiencies will again appear in areas of material reproduction, and thus they represent only 'a reification of the communicative sphere of action'. Habermas (1981b: 33) adds that:

The question is how to defend or reinstate endangered life styles, or how to put reformed life styles into practice. In short, the new conflicts are not sparked by problems of distribution, but concern the grammar of forms of life. This new type of conflict is an expression of the "silent revolution" in values and attitudes.

According to Habermas, groups that represent 'new social movements' (such as environmentalists, peace supporters, feminists, and religious movements) provide resistance and enter into conflict with the status quo.

Habermas considers the public sphere to be the place where a rational ethic develops, and it is only within the public sphere that rational objectives and requirements can be determined. Moreover, the public sphere also allows us to rationalise state and politics. In fact, 'people needed to know what the state was doing or failing to do and to influence it as far as they could' (Outhwaite, 1994: 8).

This public body of citizens spontaneously formulates criticisms that can act against a governing body. The public sphere, as a structure of mediated communication, mediates between a state and a civil community, and is a place in which any critical discussion can occur, and in which the different classes of society can freely debate the actions that a state undertakes. Indeed, the public sphere 'must be exposed through critical examination in order to emancipate society from repression' (Edgar, 2006: 108). It is under these conditions that a structure of power, such as a state, has to check and modify its actions in the light of the critical examinations by its citizens.

Habermas (2001: 80) holds that, under such conditions, the authority of states to resolve their social problems fails, and they also 'increasingly lose both their capacities for action and the stability of their collective identities'. Furthermore, the importance of public opinion begins to rise and this facilitates dialogues between different religions.

In elaborating upon the formation of public opinion, Habermas assigns two functions to the public sphere in a differentiated society:

First, it constitutes a series of "sensors" for the perception, identification, and treatment of problems affecting the whole society. Second, the public sphere creates the normative context within which law making occurs and thereby affects the operation of the subsystems without displacing them. The legal system must be legitimized, and this only occurs if the participants in society recognize themselves as the "authors" of the law (Sitton, 2003: 95).

Under an analytical assessment of Habermas's ideas regarding the two functions of the public sphere and its present status in Europe, it is clear that, given the influence of secularism (which still pervades in Europe), religion has a limited or negligible role in providing sensors or normative context. Indeed, secularism has kept religion silent by requisitioning the properties and territories held by the church, and inhibiting it from interfering in political affairs. Secularism endeavours to hold the church under control: in other words, the church (and the university) has developed into a headquarters employed by the state for legitimizing its organisations. If religion is now returning to the public sphere, it may be claimed that this restoration depends less on the mediation exercised by the church and Europe than on the revival of religion at the public and plebeian levels (something that is already growing and progressing in Asia, Africa and Latin America).

Moreover, Habermas holds that his theory of the public sphere invites us to reflect on the democratic process. The church itself constitutes one of the main elements of the public sphere, and the freedom of the church and religion play a positively progressive role for democracy.

Here, secularism is faced with a paradox. If a secular state has the capability to administer democracy, how it can control or monitor religion or the church, and drive it into isolation? Another way of posing this challenge is to ask: how can democracy be integrated with the notion of usurping the church's estates and hindering it from interfering in political affairs? In *The Postnational Constellation,* Habermas (2001: 65) alludes to the fact that:

The democratic constitutional state, by its own definition, is a political order created by the people themselves and legitimated by their opinion and will-formation, which allows the addresses of law to regard themselves at the same time as the authors of the law. But because capitalism follows a logic of its own, it is unable to conform to these demanding premises by itself: politics must see to it that the social conditions for public and private autonomy are met. Otherwise an essential condition for the legitimacy of democracy is endangered.

Habermas's thought on the role of religion in public sphere can be investigated with reference to two distinct stages.

Habermas's early thought was influenced by the Frankfurt school, which led him to take an instrumental approach to religion. He interpreted religion to be a man-made instrument that helps to resolve the dilemmas of knowledge and the problems of living in pre-modern stages of social and cultural evolution. As Asad (1993: 27) sums this view up, 'in evolutionary thought, religion was considered to be an early human condition from which modern law, science, and politics emerged and became detached'. Therefore, religion must be displaced by philosophy and communicative action in the process of modernisation. In addition, both the public and private spheres – which are construed to be the foundation of Habermas's political sociology – can be separated from each other. Given this, Mellor (2004: 151) believes that:

For Habermas the creation of the public sphere is dependent upon a post-Enlightenment commitment to a secular polity. The public sphere is an arena for 'rational-critical discourse'. The private sphere is, in contrast, associated with individual interests, which is where he locates religion.

Nevertheless, in virtue of the practical failure of separating the public and private spheres and religion's restoration to public life, Habermas has re-structured his position in an evolutionary and historical direction. He (2006a: 3-4) asserts that the state cannot anticipate people's identities by dividing them into private and public categories when they are involved in a general discourse to formulate public opinion. Consequently, he emphasises the key role played by religion in the public sphere. He declares that 'the religious traditions are the principal sources of the passions, motivations and visions of the good life that allow modern persons to flourish' (Adams, 2006: 11). Furthermore, in his lecture on religiousness (at Tehran University on 14th May 2002), Habermas (2002c: 18) states that religion has not disappeared in the arena of the public sphere in the West, and that it has maintained its importance in citizens' worldviews. Religion has an enormous effect on political public opinion, both through the doctrines of churches and through the opinions expressed by religious communities and associations. Habermas leaves no doubt that religion is returning to the public sphere and affects both social and political attitudes.

Habermas claims that irrespective of how one evaluates the facts, there is now a new cultural wave in the United States that has provided a background for an academic discussion on the role of religion in the political public sphere. He predicts that the development of religious beliefs has been reflected in the arena of internal politics. These religious beliefs are also marking their influence in the international field in different ways. 'World religions that to this very day shape the physiognomy of all major civilizations fuel the agenda of multiple modernities with requisite cultural self-esteem' (Habermas, 2005b: 3-4).

Indeed, religious meditations find ways to enter the public sphere and to influence policy, and some sociologists consider this revival of religion to be based on the crisis of identity and spirituality. It seems that this return to the public sphere is the result of an effort to revive religious doctrines and to find identity and solidarity in them, as well as to provide significance to public and private lives.

In his work *The Postmodern Condition: A Report on Knowledge,* Lyotard appeals to Wittgenstein's and Cohen's ideas to challenge the views expressed by Habermas. He claims that mutual consent is impossible in the public sphere because of a multitude of language games, which means that not all people can achieve similar results and agreement. Accordingly, he introduces a way of formulating local rules so that smaller collections of people can generally reach better forms of mutual agreement. Lyotard (1984: 65-66) adds that:

Consensus is only a particular state of discussion, not its end. Its end, on the contrary, is paralogy. This double observation (the heterogeneity of the rules and the search for dissent) destroys a belief that still underlies Habermas's research.

Luhmann also challenges Habermas's theory by arguing that societies are too complex to be governed by their citizens through a rational discourse and consensus under conditions of freedom (Pusey, 1987: 101). In an interview that I conducted with Whitehead on Sunday 26th of June 2011, he claimed that

Habermas's ideas about the public sphere are based on old media, such as television and newspapers, which people no longer pay as much attention to with the emergence of visual on-line communication, and thus that his views need some updating.

However, the utility of Habermas's ideas about the public sphere (in relation to the power of criticism, freedom of speech and intersubjective mutual understanding in an unrestricted atmosphere absent of violence) is that it provides a great lesson for both governors and individuals within a society.

Nevertheless, opponents of globalisation hold that Habermas's approach to the public sphere still leaves much to be desired. These opponents believe that his approach spuriously assigns Western ideas a worldwide application. They consider this to be incompatible with the pluralism and diversity that exists in the world, which contributes to the trend of dismantling national identities.

2.2. Globalisation

Globalisation has had considerable effects on people's lives in the modern world. Even though it is not a new phenomenon, as some have argued, the concept of globalisation has become more prominent since the end of the cold war and the collapse of the Berlin Wall in 1989. Whilst there are a variety of pessimistic and optimistic outlooks regarding globalisation, there is also an intermediate outlook on it, which can be found in the works of Robertson, Beyer, Luhmann and Habermas.

Those who oppose globalisation claim that it provides a construct for industrialised states to sustain their hegemonies. From their points of view, globalisation is only an idea or a meditation for inculcating a typical Western philosophy and identity into an empire ruled by the USA. Tight controls are exercised by leading powers in the world of commerce, information and communication to promote globalisation resulting in cultural integration. (Ehteshami, 2006: 16). For instance, Mirsepassi (2000: 24) holds that:

Hegel assembled the totalizing elements implicit in Enlightenment conceptions of modernity within a massive frame in which all civilizations were consolidated inside the West's orbit. The West, inscribed as the center and controller of every one of them, emerged with the power to assign them placement within a scheme where they could only count as peripheral and tangential.

These dissidents also contend that this phenomenon creates intensified global inequalities to which it assigns public legitimacy. The westernisation of the world culture deepens the gap between the poor and the rich and weakens the foundations of non-Western rules and governments, thus abusing freedom and aiming to renew economic colonisation. Held and McGrew (2002: 84) summarise the position that Hirst and Thompson (1999) and Petras and Veltmeyer (2001) defend, which argues that most countries in the third world are permanently marginalised by the process of globalisation because all commercial, investment and technological flows are centralised in the OECD (Organisation for Economic Co-operation and Development): 'The division of the world into core and periphery, North and South, remains very much a structural feature of the contemporary global system'. Mandaville (2007: 104) adds that:

Globalization processes can be seen to disrupt and destabilize the traditional system of knowledge production in terms of both the ontological status and the spatial location of authority ... that is, a move away from the idea that religion is the primary source from which one gains knowledge about what to do in the world when faced with a given set of circumstances.

Some ideas of globalisation do not tackle religion directly. Theorists such as Robertson, Beyer, Luhmann and Habermas not only hold 'half-way' views on the notion of globalisation, but also present theories on religion and its connection with globalisation.

Robertson has played an important role in forming and generalising a globalisation theory, and states that his studies belong to the issues that link the 20th century to that of the 21st, rather than the 19th to the 20th (Robertson, 1992: 1). Beyer (1994: 30) suggests that, for Robertson, globalisation is substantially a religious theory, and explains that:

'Humani[s]tic' concern, despite its reduction of explicitly *theological* reference, centres on the ends of humanity, the ultimate meaning of human existence, the 'deep' issues of human life (see Robertson, 1989: 14). As such, it is intrinsically religious.

Robertson (1992: 8) conceives globalisation 'as a concept refers both to the compression of the world and the intensification of consciousness of the world as a whole'. This definition is, however, related to culture rather than to economy and policy. He alludes that 'today the emphasis has shifted and it is the cultural flows between nations which above all else seem to typify the contemporary globalization process' (Ahmed and Donnan, 1994: 3). In fact, Robertson looks at the notion of globalisation in multi-dimensional manner; he cares about both increasing the acceleration of concrete global interdependence and increasing the consciousness of the global whole. Therefore, he accepts the idea of global interdependence rather than a more integrated world. He explains that:

The insistence on heterogeneity and variety in an increasingly globalized world is, as I have said, integral to globalization theory. Yet the latter resists the attempt by some "civilizationists" to cultivate at all analytical costs the "purity" of civilizational and societal traditions. It does not decline to produce (at least a sketch of) a theory of the world as a whole for fear that generalizing across the world flattens humanity into a homogenous and potentially harmonious whole (Robertson, 1987: 22).

This definition differentiates his view from that of Giddens who considers globalisation to be a consequence of modernity. However, the view of Held and McGrew (2002: 1) can be likened to that of Robertson, since they hold that:

But it [globalization] should not be read as prefiguring the emergence of a harmonious world society or as a universal process of global integration in which there is a growing convergence of cultures and civilizations. For not only does the awareness of growing interconnectedness create new animosities and conflicts, it can fuel reactionary politics and deep-seated xenophobia.

Robertson's definition has two main characteristics: the universalisation of particularism and the particularisation of universalism. This means that while human communities maintain their identities, even when they absorb some specific ingredients from other cultures, they simultaneously provide general conditions of their culture within any historical era by conveying a certain parts of their culture to others (Robertson, 1992: 155). In a nutshell, 'globalization itself produces variety more accurately; it encourages heterogeneity-within-homogeneity, or difference-within-identity' (Robertson and Garrett, 1991: 283).

Since the universalisation of particularism and the particularisation of universalism can be created in every community, Robertson (1992: 27), unlike Giddens, contends that the globalisation process is not substantially an outcome of the Western project of modernity or enlightenment, but has pre-enlightenment origins. He (1992: 58-9) introduces five phases to the globalisation process: *The Germinal, The Incipient, The Take-off, The Struggle-for-Hegemony* and *The Uncertainty*. He believes that the process of globalisation started in the early fifteenth century, but has proceeded in the last few centuries.

King (1991:88), however, argues that the notion of globalisation has a long history, reaching back at least as far as the development of the major world religions. He explains that:

Along such lines we can readily conceive of global culture as having a very long history. "The idea of humankind" is at least as old as Jasper's Axial Age, in which major world religions and metaphysical doctrines arose, many centuries before the rise of national communities or societies (ibid.).

Robertson (1992: 26-27) introduces the 'global field' or 'Global-Human Condition' model for the process of globalisation, and holds that this model is 'both multidimensional and much more global than is usually meant by social-scientific and other connotations of that word'. He holds that there are four major components in the process of globalisation – societies, individuals, international relations, and humankind – and that these four components establish new relationship (Robertson, 1992: 26-27). In other words, globalisation provides a mutual relationship between these four major reference points, and 'the world becoming a single place … does not in and of itself say anything about global unification in any idealistic respect' (Robertson and Garrett, 1991: 283).

It should be noted that all these new relationships result in cultures, identities and values becoming relative. In brief, globalization 'as a form of "compression" of the contemporary world and the basis of a new hermeneutic for world history relativizes and "equalizes" all sociocultural formations' (Robertson, 1987: 22). Moreover, these relationships act as a background for the revival of religions and their movements. To put it simply,

The anti-modernist effort to give religion a privileged status, usually as a supplier or meaning … Religion is obviously playing a crucial role in this –outside most of Europe. At the same time, however, religion appears to have become simply a lifestyle option in quite a few areas of the world. Therein lies the paradox of religion in the globalized and partly postmodernized world (Robertson and Garrett, 1991: 287, 290).

Beyer, however, criticises Robertson's theory, remarking that although Robertson considers religion and religious issues in his theory, globalisation is not primarily or substantially associated with the notion of identity: 'Robertson's emphasis on national societies and individual in the world system tends to imply that globalization is primarily an argument about identity' (Beyer, 1994: 31).

Beyer is one of the eminent theorists to have dealt with the interconnection between globalisation and religion, and may claim to have presented the first fully detailed theory regarding religion's position in modernity. His theoretical foundations are rooted in those presented by Luhmann, although, like Giddens, he considers globalisation as a continuation of modernity. He also holds that:

Modernization in the West has directly resulted in the spread of certain vital institutions of Western modernization to the rest of the global ... This global spread has resulted in a new social unit which is much more than a simple expansion of Western modernity (Beyer, 1994: 8).

According to Beyer, this does not mean that modern systems should expand throughout the world in order to survive, 'but rather because there is no longer a powerful enough hindrance to his expansion' (Beyer, 1994: 38). As a consequence, there is now a new process of globalisation that not only provokes people of non-Western cultures to play major roles in employing and transferring approaches of modernity, but also leads them to play these roles willingly (Beyer, 1994: 54). Notwithstanding, Beyer (1994: 53, 65) emphasises that it is difficult to be modernising without Westernising, and that globalisation still means Westernisation.

However, Beck, Giddens and Lash (1994: 104, 188), unlike Beyer, claim that 'the post-traditional society is quite different. It is inherently globalizing, but also reflects the intensifying of globalization. Nevertheless, on the large scale, globalization cannot today simply be understood as Westernization'.

Beyer, like Luhmann, introduces the theory of privatised religion. He alludes to the idea that religion is not eliminated in the process of modernity and globalisation, but rather loses its efficacy in the public sphere. By being pushed into people's private spheres, the result is the marginalisation of religion.

The concept of globalisation is not 'added' to the systems theory that Luhmann introduces in his work; rather it is considered to be an internal part of his work. For Luhmann, globalisation is entirely connected with modernity and the renovation of Western societies, and is connected with the process of structural transformation within Western societies. As a result, other communities have been consumed by these changes through the process of modernity. However, Luhmann believes that religion brings with it a very significant complicating factor.

Unlike group culture, religion is more than ecology of themes for social communication. It is also a specific way of communicating: religion is not just cultural; it is also (at least potentially) systemic. As such, like political, legal, economic, artistic, and other ways of communicating, it can be and to a large extent is the locus of a differentiated instrumental subsystem of modern global society (Beyer, 1994: 67).

According to Luhmann's theory, although globalisation privatises religion, it also supplies fertile grounds for its new public influence. He explains this as follows:

The globalization of society, while structurally favouring privatization in religion, also provides fertile ground for the renewed public influence of religion. By public influence, I mean that one or more religions can become the source of collective obligation ... Public influence for religion is possible primarily when, like socio-cultural particularisms, it takes on the role of cultural resource for other systems (Beyer, 1994: 71-72).

The terms 'function' and 'performance' are important in Luhmann's systems theory. 'Function' refers to religious rites such as worship, purification of the soul and the search for enlightenment or salvation:

Function is the pure, 'sacred' communication involving the transcendent and the aspect that religious institutions claim for themselves, the basis of their autonomy in modern society (Beyer, 1994: 80).

On the other hand, religious performance is used to solve difficulties of other subsystems. Luhmann holds that the religious function has an undesirable position in modernity because the social system in modernism drives social interaction out of the control of religion. It is under these circumstances that the public influence of religion is lost and religion is degenerated into a private issue. Consequently, the only way that religion can acquire a public reputation and influence is through granting its services to solve problems in the other subsystems. Examples of such problems are 'economic poverty, political oppression, familial estrangement, environmental degradation, or personal identity' (Beyer, 1994: 80).

Beyer criticises the accounts of Wallerstein, Meyer and Robertson, who focus on one of three dimensions of the global system: the economy, policy and culture, respectively. Nonetheless, he supports Luhmann's position, claiming that Luhmann not only makes his theory devoid of error, but also gives broad explanations on these focuses that contain many deviations (Kachouian, 2007: 127, 131).

However, Robertson (1991: 284) challenges Luhmann's concept of 'a single place' and asserts that:

I consciously resisted, in opting for the concept of "a single place" Luhmann's adamantly expressed claim that the only "real" society in the modern world is world society. I must now confess that I find it difficult to resist the general force of Luhmann's argument, although I do not think that he has provided reasons, nuances, and caveats sufficient to convince on a large scale.

In addition, Habermas challenges Luhmann's views during his writing in the early 1970s, and resumes his disagreements with him in the mid 1980s. In a joint seminar that Habermas invited Luhmann to hold at the University of Frankfurt, the most general objection that he raised concerning Luhmann's system theory concerned its methodological orientation. He considers the systems theory to be problematic because it is tied to empirical-analytical methods, and that, like positivism, it serves to justify the oppressive character of the status quo (Holub, 1991: 108). Moreover, as Holub (1994: 145) says:

Habermas, who advocates a consensus theory of truth, believes that Luhmann's position has rather pernicious consequences for social theory ... Luhmann's theory, Habermas implicitly contends, prohibits any emancipation because it does not allow us to critique the regressive nature of domination in individual social systems or in the social system as a whole.

Luhmann, unlike Habermas, does not think that democracy is a process of free discussion that aims at reaching an intersubjective mutual understanding. Luhmann holds that comprehensive and non-participatory planning, secure from the influence of the public and political parties, is the only acceptable pattern for Western communities. In fact,

Luhmann's option for the type of non-participatory, global, system planning that is realized in a self-reflective administration removed from politics cannot, at the present stage of the planning discussion, be grounded with compelling arguments. Indeed, the empirical evidence that today can be marshalled speaks rather against Luhmann's option (Habermas, 1976: 139).

According to Holub (1991: 115), Habermas claimed Luhmann's selection of meditations would eliminate the last bastions of democracy through aggravated rationalisation.

From Luhmann's point of view, we are moving towards a global society that is not conceived of as a world political system. The global society, which is founded on a post-metaphysical idea, is not formed on the basis of reason, but on the basis of relinquishing reason (Harrison, 1995: 45).

In *The Postnational Constellation* (2001: 58-112), Habermas deals with globalisation and the future of democracy. Here, he uses a simple theory to promote a global policy up to the level of a global economy. He does this by recommending the establishment a 'world domestic policy' that corresponds to the principle of democratic decision-making, in contrast to current globalisation principles, which seek to integrate policy with economy in a way that allows policy to serve a global system of economy. Habermas chooses the concept of 'world domestic policy' to replace that of the current 'international relations'. Under such conditions, he notes that world problems would be organised in a similar way to the domestic problems of a national unit, based on a social democratic principle. As he puts it:

Global powers have to be willing to broaden their perspectives on what counts as the "national interest" into a viewpoint of "global governance." But this changed perspective, from "international relations" to a world domestic policy, cannot be expected from governments if their populations themselves do not reward them for it (Habermas, 2001: 111).

According to Habermas (2001: 38-57), in the process of globalisation, one can no longer restrict social solidarity within the limited framework of nation-state. Unity based on cosmopolitan principles needs to be replaced with unity based on a national sovereignty. The basis of a cosmopolitan solidarity is grounded in the general abstracted principle of equal freedom for all under equal law. That is, human right is the basis of a cosmopolitan solidarity.

It is probably fair to say that, as Habermas sees it, globalisation acts as an opportunity for nations on the one hand, and a threat for them on the other. For instance, he construes considerable economic growth as an opportunity for nations, and believes that the globalisation of the economy is the most important form that globalisation takes:

But the most significant dimension is economic globalization, whose new quality can hardly be doubted: "Global economic transactions, if measured against nationally limited economic activity, are reaching a level achieved in no other previous epoch, and directly affect national economies on a previously unknown scale" (Habermas, 2001: 66).

On the other hand, Habermas (2001: 67) is pessimistic about how a democracy may evolve within a nation-state as he believes that the nation-state is losing its power. Thus, because the states have been weakened under globalisation, and because today's communities are growing more and more complicated, the realisation of a democracy seems difficult. However, in *Globalization/Anti-Globalization,* Held and McGrew (2002: 124) assert that:

The simple formulations of the loss, diminution or erosion of state power can misrepresent this change [the roles and performances of state are being re-organised and re-stabilised]. Indeed, such a language involves a failure to conceptualize adequately the nature of power and its complex manifestations, since it represents a crude zero-sum view of power.

Furthermore, in emphasising the pivotal role that nation-states can play and the fact that they can survive after being globalised, Giddens and Huntington have both talked about developed democratic structures following the new global changes. Huntington (1993: 22) also holds that nation-states will remain the most powerful actors in world affairs.

Interestingly, Habermas (2001: 81) considers the balanced approach towards globalisation. He declares that: 'neither of these positions, neither the uncritical welcome of the globalization process nor its uncritical demonization, goes for enough, of course'.

Habermas (2001: 68) prefers to investigate globalisation's affects through the following questions:

How does globalization affect (a) the security of the rule of law and the effectiveness of the administrative state, (b) the sovereignty of the territorial state, (c) collective identity, and (d) the democratic legitimacy of the nation-state?

Habermas (2001: 75) agrees that the commodified and homogenous culture that has been shaped by the USA not only imposes itself on distant lands, but also homogenises the most significant differences and weakens the strongest local traditions in the West. Nevertheless, he also holds that not only differences will remain, but also that some differentiations can be created.

It is important to emphasise that, according to the view that Robertson, Beyer, Luhmann and Giddens hold, religion is marginalised as the result of the expansion of globalisation and modernity. In fact, their ideas concerning the notion of globalisation serve to secularise public life. However, in the Holberg Prize Seminar, held to tackle "Religion in the Public Sphere", Habermas (2005b: 2) emphasised the revival of religious traditions in the process of globalisation stating that 'we can hardly fail to notice the fact that religious traditions, and communities of faith have gained a new, hitherto unexpected political importance ... Apart from Hindu nationalism, Islam and Christianity are at present the two vital religious sources'.

Habermas goes on to observe that, what is more surprising than religion's revival within the process of globalisation is its reclamation of a political role at the heart of Western society. Although statistical evidence shows the development of secularisation in nearly all European countries (especially after the Second World War), all the data in the United States indicates that the majority of its population is constituted of devout and religiously active citizens, and that this has remained constant over the last six decades. 'The Occident's own image of modernity seems, as in a psychological experiment, to undergo a switchover: what has been the supposedly "normal" model for the future of all other cultures suddenly changes into a special-case scenario' (Habermas, 2005b: 4).

Habermas's idea here represents a realisation of global or local communities based on communicative action, mutual understanding and finally a consensus between two powerful and effective poles of secular and religious adherents. His recommendations to both of these are as follows:

1. To amend the epistemological foundations of secularism and promote it to a post-secular stage, as well as to produce changes in the philosophical and epistemological foundations of religion by adopting a hermeneutic and pluralistic approach to it, and heightening it to the point of post-metaphysics.

2. To recognise the existence of secularism and religion in the process of globalisation.

3. To accept the utilitarian nature of modernity and its achievements for religious people, as well as the utilitarianism of piety and original spiritual doctrines to improve ethical soundness in the modern age.

4. To secure the freedom for all citizens to draw on the possibilities and opportunities existing in a society and state.

5. To enter into dialogue in order to learn from each other, and reach a mutual understanding in a democratic and just space (Habermas, 2005b: 1-14).

Habermas believes that human beings can get closer to the truth during the process of globalisation by being impartially involved in intercultural dialogue. Only by free participation and mutual conversation can people reach a global consensus; and a conciliatory world can only be found by relying on rationality and communicative action, and an absence of force and hegemony.

2.3. Modernity

In *The Postnational Constellation,* Habermas (2001: 131) suggests that the term *modern,* from the Latin root *modernus,* was first employed in the late fifth century in order to distinguish the current Christian age from the Roman age, and the old age of blasphemy. Since that time, this term has indicated a separation of the new period from the old one. 'The Renaissance, with which our own conception of the modern age begins, referred back to classical Greece in this manner'. Edgar (2006: 96) points out that 'Modernity began with the end of the Renaissance (and thus around the beginning of the seventeenth century), and therefore 'modernism' is the culture that is characteristic of this period'. Mirsepassi (2000: 24) observes that:

According to Jurgen Habermas, "Hegel was the first philosopher to develop a clear concept of modernity"... As Peter Singer has claimed, "[W]ithout Hegel, neither the intellectual nor the political developments of the last 150 years would have taken the path they did".

Habermas asserts that the spell of the classics of the ancient world on the soul of later periods was first broken through the ideals of the Enlightenment periods in France. 'Specifically, the idea of being 'modern' by looking back to the ancients changed with the belief, inspired by modern science, in the infinite progress of knowledge and in the infinite advance towards social and moral betterment' (Habermas, 1981a: 4).

The "modern" spirit has to devalue its own immediate prehistory, distancing itself from it as a way of grounding itself normatively from its own resources ... For this new consciousness, the "modern" now stands opposed to the "old" world insofar as it is radically open to the future. The transient moment of the present thus gains significance as the point of departure for each new generation's embrace of the whole of history (Habermas, 2001: 131-2).

Weber has dealt in detail with the definition and illustration of modernity, as well as the relationship between religion and rationality. Weber considers modernity to be a rational process that has disenchanted the world and emancipated people from religious hallucinations. He has discussed how it is possible to separate the three realms of science, religion and art from one another, and that this is a positive aspect of modernity. On the other hand, he likens the process of rationalisation to an "iron cage" that has captured human beings. In the introduction to *The Theory of Communicative Action* (Habermas, 1984: xx), McCarthy explains that, for Weber, the realisation of rationality – which was construed by 18th century philosophers as 'God's domain on the earth'– has degenerated into an "iron cage" in which we are still condemned to live. Disenchantment and rationalisation cannot be restored in the same way as the losses of meaning and freedom that correlate to them. Shilling and Mellor (2001: 10) believe that, for Weber, 'there was little room for religion within modernity'. Weber (1948: 139) illustrates the encounter of tradition and modernity as follows. Under modernity, there are no substantially unknown or mysterious forces that command the world, and mankind can preside over all things by calculation. This means that the world is disenchanted, with magical means no longer being necessary for subduing or beseeching the spirits. Technical tools and calculation devices perform this service instead, which creates the intellectualisation of the modern world. According to Weber, this intellectualisation was manifested when science, ethics and art were separated from one another, and this led to human beings being trapped within an "iron cage" – a rootless world without any meaning. Weber believes that these three areas of value cannot be unified, and thus individuals are forced to select contradictory or conflicting values. Bernstein (1985: 5) alleges that: 'Weber argued that the hope and expectation of the Enlightenment thinkers was a bitter and ironic illusion'. They believed that human emancipation depended on the growth of science and rationality, but this growth led to what Weber called 'instrumental rationality': 'The growth of *zweckrationalitat* does not lead to the concrete realization of universal freedom but to the creation of an "iron cage" of bureaucratic rationality from which there is no escape' (ibid.).

Modernity can be divided into three stages. In its first stage during the Middle Ages, there was a vigorous contrast between religion and science. The schism between new scientific data and religious texts and scriptures contributed to the negation of any religious and metaphysical meditations. The doctrines and teachings of Christianity in the Augustinian fashion, with its dominant pattern for understanding and interpreting everything, were replaced by the adoption of rationality as a final judge for everything. It was on this basis that Protestant ethics emerged, rejecting those of Roman Catholicism, and challenging its authority in doing so:

It [Protestantism] demanded of the believer not celibacy, as in the case of the monk, but the elimination of all erotic pleasure or desire; not poverty, but the elimination of all idle enjoyment of unearned wealth and income, and the avoidance of all feudalistic, life-loving ostentation of wealth; not the ascetic death-in-life of the cloister (Pusey, 1987: 49-50).

After a while, this approach provided the background for the appearance of secularism and modernity by denying any authority to revelation. As a result, both rationalism and humanism reached an unbreakable unity, whilst the church and religion became noticeably weakened, withdrawing from the social and political arenas and progressively entering into privacy. In fact, these two incidents – the conflict between science and religion and the birth of Protestantism from Catholicism – made the Christian church so weak that it was driven out of both the political and the public sphere.

In the second stage of modernity, Habermas (2001: 132) argues that it comes to understand itself in opposition to tradition and tries to seek a pretext in reason. It also tries to select its pattern by means of its own criteria, and to produce its normativity from within. Modernity had to stabilise itself through reason, and it was only in the name of the Enlightenment that it could devaluate tradition and overcome it:

Thus modernity prides itself on its critical spirit, which accepts nothing as self-evident except in light of good reasons. "Subjectivity" has both a universalistic and an individualistic meaning. Each person deserves the equal respect of all. At the same time, each person should be recognized as the source and the final judge of her own particular claims to happiness (Habermas, 2001: 133).

When the possibilities for facilitating learning expanded in modernity, and the sciences became specialised, a new stage was reached in which the culture-value domains of science, ethics and art were separated from each another.

Habermas (1981a: 8-9) argues that, for Weber, the unique characteristic of cultural modernity is the differentiation of the "substantive reason" of religious and metaphysical systems into the three independent areas of science, ethics and art. The reason for this separation was the collapse of an overarching religious and metaphysical worldview. Since the 18th century, the issues that had previously been part of the framework of religion and metaphysics had been divided into the three categories of validity truth, normative rightness, and authenticity or beauty. In other words, they have been debated as questions of knowledge, morality or justice, and taste. This division represents one side of the second stage of modernity. However, the other side of this stage is represented by the distance that has developed between the culture of experts and that of the populace. The risk associated with this form of rationalisation is that the lifeworld will be impoverished with the loss of its traditional content.

Habermas's analysis of Weber's ideas regarding the self-understanding of modernity reflects Kant's three critiques, which consist of the critique of pure reason (epistemology), the critique of practical reason (morality), and the critique of judgement (aesthetics). Habermas (1981a: 11), unlike Weber, believes that:

A reified everyday praxis can be cured only by creating unconstrained interaction of the cognitive with the moral-practical and the aesthetic-expressive elements. Reification cannot be overcome by forcing just one of those highly stylized cultural spheres to open up and become more accessible. Instead, we see under certain circumstances a relationship emerge between terroristic activities and the over-extension of any one of these spheres into other domains.

However, Burger criticises Habermas's view, arguing that his 'hope for a simultaneous reintegration of the three spheres into a rationalised life-world seems highly unrealistic' (Bernstein, 1985: 135).

In the third stage, modernity begins to promote its power and ascendancy over existence by way of law. Law is rationalised and practiced by jurists who are well-trained and control the historical changes in culture and ethics. In the 20th century, postmodernists (the inheritors of Right Hegelianism who thought that there was no real need for further change), the Frankfurt school, Heidegger and Foucault attempted to discredit modernity, arguing that modernity had lost its power and importance and thus needed to be abandoned. Having criticised and rejected their arguments, Habermas (the inheritor of Left Hegelianism who holds that the thrust of Hegel's philosophy aims for a much more far-reaching revolutionary change) 'has sought to defend the modern project by arguing that postmodernism is often the expression of an ideological opposition to modernist principles of authentic self-experience and self-realisation' (Mellor and shilling, 1997: 188).

Habermas presents himself as the supporter of the 'unfinished project' of modernity. He holds that if it were completed, it would lead to the deliverance of humanity from instrumental rationality. He believes that instrumental reason, positivism and mass culture have deviated the project of modernity from its course: 'for Habermas's mentors, science had been absorbed by instrumental reason, while morality had been absorbed by the positivist understanding of science. Even art, corrupted by mass culture, had been emptied of all critical and utopian content' (Rasmussen, 1990: 15).

As a result of these obstacles to modernity, capitalism has predominated over cultural and objective conditions and human autonomy through the media held by power and money. Habermas is 'seeking to diagnose the roots of political repression as a means to the realisation of a political emancipation' (Edgar, 2006: 98). His recommendation is the expansion of the public sphere and communicative action. Habermas (1981a: 6) also declares that:

In this manner, Bell places the burden of responsibility for the dissolution of the Protestant ethic (a phenomenon which has already disturbed Max Weber), on the "adversary culture". Culture, in its modern form, stirs up hatred against the conventions and virtues of an every day life, which has become rationalized under the pressures of economic and administrative imperatives ... Bell sees a religious revival to be the only solution. Religious faith tied to a faith in tradition will provide individuals with clearly defined identities, and with existential security.

In Habermas's view, although modernity has brought some forms of development in economic, political and cultural areas, it has also left a vacuum in human identity and direction by removing the chains of tradition and the metaphysical element from the person. Nevertheless, Habermas has recently come to believe that it is impossible to wholly eliminate religion from public life and, as a result, has sought to recognise the public role of religion. Interestingly, Habermas (2008: 108) notes that the thesis 'that a religious orientation to a transcendent reality alone can show a contrite modernity the way out of its impasse is once again gaining adherents'. In an interview with Pope Benedict XVI (2004, 19th January), Habermas (2005a: 2) asserts that:

Religions and secular rationalities need to engage in a mutual process of dialogue in order to learn from each other and to protect the planet from the destructive potential of the uncoupling of faith and reason in the modern world ... The modern secular state, in order truly to guarantee impartiality in its decisions, must take religious arguments as valid interventions in public debates.

Furthermore, in his speech at Tehran University, 'Religiousness in a Secular Context', Habermas (2002c: 19) said that religion could remain stable within the framework of modernity if it could make its position clear in three directions:

1. In its challenge with other religions that are epistemologically different from one another, the religious consciousness must be able to settle this challenge rationally.

2. In areas in which there is scientific authority, it must adapt itself to sciences, which possess social monopoly of mundane knowledge.

3. From the religious point of view, it must seek to link itself to the sovereignty of the people and to the human right.

Habermas goes on to explain that post-secular communities have adapted to the continuation of religion, which can survive only when it addresses individuals in society without resorting to political authority, and only by relying on its own words as its instruments. In democratic communities, both religious and non-religious citizens take advantage of political challenges.

Thus, a religious community can exercise its views on cultural, social and political areas through institutions such as associations and religious centres.

2.4. Democracy

Democracy is originally a Greek term, which entered into the English language in the 16th century from the French word *democratie*. It is etymologically derived from the term *demokratia*. It is collocated from two morphemes: *demos* (people), and *kratos* (rule). Based on this derivative collocation, democracy suggests a government in which the people rule, and is in obvious contrast with monarchies and aristocracies: 'Democracy entails a state in which there is some forms of political equality among the people' (Held, 1987: 2).

A democratic mode of thinking emphasises the social human, who is involved in ruling, accepts all social obligations in an urban community, and embraces a community life in order to obtain peace, tranquillity and security. On this basis, Carl Cohen (1973: 7) defines democracy as follows:

Democracy is that system of community government in which, by and large, the members of a community participate, or may participate, directly or indirectly, in the making decisions which affect them all.

In the *Social Roots of Dictatorship and Democracy*, Moor (1991: 9) holds that democracy has grown in order to achieve three purposes:

1. Narrowing the powers of arbitrary rulers;

2.   Replacing arbitrary legislations with rational and just laws and regulations; and,

3.   Allowing lower classes of society to share in the making of decisions.

Two factors that vitally influence the achievement of the objectives mentioned above are liberty and equality. Locke (1972: 452) says that:

And reason, which is that law, teaches all mankind who will but consult in that, being all equal and independent, no one ought to harm another in his life, health, liberty, or possessions.

Moreover, Mill (1996: 59), who defends a complete freedom of thought and representative democracy, argues that it is a moral fact that suppressing and succumbing a creed is detrimental to humanity. If a suppressed idea is right, then what is lost shall be made obvious. If it is wrong, people will lose the opportunity to develop better ideas and receive a more lively feeling of a reality that is provided through a contrast between right and wrong.

The focus of Habermas's meditations is the notion of 'deliberative democracy'. Habermas (1996: 287-328) examines three models of democracy – the normative, empiricist and deliberative – and argues that deliberative democracy is the best solution for a compromise between facts and norms. He also holds that:

Empiricist redefinitions ... do not give us a way to avoid the question of how norm and reality are related. If this is the case, then we must return to those normative models of democracy already introduced and ask whether their implicit conceptions of society offer any points of contact with available sociological analyses. Our reflections from the standpoint of legal theory revealed that the central element of the democratic process resides in the procedure of deliberative politics (Habermas, 1996: 296).

According to Habermas, the deliberative or discursive model of democracy can rescue the modern world from the problems of disruption and arbitrary individuality. This is because:

Deliberative democracy acquires empirical relevance only when we take into account the multiplicity of forms of communication in which a common will is produced, that is, not just ethical self-clarification but also the balancing of interests and compromise, the purposive choice of means, moral justification, and legal consistency-testing (Matustik, 2001: 209).

In fact, deliberative democracy places an emphasis on people involving themselves in the processes of free discussion and unrestricted conversation in order to reach an intersubjective mutual understanding.

Joshua Cohen (1995) has dealt with the notion of deliberative democracy in detail, and argues that 'within an egalitarian-democratic order, political decision-making must be deliberative. Public decision-making is deliberative when it is framed by different conceptions of the common good, and public initiatives are defended ultimately by reference to an openly acknowledged conception of the public interest' (Cohen, 1995: 38).

Habermas holds that deliberative democracy is achieved within the public sphere, and that any extended criticism of government policies that issues from the public sphere results in political expansion to the detriment of a closed domain of power. In other words, according to Habermas:

For a democracy to function on a more than formal basis, it is necessary for its citizenry to reflect critically on the policies and directions of its government. Any endeavour to curtail such reflection undermines the fundamental structures on which democratic institutions are built (Holub, 1991: 186).

To put it simply, the public sphere is not only an open arena for political decision-making, but also an arena in which rational aims can be highlighted and demands made. As such, it is an arena in which both the state and politics can be rationalised. This crucial outcome can only be gained through free communication, and language is the tool through which one can freely and openly exchange ideas with others. Thus language plays a liberating role and provides a special efficiency to the public sphere. Once again, Habermas furnishes important clues that a deliberative democracy and emancipation are shaped on the condition that all individuals involve themselves in dialogue and open discussion that is free from any type of pressure and constraints, and come to mutual understanding through the power of reasoned argument. In *Moral Consciousness and Communicative Action,* Habermas (1990a: 89) talks about the importance of following rules of discourse in order to guarantee discursive equality and freedom:

(3.1) Every subject with the competence to speak and act is allowed to take part in a discourse; (3.2) a. Everyone is allowed to question any assertion whatever. b. Everyone is allowed to introduce any assertion whatever into the discourse. c. Everyone is allowed to express his attitudes, desires, and needs; (3.3) No speaker may be prevented, by internal or external coercion, from exercising his rights as laid down in (3.1) and (3.2).

Discourse under the aforementioned conditions will be successful only if participants adopt attitudes of equal respect and impartiality. It is exactly this position that produced *The Theory of Communicative Action* in which Habermas's theoretical foundation of deliberative democracy is developed:

The aim of communicative action is to reach agreement over facts about the world and over norms of social interaction and to achieve dependable mutual understanding by people about their unique world views and perception of themselves (Cunningham, 2002: 175).

In other words, Habermas (1972: 191-192) claims that human beings interact with one another as social creatures and, as such, they need to understand each other. They use their common language for their interaction, and he calls this 'communicative action'. Therefore, in illustrating this interaction, he considers the concept of the ideal speech situation to be a fundamental prerequisite for communicative action. The ideal speech situation consists of equal rights and powers between participants in a discourse. Within the ideal speech situation, any idea can be expressed and criticised, and it is thus possible to reach an intersubjective understanding and consensus through this process. Indeed, it anticipates a form of life in which truth, freedom and justice are possible. On this basis, Gutmann and Thompson (1996: 351-352) remark that within deliberation:

Representatives must give reasons to their constituents and respond to criticisms from them. Citizens should use reciprocity in their reasoning not only to judge other principles but also to judge its own adequacy. Deliberative democracy expresses a bootstrap conception of the political process: the conditions of reciprocity, publicity, and accountability that define the process pull themselves up by means of the process itself.

As a result of the above situation, all the conflicts between participants are resolved, and they come to an agreement with one another.

In developing this theory, Habermas pays attention to what provides laws with their legitimacy in order to conform his theories to democracy. He holds that democracy involves institutionalising a theory of argumentation through a system of law that guarantees an equal right of partnership for every individual in the legislating process. In *Between Fact and Norms*, Habermas (1996: 110) explains that:

On the premise that rational political opinion and will-formation is at all possible, the principle of democracy only tells us how this can be institutionalized, namely, through a system of rights that secures for each person an equal participation in a process of legislation whose communicative presuppositions are guaranteed to being with.

Habermas (1996: 458) also states that the doctrine of democracy holds that only those laws that are able to win the approval and satisfaction of all citizens in a process of dialogue aimed at producing legislation can claim to be legitimate. To put it simply, 'only those laws can claim legitimate validity which can achieve the agreement of all citizens in a discursive process of legislation which is itself legally constituted' (Outhwaite, 1994: 141).

Although Habermas's theory considers the agreements of citizens within a society to be the basis for the legitimacy of that society's laws (as liberal democracy does), it diverges from liberal democracy with respect to how this consensus is achieved. For Habermas, consent is based on the outcome of the rational argumentation that participants engaging in the decision-making process make. Free and equal citizens defend their theories by presenting their arguments, and finally they achieve an agreement. Thus, reaching consensus depends on reaching an understanding that lies inherently in human language.

The legitimacy of decision-making during the process of liberal democracy is based on individual reason, not collective reason as it is in deliberative democracy, and relies on experimentation (which is influenced by positivism). Hence, religion loses its authority in liberal democracy, and public life is released from the authoritative domain of religion.

Habermas argues that, under the deliberative approach, 'democracy is the exercise of sovereignty by the people, while for liberal democracy it is voting in accord with constitutionally prescribed procedures and constraints' (Cunningham, 2002: 179). Furthermore, in liberal democracy, the majority vote is the most important instrument for decision-making. Minority interests are ignored, with the aims and values of the majority being imposed upon those of the minority. However, Habermas's deliberative democracy focuses on the interests of all people in the process of decision-making, and he believes that the majority's decision can be fallible, and thus that, even after a process of argumentation and a majority vote, the interests of minorities are not ignored:

Such doubts are based on the view that the outnumbered minority give their consent to the empowerment of the majority only with the proviso that they themselves retain the opportunity in the future of winning over the majority with better argument and thus of revising the previous decision (Habermas, 1996: 179).

Lyotard criticises Habermas's theories in several ways:

First, the legitimizing narrative of emancipation is no longer plausible because of the plethora of incommensurable language games that make up social life. Second, Habermas misconceives language when he argues that it is grounded on an attempt to reach understanding with each other. On the contrary, the use of utterances is actually conflictual, provocative, displacing, in a word, agonistic. Third, attempts at achieving consensus in this circumstance must necessarily be oppressive, a silencing or denial of practices that expose and pursue the different (Sitton, 2003: 101-102).

Goode (2005: 49) contends that Habermas's idea 'may have fit the ancient Greek agora but not modern societies'. Thus, it seems that although the communication in a deliberative democracy takes place within idealised conditions, and no such form of communication and consensus ever actually occurs, its importance cannot be ignored. In any case, this theory presents a notable model for democratic structures in society to be used as a guarantee for popular contribution and deliberative democracy. Indeed, as far as no democracy in its true sense has ever existed in the West, this theory can be used and identified as a better form of democracy.

2.5. Positivism

Empirical science noticeably advanced from the time of Galileo and later showed itself in the form of positivism. The most eminent and famous philosophical representatives of positivism were Comte (1798-1857), Peirce (1839-1914), Dewey (1859-1952) and the members of the Vienna School in the 1920s and 1930s. Positivism involved a direct attack on the truth of religious and metaphysical concepts. Put simply, positivism is 'the rejection of all religious and theological language as nonsense, and the rejection of all value statements, including those in ethics and aesthetics' (Edgar, 2006: 106).

Comte used the investigation of positive facts to observe phenomena and discover laws through induction, and held that this methodology was superior to metaphysical meditations and religious dogmas, which cannot be proved. Furthermore,

Comte's suggestion is that positive polity must re-establish this distinction [between the temporal and the spiritual], shorn of any supernatural referents, in a sociological 'religion of humanity'... Durkheim criticised Comte, however, for focusing on 'Society' rather than 'societies' and for using the words 'humanity' and 'society' interchangeably. In other words, he found Comte's notion of society too abstract, and too prone to conflate different aspects of human experience into one overarching narrative (Mellor, 2004: 126-127).

Since Comte, positivism has been used in all branches of the sciences, and for the generalisation of natural science methodologies into social sciences.

Habermas (1974b: 272) argues that under the criteria of positivism, the precedent systems of value can change and, above all this leads to 'the reformulation or even total devaluation of traditional norms, which fail to function as principles of orientation for a technical realization of concrete goals'.

In his two best-known works, *Knowledge and Human Interests* and *Theory and Practice* (which provide the best entrance into his other works), Habermas takes an extremely anti-positivistic position. He wants to attack a typical conception of science that is improper and arrogant, rather than attacking science itself. This scientism claims that the model of the natural sciences is the only valid approach, and that it is the proper measure for all scientific inquiry. The main reason for Habermas's attack on positivism is due to his antipathy to the positivists' claim that they are the only authors who hold rationally valid social knowledge.

As Habermas notes, positivism holds that all human knowledge of reality originates from experience or observation. Since scientific knowledge is real knowledge, and this knowledge has been applied successfully in the sphere of nature, it must also be applied in social world. In addition, this real knowledge cannot include a knowledge of values – such as moral values – because value judgements cannot be verified by scientific methods. As a result, sciences (including the social sciences) are necessarily devoid of value.

In other words, positivism has deviated the link between theory and practice by only studying "is" and avoiding the ideal "ought to", and this enables it to be used by ideology that is all the ideas that conceal any arbitrary power or add legitimacy to it. Therefore, it has provided stifling conditions for populations through adopting an instrumental rationality that reduces human beings to objects with no identity and ignoring the relationship between knowledge and human interests, which has led to the decline of the public sphere. According to Weber, the domination of positivism in our era has resulted in a loss of meaning and freedom, and the fall of an "Iron Cage" over human beings.

Habermas, however, criticises Weber's pessimistic approach, considering enlightenment to be an unfinished project, the actualisation of which would lead to human beings being freed from the "iron cage". Habermas's solution for freeing people from Weber's iron cage can be found in his critical theory. He believes that 'it will be the task of critical reflection to grub out the positivist root and thus to once again put science back into the service of human rationality' (Pusey, 1987: 26).

This critical theory can be self-reflection, the process of which 'is determined by an emancipatory cognitive interest' (Habermas, 1972: 310). To put it another way, a process of self-reflection results in a knowledge of positivism's restrictions whilst liberating human beings from their dependency on embodied powers. However, unlike Marx, Habermas does not promote violence or revolution as a means to achieving this liberation, but promotes 'intersubjectivity of action-orienting mutual understanding' (Habermas, 1972: 195).

Briefly, the critical theory is based on an open society and strengthens the same type of society:

A society, that is, where incompatible views can be expressed; where everyone is free to propose solutions and to criticize the proposed solutions of others; and where government policies are changed in the light of criticism (Connerton, 1976: 33-34).

In addition, Habermas asserts that values are not separate from science. Like Kant, he explains that even time and space are not only the products of experience. However, Habermas, unlike Kant, believes that all knowledge is mediated by social experience rather than by individual rationality.

On the other hand, studying a social and historical world requires the application of methods that differ significantly from those of the natural sciences: 'Whilst the natural scientists can only describe how nature works, the historian who studies history is the same as he who makes history' (Habermas, 1972: 149).

The social sciences need to use hermeneutic methodology, that is, the sciences of interpretation. Hermeneutic is a part of the criticisms that are applied to positivism. However, Habermas claims that hermeneutics is incomplete and that 'the problem for hermeneutic theory is not just that communication may be systematically distorted by extraneous causal influences, but that linguistic communication in anyway part of more general social process, which should not be reduced to communication alone' (Outhwaite: 1987: 75).

2.6. Hermeneutics

Hermeneutics has its root in a Greek verb *Hermeneuein*, which is generally translated as 'to interpret' or 'to paraphrase'. Aristotle attributed such a high value to hermeneutics that he dealt specifically with it in a large dissertation in his *Organon* (Palmer, 2005: 19). Hermeneutics is an approach that deals with the interpretation of texts (religious or non-religious) in order to uncover their original and latent meanings, and thus to enable individual behaviours and social lives to be perceived. In other words, 'hermeneutic understanding is the interpretation of texts with the knowledge of texts that have already been understood' (Habermas, 1988: 153).

Before the 19th century, hermeneutics was used solely for interpreting the meanings and spiritual reality of scripture so that new generations were capable of understanding it. However, in the early 19th century, Ast (1778-1841) presented his theory of hermeneutics, and this was subsequently developed by Schleiermacher (1768-1834), founder of the newly-developed hermeneutic tradition. In the late 19th century, Dilthey (1833-1911) generalised hermeneutic theory, moving it away from the purely theological sphere into the philosophical sphere. In the 20th century, the prominent innovators in the arena of hermeneutic theory were Heidegger (1889-1976) and his disciple, Gadamer (1900-2002). Heidegger's and Gadamer's thought on hermeneutics can be divided into three categories:

1- Hermeneutics no longer concerns itself exclusively with the understanding and interpretation of written documents or speech. 2- The aim of understanding is not focused on communication with, or the psychology of, another person. 3- Ontological hermeneutics thus replaces the question of understanding as knowledge about the world with the question of being-in-the world (Holub, 1991: 51-52).

It is important to bear in mind that while positivism recognises just one form of sciences – the natural sciences – Habermas identifies three forms: the natural, cultural and critical sciences. However, when it comes to discussing theology:

Habermas's theory of social evolution allied to his insistence three – and three only – modern kinds of autonomous claims (scientific, social, aesthetic), which suggests his relative lack of attention to religious thought and practice in modernity (Browning and Fiorenza, 1992: 35).

In 1964, Habermas introduced his theory of 'knowledge constitutive interests' in *Knowledge and Human Interest* (1972: 308-11). This plays a pivotal role in all his later works. In relation to the views of Peirce, Dilthey and Freud, Habermas divides human knowledge into three parts – the natural, cultural and critical sciences – and holds that any of these three categories of human knowledge is based on any one of the three interests: technical interests in the empirical-analytic sciences; practical interests in the historical-hermeneutic sciences; and emancipation autonomy interests in the critical sciences. These three interests, respectively, govern the three types of approaches distinguished from one another in sociological studies, which consist of positivistic, hermeneutic and critical approaches.

The Hermeneutic approach represents an understanding and recovering of the meanings of texts, human actions, and cultural products. It shows human beings' practical interests in establishing an intersubjective understanding about the common concerns of human life through language and the attainment of a social consensus. Habermas says that:

Socialization is a universal precondition for individual identity: the specific contents of my subjective world may be very different to those of your inner world but, like it or not, I can have no coherent identity unless I can enter your experience in a way that allows me to understand what you mean. The same is true for you and so we share with all other human beings, in every place and time, a universal interest in the mutual self-understanding that underpins all social action. Habermas calls this the 'practical' interest that constitutes knowledge in the 'historical-hermeneutic' sciences (Pusey, 1987: 25).

Habermas's conception of hermeneutics is summarised in the following five points:

1.   Meaning can only be perceived 'from the inside out' and, according to Weber, it can be understood as 'meaningful social action'. Both Habermas and Gadamer agree that the process of comprehending a tradition, a culture, or a text requires that a special type of communication be conducted with the mental universe of the other person, culture or tradition. That is, both Habermas and Gadamer emphasise the intersubjectivity of this process. Habermas uses Gadamer's metaphor of a 'fusion of horizons' to explain this, which postulates that every position has a horizon, and the horizon of everything is the encircling limit of understanding.

2.   Habermas draws three conclusions relating to the 'fusion of horizons'. The first is that the 'fusion of horizons' results in an interpretation that is more comprehensive, profound and rational. The second is that the process of hermeneutic understanding directs the commentator beyond his or her personal perceptions. The third is that, not only does the fusion of horizons causes experiences to continue, but also gives orientation to the commentator's actions, and maintains an 'action-orienting understanding' from generation to generation.

3.   The important point about the interpretation of texts is the fact that the meaning and validity are internally connected with each other, and created together in the process of interpretation.

4.   According to Habermas, the hermeneutic methodology carries universal importance because it highlights how norms

are transferred from generation to generation, and from culture to culture. This undermines the prejudgement of empiricists, who held that values are merely sensations or common practices.

5.   The theory of hermeneutics has played an essential role in introducing Habermas's later ideas on the 'linguistic turn'. Habermas accepts Gadamer's view that 'language is not only an object in our hands, it is the reservoir of tradition and the medium in and through which we exist' (Pusey, 1987: 61-64). However, Habermas also holds that language can supply power and repression.

Habermas has acknowledged the achievements of hermeneutic theory, and states that this theory has demonstrated that the objective patterns of natural science are insufficient. He holds that it is also concerned with a rational process and intersubjective communication.

However, Habermas claims that the hermeneutic sphere in Gadamer's ideas is not comprehensive, and only serves the purposes of social and historical sciences. To put it simply, 'While Habermas accepts the core of the hermeneutical analysis of meaning and history, he rejects its claims to universality as forwarded by Gadamer' (Bernstein, 1995: 58). Habermas asserts that this hermeneutic accepts existing traditions as right, and can act as a medium to provide either power or suppression. On this basis, traditions withdraw from criticism. In general, Habermas holds that Gadamer's hermeneutic sphere is problematic because it does not represent a critical approach, and because it leads to relativism and ideology. Moreover, Habermas (1984: 134-135) also believes that:

Gadamer remains bound to the experience of the philologist who deals with classical tests: "The classic is that which stands up in the face of historical criticism." The knowledge embodied in the text is, Gadamer believes, fundamentally superior to the interpreter's ... Gadamer endangers his fundamental hermeneutic insight because hidden behind his preferred model of philological concern with canonical texts lies the really problematic case of the *dogmatic interpretation of sacred scriptures.*

It appears, however, that the critical hermeneutic introduced by Habermas has the following problems:

1.   A tradition cannot be criticised in an absolute way. If criticism and scepticism towards religion and tradition are designed from various materials to make a special point, hermeneutics can be used to ponder over texts and human minds and practices, as well as to criticise them. However, if this criticism is undertaken in such a way that it calls into question all the necessities that are embedded within religion, and conceives them as nothing but deceit of ideology, it has adopted an erroneous position. Using his own critical hermeneutics, Habermas attempts to question all absolute cultural and religious truths in order to pursue his unfinished project of modernity. Despite a number of worthy criticisms against philosophical hermeneutics, Habermas created a groundwork to attack religious knowledge. His theory follows Marx's, Nietzsche's and Freud's hermeneutic theories, which negate theology.

2.   Habermas has borrowed the notion of a "fusion of horizons" from Gadamer. This notion requires that interpretation should involve a combination of one's intelligence horizon and that of text. That is, understanding is

the product of a continued dialogue that the interpreter conducts with the text. Under Habermas's view, the role of an author begins to fade because, in practice, the discovery of an author's intention is ignored.

In summary, utilising the key themes above, Habermas tries to capture a situation in which conflicts are rationally resolved through a mode of the intersubjectivity of mutual understanding within his model of the public sphere. This communication needs to be free of coercion for the best argument to succeed. Habermas emphasises that reaching a mutual understanding and a final consensus are the inherent *telos* of human speech and communication. Put differently, he believes that human beings can get closer to the truth during the process of globalisation by being impartially involved in intercultural dialogue. The rational dialogue that is free from domination, and oriented towards intersubjective understanding and consensus is the type of activity appropriate for global and local communities. Thus, Habermas aims to overthrow the monological individualism of liberal democracy and to introduce deliberative democracy. Deliberative democracy places an emphasis on people involving themselves in the processes of free discussion and unrestricted conversation in order to reach an intersubjective mutual understanding. In this regard, Habermas holds that the validity of social norms is grounded only in the intersubjectivity of mutual understanding of intentions, and secured by the general recognition of obligations. This might be thought to undermine the need for religion, pronouncing its theoretical and social-developmental death. Nevertheless, because the separation between the public and private spheres that much secular philosophy (including his own earlier work) envisages has not occurred in practical, and religion has been restored to public life, a further stage of Habermas's thought seeks to re-structure his position with reference to a different evolutionary and historical direction. He asserts that the liberal state must not assume a simple division of peoples' identities into private and public categories when they are involved in a general discourse to formulate public opinion, and as a result he emphasises the key role played by religion in the public sphere.

Habermas (2001: 132) holds that modernity understands itself through its opposition to tradition, precisely because it grounds itself in reason and tries to define its nature and trajectory by means of its own criteria rather than through mythical or metaphysical references, thereby seeking to produce its normativity from within. Through the Enlightenment, for example, modernity sought to devalue and overcome tradition via its commitment to reason. However, while Habermas is well-known for his commitment to modernity as an 'unfinished project', he is also highly critical of what modernity has become, particularly with regard to what he calls the 'goal-directed rationality of the social system'. In light of this, Habermas seeks to reconstruct the project of modernity, releasing it from the control of goal-directed rationality. It is this desire to reconstruct modernity that, in his later thought at least, allows Habermas to recognise the importance of religion even within advanced modern societies.

In fact, Habermas describes how positivism has developed 'one-sidedly' in modernity, and in a way that selectively favours the institutionalisation of goal-directed rationality alone. He considers hermeneutics to be an intersubjective process, and a powerful weapon against positivism. Therefore, hermeneutics 'play an important role in what Habermas would later develop in his theory of communicative action. By mediating understanding from the past as well as between present cultures and groups, it proves itself essential for assisting in the formation of consensus' (Holub, 1991: 64).

Chapter 3: Religiosity and Rationality

This chapter has two main agendas. First, it explores the arguments and assumptions of sociological and philosophical thinkers who have had a significant influence on Habermas's view of modernity in general, and his view of religion in modernity in particular. In exploring the works of Marx and Weber, amongst others, this chapter will note the effects and implications of these works for sociological accounts of both Christianity and Islam in the modern West. Secondly, I aim to develop my engagement with Habermas's work further. What Marx and Weber in particular, bequeathed to Habermas was a critical view of the influence and impact of patterns of instrumental rationality in modernity. It is this instrumental rationalisation that is understood to undermine the importance of religion in modernity, but, more broadly, it also a phenomenon that is central to Habermas's account of the most damaging aspects of modernity as it has developed in the West, which he seeks to confront and overcome through his theory of communicative action. This theory will be explored in the latter part of this chapter.

3.1. Different Theories on Religion: Christianity and Islam

Since the beginning of scientific and sociological research into religion, there have been various theories on religion. In the interim, great theorists such as Marx and Weber introduced fundamental concepts to the area of religious sociology, and produced many important changes and effects. It is worth pointing out that, 'if Max Weber has been described as a bourgeois Marx, Habermas might be summarily characterized as a Marxist Weber' (Outhwaite, 1994: 3).

3.1.1. Karl Marx and Christianity

Karl Marx was born in Germany in 1818, and died in England in 1883. His doctoral dissertation (1841) was on the difference between the philosophies of nature in Democritus and Epicurus. Marx regarded *Capital* to be his most important work, and it was one of the most influential books of the nineteenth century. Habermas (1990b: 62) says that, 'for Marx, society – "the modern political-social reality" – is the ground from which religious life, philosophy, and the bourgeois state have become detached as abstractions'.

Marx was fundamentally and vocally opposed to religion. He announced himself to be an atheist, and held that human nature does not inherently tend to religion, but that religion is the output of social circumstances; namely, it is the same man who creates religion that creates other social institutions. 'For Marx, God is a fantasy, and the happiness offered by religion "illusory"' (Parekh, 1982: 202). Thus, he remarks that the criticism of religion is the premise of all criticism, because:

The Church persecuted the greatest scientists with blind cruelty, torturing them, burning them at the stake, forbidding or destroying their works. The Catholic Church, whose instrument was the Inquisition, was particularly Zealous in this respect. For centuries the Church played an extremely reactionary role and fought pitilessly against the scientific conception of the world and against the democratic and socialist movement. But the development of natural science inevitably caused more and more breaches in the religious and idealistic outlook. That is why the founders of Marxism considered scientific and materialist propaganda as the most powerful weapon in the fight against religion (Marx and Engels, 1957: 9).

Marx was influenced by Hegel, the Young Hegelians, and Feuerbach. Marx believed that Feuerbach had demonstrated that gods have the same characteristics as human beings do, and that religion is an outcome of projecting the human essence onto a divine being that is invested with power over human beings to hold them under control. In religion, people create God, who then appears to them as their creator. Impressed by Feuerbach's theory, Marx defines religion as follows:

The basis of irreligious criticism is: Man makes religion, religion does not make man. In other words, religion is the self-consciousness and self-feeling of man who has either not yet found himself or has already lost himself again (Marx and Engels, 1957: 37). But man is no abstract being encamped outside the world. Man is *the world of man,* the state, society. This state, this society, produces religion, an inverted world-consciousness, because they are an inverted world (Kee, 1990: 46). Religion is the sigh of the oppressed creature, the heart of a heartless world, just as it is the spirit of spiritless conditions. It is the opium of the people (Elster, 1986: 182).

Unlike Hegel, who terms "absolute spirit" or "absolute idea" as "ultimate reality", Marx searches for a fundamental reality in material forces. Man's material production, Marx contends, serves as an infrastructure for a community, with ethics, religion, and metaphysics as parts of its subordination. These subordinate phenomena have no independent existence, and it is people who gradually transform their intellectual outputs, based on progressing their material production. In fact, Marx claims that economic realities form human behaviour:

The simple fact [is] that human beings must have food, drink, clothing and shelter first of all, before they can interest themselves in politics, science, art, religion and the like. This implies that the production of the immediate material means of subsistence, and consequently the degree of economic development of a given people or epoch, form the foundation upon which the state institutions, the legal conceptions, the art, and even religious ideas are built up. It implies that these latter must be explained out of the former, whereas the former have usually been explained as issuing from the latter (Worsley, 1982: 48).

However, Weber challenges Marx with overemphasising religious variables that contribute to all historical evolutions and diversifications. He considers religion as foundational, and economics as a subordinate phenomenon. He believes that Protestantism acted as a prior cause of emerging capitalism, although other conditions have also intervened to promote it, and holds that there was 'mutual reinforcement' between these two variables. At the end of *The Protestant Ethic and the Spirit of Capitalism,* Weber (1930: 183) characterises the notion of 'mutual reinforcement' as follows:

Here we have only attempted to trace the fact and the direction of its influence to their motives in one, though a very important point. But it would also further be necessary to investigate how Protestant Asceticism was in turn influenced in its development and its character by the totality of social conditions, especially economic.

It should be noted that Weber is 'sometimes mistakenly interpreted as suggesting that Protestantism alone transformed the ethical basis of economic life, but he highlighted a variety of other extra-economic factors conductive to the rise of rational capitalism' (Shilling and Mellor, 2001: 80). Craib (1992: 188) also alleges that 'for the Frankfurt School, however, the roots of instrumental reason go much further back than the development of capitalism. Rather as Max Weber traced the origins of the Spirit of Capitalism back through Christianity to Judaic beliefs, so Adorno and Horkheimer find the origins of instrumental reason in Judaism'. Nevertheless, 'Ferdinand Kolegar, having rejected the fallacy of Weber's critics, of linking causally Protestantism and capitalism, referred to the "mutual reinforcement" and "elective affinity" between the economic ethic of modern capitalism and the religious ethic of radical Protestantism, both of which rest upon common "spirit" or ethos' (Turner, 1974: 11).

It appears that Marx can be criticised on the grounds that, whilst the economy serves as an important contributor to human society, it cannot be concluded that the economy stands alone as an infrastructure. In most instances, as historical evidence shows, ethics and policy, religion and metaphysics, and arts and literature have affected economies and fixed their directions, although they have also, from time to time, been influenced by economies.

Marx alleges that human history is the story of class struggles. All these perpetual conflicts and class struggles occur among those who possess objects (usually the wealthy), and those who need to work to survive (usually the poor). Marx believes that religion has led to the submission of poor and oppressed people in the course of history, whilst enabling them to evade the harsh realities of their existences. However, for the rich, who possess the tools of production, he holds that it has also presented a far better thing – an ideology. Relying on this meditation, Marx defines the social principles of Christianity as follows in *The Holy Family, or Critique of Critical Criticism: against Bruno Bauer and Company:*

The social principles of Christianity justified the slavery of Antiquity, glorified the serfdom of the Middle Ages and equally know, when necessary, how to defend the oppression of the proletariat, although they make a pitiful face over it. The social principles of Christianity preach the necessity of a ruling and an oppressed class, and they have for the latter is the pious wish the former will be charitable. The social principles of Christianity declare all vile acts of the oppressors against the oppressed to be either the just punishment of original sin and other sins or trials that the Lord in his infinite wisdom imposes on those redeemed. The social principles of Christianity preach cowardice, self-contempt, abasement, submission, dejection (Marx and Engels, 1957: 74).

However, in contrast to the characterisation of Christianity that Marx provides, the world's major religions, in particular Islam, have also had a record of opposing tyrants and colonisers and creating highly positive changes in society. Thus, religion can be a protest against domination and exploitation. Certainly, where those who advocated these religions were workers, peasants, and the impoverished, there has been an emphasis on fighting rather than reinforcing social injustice. In this regard it can be noted that Almighty God promised them a final victory over the arrogant of the Earth, as evidenced by the Glorious Koran, chapter 28 verse 5: 'And we wished to be Gracious to those who were Being depressed on the land. To make them leaders and make them heir'. Furthermore, while tracing the relationship between society and religious life in both Indonesia and Morocco, Geertz concludes (in *Islam Observed*) that Islam has a revolutionary character that opposes oppression and injustice. He also holds that 'Islam is basically the Islam of saint worship and moral severity, magical power and aggressive piety' (Geertz, 1971: 9).

Another point to note is that Marx conceives of religion as an ideology whose chief function is to justify the injustices inflicted on lower classes of society. He also termed religion as the 'opium of the people', which means that religion is a means for deducting aggressive revolts and legitimating a ruling system. Indeed, it hinders the oppressed from revolting against their government. In addition to this, Habermas (1972: 282) contends that power and ideology also distort communication.

It is reasonable to accept that, during different historical periods, many superstitions, illusions, and hallucinations entered into religion, and that these have distorted some religious truths and let religion fall into continuous abuse by authorities. Religion has often become an instrument for rich aristocrats. By overemphasising particular aspects of religion, and obliterating other dimensions of it, oppressors have sought to delude people and to take advantage of their simplicity. By focussing on this aspect of the use of religion, scholars such as Marx and Habermas came to attribute social disorders and injustices to the intermediation of religion in the public sphere, but they did not consider that this can be more accurately seen as representing religion's mismanagement by theologians and ruling institutions:

In this way, the intellectuals of the 17th, 18th and 19th centuries, especially those of the 19th century who said, "Religion has continuously been the opium of the people," are correct. What religion are they speaking about? They are referring to a religion which existed in history and they analyze that. They see that the religion narcotized the masses of the people. We must say that those who say that religion was a factor to justify the social and economic domination of the minority over the majority are correct. It is Ali [the first leader of the Shiite faith] who calls these religions, the religions of multitheism [*shirk*], 'merchantile religion', 'the religion of those who are afraid'. Thus what worship is the worship of "*My religion...*"? (Shariati, 1988: 49, 58).

As Marx comments, religion is the 'opium of the people': a reflection of human misery that gives illusory comfort and dissuades people from struggling for social equality. That is, religion does not heal any disease, but provides an interim relief that bestows a false happiness. Religion provokes people to avoid comprehending real life and estranges human beings from themselves: 'Thus Marx's concept of alienation embraces the manifestations of "man's estrangement from-*nature* and from *himself*" on the one hand, and the expressions of this process in the relationship of *man-mankind* and man and man on the other' (Meszaros, 2005: 15). To put it another way:

How will they organize, plan their attack, and begin their revolt if their hope of heaven leaves them no more wish to change their life than the "sigh of protest" we find in otherworldly rituals and ceremonies? Religion shifts their gaze upward to God, when it should really be turned downward to the injustice of their material, physical situation ... For him, belief in God and in some heavenly salvation is not just an illusion; it is an illusion that paralyzes and imprisons. It paralyzes workers by drawing off into fantasy the very motives of anger and frustration they need to organize a revolt. Desire for heaven makes them content with earth. At the same time, religion also imprisons; it promotes oppression by presenting a system of belief which declares that poverty and misery are facts of life which ordinary people must simply accept and embrace (Pals, 1996: 142-143).

What such a view fails to account for, however, is the degree to which religion can actively encourage people to initiate and embrace change: according to the Koran (chapter 13, verse 11), 'Verily never will Allah [God] change the condition of a people until they change it themselves'.

Marx considers alienation to be displayed by the fact that religious people insist on calling themselves miserable sinners and attribute all glory and ethical ideals to God. The lack of self-realisation is one of the main forms of alienation, which emanates from economic estrangement. Rather, 'religious distress is at the same time the expression of real [economic] distress and the *protest* against real distress ... The abolition of religion as the illusory happiness of the people is required for their real happiness' (Marx and Engels, 1957: 38).

Although it might be assumed that Marx challenges all religions, his criticism focuses solely on Christianity (whether it is the Catholic or the Protestant faith) in a particular historical period of the 18th century. His comments do not apply to the other religions, particularly Islam. According to Turner (1974: 7), Marx had little or nothing to say about Islam. In fact, his theories cannot be generalised as he expected, and thus fail to be comprehensive. From an Islamic perspective, Marx's criticism of religion is unrealistic; it is 'too narrow, too exclusive, too shortsighted in its conception of human potential' (McLellan, 1987: 170).

Marx expounds that: 'the Church with its sacred institutions often legitimized and solidified the State and other parts of the social fabric, society was frequently conceived as an affair of divine ordinance rather a product of human freedom' (Davis, 1994: 22). Acknowledging that policy is separate from religion, Marx believes that no government must be founded on religion because there is no future for religion. He anticipates that the 'forces of the industrial proletariat, at first merely in revolt, will, under the leadership of a theoretically enlightened avant-garde, form themselves into a movement that seizes political power for the purpose of revolutionizing society' (Habermas, 1987: 340). It cannot be ignored that Marx's notion of alienation furnishes an important and valuable insight into the modern world, which is that:

In modern, industrial societies, people are seen as isolated individuals or as a conglomerate mass, but in either case everything that is good about individuality is seen as having disappeared. The modern world is seen as a spiritual desert, any meaning attached of life as disappearing, and people are empty and lost souls in a world they cannot understand. These themes appear in different ways in the work of the founding figures of sociology, in Marx as alienation, in Durkheim as anomie and in Weber as disenchantment. In the work of the Frankfurt School, the bleak landscape has turned into a nightmare: the social world becomes an electronic monster feeding off its own members, manipulating and absorbing any resistance that may be offered (Craib, 1992: 183).

However, Marx's expectations have not proven correct, and have thoroughly failed because, during recent decades, communist systems have begun to collapse, and religion has started to become restored to the public sphere. Indeed, there is a type of post-secularism at the level of world community. For example, if Marx had lived in the 20th century, he would not have been able to account for the collapse of the Soviet Union in 1989. Nor would he have been able to explain anti-colonisation and the anti-despotic Iranian religious revolution that took place in 1978, because he held that 'there is a correlation between the advance of socialism and the decline of religion. Since socialism is the creation of the working class, it is there that irreligion should increasingly be concentrated' (McLellan, 1987: 169). Consequently, Marx was truly unable to perceive real religion as a stimulating force for exercising any social changes. According to Shariati, Marx was also unable to understand that religion cannot be eradicated for good because it remains stable and alive as a 'school of thought and action' forever. The most striking thing about school of thought and action is that, from the time when religion turned from a school of thought and action to 'cultural knowledge and a collection of religious sciences, it lost its ability and power for creating movement, commitment, responsibility and social awareness and it was held back from having any effect or influence upon the fate of human society' (Shariati, 1989: 26).

3.1.2. Max Weber and Christianity

No one knows who will live in this cage in the future, or whether at the end of this tremendous development entirely new prophets will arise, or there will be a great rebirth of old ideas and ideals, or, if neither, mechanized petrification, embellished with a sort of convulsive self-importance. For of the last stage of this cultural development, it might well be truly said: "Specialists without spirit, sensualists without heart; this nullity imagines that it has attained a level of civilization never before achieved" (Weber, 1930: 182).

Weber (1864-1920) was one of the great German classical sociologists. Building on the '*Geisteswissenschaft* tradition of Heinrich Rickert and Wilhelm Dilthey, Weber developed a method of sociological analysis which focused on the subjective meaning of action from the point of view of the social actor rather than on behaviour' (Turner, 1974: 39). Weber grew up within a Protestant family, and his most important work on religion is *The Protestant Ethic and the Spirit of Capitalism.* He is referred to as the initiator of the hermeneutic methodology, and considered to be the founder of comparative sociology. He wrote on Christianity, Islam, Judaism, Hinduism, Buddhism, and Confucianism, although he had a poor and sometimes flawed knowledge of Islam: 'Weber's treatment and interpretation of Islam is in fact very weakly connected with the specific thesis about Calvinism which Weber first developed in *The Protestant Ethic and the Spirit of Capitalism* and died before his Religions-soziologie was completed by a full study of Islam' (Turner, 1974: 7-8). Like Comte, Spencer, Marx, Durkheim and Freud, Weber believed in the secularisation thesis, and held that illogical constructions such as religion were losing their preponderance and social penetration, and would eventually be driven to the margins with the development of logical and modern societies. In this respect, Habermas (1992: 120) believes that:

Metaphysics also belongs to the world-historical process described by Max Weber from the perspective of the sociology of religion as rationalization and by Karl Jaspers as the cognitive advance of the 'axial period' (extended from Buddha via Socrates and Jesus up to Mohammed).

Weber, like Marx, believed religion to be man-made and that divine credence and rites are all products of historical circumstances that will be put aside in the modern period. Nevertheless, Weber noted the way that religion produces changes in society, and looked at religion less negatively than Marx did. Unlike Marx, Weber disapproved of the fact that religious conceptions are only reflections of materialistic opportunities and the interests of social groups. Indeed, he held that ideal interests constitute fundamental aspects of the human position rather than his materialistic interests. From the above sketch, it can be seen that Weber inclined to give a greater autonomy to religion than did Marx. He emphatically rejected the view that 'the specific nature of a religion is a simple "function" of the social stratum which appears as its characteristic bearer, or that it represents the stratum's "ideology", or that it is a "reflection" of the stratum's material or ideal interest-situation' (McLellan, 1987: 164).

Moreover, 'many people know that it was Weber who first connected Protestantism with capitalist economics in the essays of his well-known book *The Protestant Ethics and the Spirit of Capitalism*' (Pals, 1996: 239). In *The Protestant Ethics and the Spirit of Capitalism,* Weber tried to demarcate the influences of religion over capitalism, and did not seek to prove that the spirit of capitalism has only emanated from a Protestant ethic. He (1930: 91) explains that:

We have no intention whatever of maintaining such a foolish and doctrinaire thesis as that the spirit of capitalism ... could only have arisen as the result of certain effects of the Reformation, or even that capitalism as an economic system is a creation of the reformation. In itself, the fact that certain important forms of capitalistic business organization are known to be considerably older than the Reformation is a sufficient refutation of such a claim. On the contrary, we only wish to ascertain whether and to what extent religious forces have taken part in the qualitative formation and the quantitative expansion of that spirit over the world.

Rationality is one of the fundamental concepts in Weber sociology. He considered instrumental rationality to be rooted in a Protestant ethic. He held that Protestantism, or the religious viewpoint developed by Calvin, had brought about a spirit of contentment and asceticism that did not contrast with the principles of capitalism. In fact:

The Protestant 'calling' was not part of Catholic theology but was introduced by Luther [1483-1546], who suggested that individuals were religiously obliged to fulfil their duty in worldly affairs. Work was no longer religiously neutral but a religious duty. There developed, however, two major versions of the calling; the Lutheran and the Calvinist. Luther's conception was relatively traditionalist, in that it emphasised that people should accept and adapt to their labours as a 'divine ordinance' (Weber, 1904-5: 85). Calvin's conception of the calling, in contrast, p Capitalism laced priority on the *doing* of work rather on adaptation. As Weber (1904-5: 160) emphasises, 'this calling is not, as it was for the Lutheran, a fate to which he must submit ... but God's commandment to the individual to work for the divine glory' (Shilling and Mellor, 2001: 80).

In other words, Weber argues that Catholics consider monastic life to be the highest form of living because they believe that a holy life cannot be linked to mundane affairs. Monks and nuns avoid mundane affairs by sacrificing and devoting their whole lives to God. Moreover, Catholics believe that priests and the others of the Christian church intercede with God on behalf of people, and their sins can be forgiven only if they are interceded to God. In his attack on the Pope and Catholic rules, Luther criticised this intercession and announced a monastic life to be indecent. Luther's conception of the calling explains that:

The only way of living acceptably to God was not to surpass worldly morality in monastic asceticism, but solely through the fulfilment of the obligations imposed upon the individual by his position in the world ... It and it alone is the will of God, and hence every legitimate calling has exactly the same worth in the sight of God (Weber, 1930: 80-81).

However, Luther also interprets a social life in a conventional way since he believes that one's belief in God is the origin of salvation and, thus, 'for Luther the concept of the calling remained traditionalistic. His calling is something which man has to accept as a divine ordinance, to which he must adopt himself' (Weber, 1930: 85).

Calvin, who followed Luther, put aside this traditionalistic understanding, and announced that work is the only way to prove one's faith and achieve salvation. In the Calvinistic movement, work was counted as worship, and one 'who performed no good works was not a true believer' (Weber, 1930: 141). Consequently, Calvinists amassed vast wealth from their hard labour and, finally, the huge monastery that was built by Calvinism developed into a large factory, which aimed at a voluminous production, but resulted in a voluminous consumption that was not in keeping with God's commandments (Abazari, 1998: 143-145).

Weber aimed to show that the concept of a duty was originally yielded by the religious reform movement, and that fulfilment of function in mundane affairs is the uppermost form of an individual's moral activity. To put it simply, 'the valuation of the fulfilment of duty in worldly affairs is the highest form which the moral activity of the individual could assume' (Weber, 1930: 80). In *The Protestant Ethic*, Weber (1930: 176-177) alludes:

As far as the influence of the Puritan outlook extended ... it favoured the development of a rational bourgeois economic life; it was the most important, and above all the only consistent influence in the development of that life. It stood at the cradle of the modern economic man (1930: 174). A specifically bourgeois economic ethics had grown up. With the consciousness of standing in the fullness of God's grace and being visibly blessed by Him, the Bourgeois business man, as long as he remained within the bounds of formal correctness, as long as moral conduct was spotless and the use to which he put his wealth was not objectionable, could follow his pecuniary interests as he would and feel that he was fulfilling a duty in doing so. The power of religious asceticism provided him in addition with sober, conscientious, and unusually industrious workmen, who clung to their work as to a life purpose willed by God. Finally, it gave him the comforting assurance that the unequal distribution of Divine Providence, which in these differences, as in particular grace, pursued secret ends unknown to men. Calvin himself had made the much-quoted statement that only when the people, i.e. the mass of labourers and craftsmen, were poor did they remain obedient to God.

According to Weber, this Protestant attitude to duty (unlike the Catholic one) holds that a piece of work must be orderly and earnestly engaged in, and must not lead to extreme consumption. This idea has provided the best cultural grounds for private investment and bourgeoisie capitalism in the West. Finally, Weber construes the spirit of capitalism as resulting in a loss of meaning and freedom, and the fall of an 'iron cage' over man. In fact, 'Lukacs brings together Marx and Weber, reification and rationalization. Just as, for Hobbes, man is a wolf to man, in developed capitalism men and women become commodities for one another, trapped in a nexus of apparently objective and increasingly instrumental relations' (Outhwaite, 1994: 80). In approaching Weber's ideas, Habermas (1984: 228) argues that:

The Protestant ethics of the calling fulfils necessary conditions for the emergence of a motivational basis for purposive-rational action in the sphere of social labour. With the value-rational anchoring of purposive-rational action orientation, it satisfies, to be sure, only the starting conditions of capitalist society; it gets capitalism underway, without, however, being able to secure the conditions for its own stabilization. In Weber's view, the subsystems of purposive-rational action form an environment that is destructive of the Protestant ethic in the long run; this is all the more so, the more these systems develop in accord with the immanent laws of capitalist growth and of the reproduction of state power.

Like Weber, Charles Davis also considers Christianity to be a source of secularism and capitalism. Davis (1994: 6, 23) holds that 'the last phase of theology's dalliance with the rationalism of the Enlightenment was the theology of secularization, which frees the secular to do its own thing without any check from the supernatural. Reason, once hailed as an instrument of liberation, has become (it is argued) a means of entrapping us in an iron cage of unfreedom, pushing us towards a totally administered, bureaucratized society'. As Habermas (2006b: 150) sums up, 'in the West, Christianity not only fulfilled the initial cognitive conditions for modern structures of consciousness; it also fostered a range of motivations that formed the major theme of the economic and ethical research of Max Weber'.

Weber's views can be challenged on the grounds that he failed to notice that one of the important factors that causes a social economy to be driven for the better in a capitalist system is its misplaced culture of extremely broad ways of consumption, which is itself an 'iron cage'. Furthermore, as Habermas holds, there are two types of instrumental and communicative rationality, and the main problem is the disproportionate growth of instrumental rationality. This 'instrumental rationality surges beyond the bounds of the economy and state into other, communicatively structured areas of life and achieves dominance there at the expense of moral-political and aesthetic-practical rationality, and this produces disturbances in the symbolic reproduction of the lifeworld' (Habermas, 1987: 304-305). On this basis, it can be concluded that Weber understands the notion of rationality in a limited way, and is unable to identify communicative rationality. Challenging Weber, Habermas (1987: 303) points out that: 'Weber, hampered by bottlenecks in the formation of his action-theoretical concepts, equated the capitalist pattern of modernization with societal rationalization generally. Thus, he could not trace the symptomatic manifestations he noted back to the selective exploitation of culturally available cognitive potential'.

3.1.3. Max Weber, Bryan S. Turner and Islam

Weber and Islam, written by Turner, deals with Weber's viewpoints about Islam. This book has brought together and explained Weber's dispersed connotations of Islam in an interesting way. Undoubtedly, an awareness of Weber's views on Islam is important to this book.

However, *Weber and Islam* contains serious deficiencies and inconsistencies in its analysis of Islam. Despite the merit of some of Turner's arguments, which I use as evidence against Weber here, neither Weber nor Turner have understood and appraised Islam properly. As Turner himself admits, both of them are hampered by a deficit of original Islamic resources. Turner (1974: 1, 36) holds that:

This study of Islam grew out of the context of teaching comparative sociology of religion against the background of scarce, inadequate and over-specialized literature on Islam ... It is perfectly proper to point out that Weber did not have access to this factual information and contemporary Koranic interpretation.

Another important point to note is that, whilst Turner repeatedly criticises Weber for ignoring Muslims' interpretations of Islamic realities, Turner also provides incorrect characterisations of Islamic concepts. In short, Weber and Turner regard the outward features of Islam and Islamic nations, with no deliberation or understanding of its other aspects. Drawing conclusions based on such an approach has produced severe deficiencies in Weber's and Turner's work in this area. On this basis, Turner points out that:

Weber's account of Muhammad and the rise of Islam is a totally reductionist argument ... First, there are factual problems in his emphasis on the warrior group in Islam and second, by ignoring the Koranic and other Muslim accounts of early Islam, Weber in effect ignored some basic principles of his own *verstehende* sociology (1974: 32, 34-35).

Another objection that has been raised against Weber regards his failure to study Islam more carefully and comprehensively, as he attempted to learn about Islam solely through the Ottoman Empire and modern Turkish states. In other words, he does not distinguish accurately between Shar'ia (religious law), Muslim's opinions, and the Islamic community. As a result of this, Turner (1974: 8) elucidates that 'because of the problems of consistency within Weber's sociology, no definitive or authoritative interpretation of Weber is genuinely possible'. Turner (1974: 1-2), at the outset of *Weber and Islam* claims that:

As examination of any sociology of religion text-book published in the last fifty years will show the recurrent and depressing fact that sociologists are either not interested in Islam or have nothing to contribute to Islamic scholarship ... There is no major tradition of sociology of Islam and modern research and publication on Islamic issues are minimal. Most sociological comparisons are slanted, therefore, towards such combinations as Christianity and Buddhism, Christianity and Judaism or Hinduism and Buddhism ... All too often major land-marks in Islamic scholarship remain untranslated. Many studies are too specialized to give an adequate coverage of the central sociological issues of Islamic phenomena ... There is consequently a need for studies of Islam which will raise important issues in Islamic history and social structure within a broad sociological framework which is relevant to contemporary theoretical issues.

In the introduction to *Allahs Sonne uber dem abendland; unser arabisches Erbe*, Sigrid Hunke (1975: 1- 4) observes that although the world of Islam has been open to Europeans for over 1,300 years, they have less information on Islam than they do concerning some declined and overthrown civilisations and nations, and the little knowledge that Europeans do have regarding Islam is mostly incorrect. Europeans largely ignore what occurred in their closest neighbourhood during the Middle Ages, that is, period of approximately 800 years during which Muslims had the most advanced civilisation on Earth. The progress made by the Islamic civilisation during this period was greater than that of Greek civilisation. It was Muslims who influenced the Western world much more immediately and multilaterally than the Greeks. This glossing over of history from the appearance of Islam until now is a classic example of how (and the extent to which) a chronology can be substantially impressed by emotions and inclination. Perhaps, as in the past, when Muslims changed the features of the earth, Muslims will be responsible for shaping our destinies in the future. Must not we finally inquire about what we have in common and what connects us, after all these divisions and disparities? This book wishes to extend its thanks to Muslims whom we have long owed.

Moreover, at a roundtable in The Civilisations Dialogues Centre in Tehran, Habermas (2002e: 9) claimed that not only are the opinions about the East and the Middle East expressed by Marx and Weber erroneous, but that they also raise wide range of disputes among scholars. There is not only a traditional perspective that belongs to the West, but also a corresponding culture of criticism and self-criticism, e.g. the European criticism of modernity, and the criticism of rationality in Europe.

Thus, Weber's and Turner's views relating to Islam contain factually misleading errors, which can be summarised as follows:

1- Weber's religious sociology represents the interconnection of religious ethics with an economic order. That is to say, Weber seeks to answer the question: Why did modern rational bourgeois capitalism evolve as a dominant phenomenon only in the West, not in the Islamic communities? To answer this question,

Weber regards Islam as, in many respects, the polar opposite of Puritanism. For Weber, Islam accepts a purely hedonist spirit, especially towards women, luxuries and property. Given the accommodating ethic of the Qur'an, there was no conflict between moral injunctions and the world and it follows that no ascetic ethic of world-mastery could emerge in Islam (Turner, 1974: 12).

It can be conclusively asserted that Weber is not familiar with the content of the Glorious Koran and Islam because neither the Koran nor the morality of earlier Islam advised men to seek pleasure from women, luxuries, and property. Furthermore, if, as Weber thinks, the lack of capitalism in Islamic societies is caused by the lack of ascetic spirit, and if there is no disagreement between the ethical law and that of the mundane in Islam, then Muslims would be motivated towards a profit-seeking morality. However, the economic values of Islam contrast noticeably with those of Western capitalism. Islam emphasises values such as justice and egalitarian; sympathy and charity; and abstention from vices and their evil consequences, such as usury, the amassing of wealth, colonisation, oppression and exploitation – things that are never reconciled with in the values of Western capitalism. The Koran (2: 275) declares that 'those who devour usury will not stand except as stands one whom the Evil One by his touch hath driven to madness. That is because they say: "Trade is like usury," but Allah [God] hath permitted trade and forbidden usury'. Indeed, unlike Weber, Turner (2003: 95-96) himself confesses that:

Islam has an egalitarian appeal, an ascetic world-view, a dynamic conception of social change and through its history provides an alternative therefore to the western model which was imposed by colonization. Islam through its prayer meetings and other religious institutions provided an alternative political and social platform to state institutions, and therefore in Iran and elsewhere religion provided a vehicle for the expression of oppositional and critical viewpoints which governments could not silence, because religion had deep popular roots in the broader community.

The basic point is that, although Islam is opposed to Western capitalism, it is not inconsistent with all of its elements; in particular, Islam does not disagree with industrialisation and with certain features of Western modernity, which can be seen from the flourishing industry during the earlier centuries of Islamic culture. Islam has a lively and creative spirit, and religious views have never barred the expansion of industrial and commercial activities. Turner (1974: 172) believes that:

Islam was, and continued to be, an urban religion of merchants and state officials; many of its key concepts reflect the urban life of a mercantile society in opposition to the values of the desert and of the warrior.

Rodinson (1974: 117) also criticises Weber's views on Islam and alleges that: 'There is nothing to indicate in a compelling way that the Muslim religion prevented the Muslim world from developing along the road to modern capitalism'. Rodinson continues by noting that the growth of financial and commercial capitalism, as well as the production of the partial goods that had been grown in the Middle Ages of Islam, stood at the same ranges of growth as those of the capitalism in feudal Europe. However, this sector stopped growing within Islamic society as a result of the rush of European goods during the period of Western imperialistic expansionism.

As a matter of fact, the most important condition for the development of Western capitalism was the isolation of religion – Protestantism influenced capitalism only when traditional Christianity (or Catholicism) was driven into isolation. Thus, Western capitalism led to the decline of Christianity and stripped the church of any authority to play a role in the public sphere and political affairs. Specifically:

Everyone agrees that economic development and the expansion of market relations has been accompanied everywhere by the disintegration of local community neighbourhoods, of extended family structures, and of the more settled forms of church and religion. Together with the residues of traditional worldviews, all these institutions *once used to* guarantee social reproduction and social integration. Habermas's argument is that now they are either spent or endangered sources of social integration and, accordingly, that motivation and legitimation deficits accrue in several ways (Pusey, 1987: 98-99).

Interestingly, it can be argued that the isolation of religion has played a major part in the creation of Western capitalism on the one hand, but on the other, the isolation of religion can be considered to be a social product of Western capitalism. In fact, 'religion has been shifted into the realm of what is – from the standpoint of the intellectual articulation of a worldview – the irrational; and this has been all the more the case, the further this particular type of rationalization has progressed'

(Habermas, 1984: 229). Turner (1974: 156) can be seen to support this argument when he claims that:

In a secular world, the only place for religion is in the area of interpersonal, rather than public, relations. Paradoxically, the demise of religion as a social bond connecting all aspects of human life was prepared by the reformation itself. Weber's thesis that secularization involves pluralism of conflicting values and the institutional relegation of religion to purely private choices, on the one hand, and that secularization was the social product of capitalism and Protestantism, on the other, has become the base-line of much contemporary sociological research.

Accordingly, John Tomilson suggests that 'the sort of modernity that the West has developed and passed on to the "developing world" is not the only possible historical route out of the chains of tradition ... Modernity as both an intellectual and a political project has a long history of differentiating, excluding and dominating the non-Western parts of the world' (Mirsepassi, 2000: 3-4).

In the same way, Habermas challenges capitalism, and seeks to persuade us that later capitalism brings with it a deepening irrationality; a manipulation of public opinion through the mass media of money and power; a technocratic consciousness (in Weber's negative sense of the iron cage); a repression of ethics, tradition and deliberative democracy; an exploitation of one class for the advantage of another; capital accumulation geared to partial interests rather than to collective needs; and a forced articulation of social needs through large organisations.

It is difficult not to think of Foucault's work and his image of an increasingly "carceral" society. Habermas's description of the role of reification and expertise in defining categorizing and organizing everyday life bears a strong similarity to Foucault's analysis of how the "discourses" associated with the growing organization of modern life create new ways of subjugating people, while ostensibly enhancing their freedom and well-being (White, 1988: 113).

In *Legitimation Crisis*, which is Habermas's best-known statement of his political sociology of advanced capitalist societies, Habermas (1976: 41-94) points to a number of problems that result from advanced capitalist growth: the disturbance to ecological balance; alienation; the self-destructive dangers of international relations; the administrative manipulation of cultural traditions; economic crisis – the requisite quantity of consumable goods is not produced; rationality crisis – the requisite quantity of rational administrative decisions is not forthcoming; legitimation crisis – the requisite quantity of motivations is not generalised; and motivational crisis – the requisite conception of meaning that motivates action is not created. In brief, the penalty for these failures is the withdrawal of legitimation. Indeed, capitalism 'could only be overcome, therefore, through a restoration of the dimension of the practical as such. For Horkheimer and Adorno (and Marcuse), human emancipation could be conceived only as a radical break with "instrumental" or "one-dimensional" thought' (Habermas, 1976: xxi).

2- Weber implicitly suggested that ... the original adherents to Islam were motivated solely in terms of the prospects of booty and conquest ... Therefore, between leader [Muhammad] and followers is not so much a discipleship relation but a patron-client pattern in which a leader supplies booty in return for adherence. Again, we see that even in Weber's account the 'economic factor' is crucial in the acceptance of charisma (Turner, 1974: 23-24).

All Muslims believe that Muhammad, peace be upon him, was a human being, but they also believe that he was the most perfect of God's creatures. For Muslims, Muhammad is located at the heart of Islam. He is the manifestation of all the virtues, such as piety, modesty, honesty, nobility, sincerity, magnanimity, generosity, and dignity. Muslims consider him as their desideratum, and love Muhammad whole-heartedly. This love, Muslims believe, is the key to loving Almighty God. Respect for Muhammad is like respect for Jesus Christ, Moses, and the Prophets before Muhammad. Furthermore, Muslims in the earlier period of Islam never coveted to seize booties or conquer nations. They were never stimulated by any economic interest whatsoever, but only for the love of their prophet and Islam, for whom they suffered much torture and pain. In fact, 'this distorted interpretation arose from the fact that Muhammad was a more successful political leader than any other human founder of a world religion' (Forward, 1997: 63).

3- The prophet, who was for Weber the epitome of charismatic leadership, based his message on an appeal to an idealized past in order to break with a corrupt present. Charisma may, therefore, be based on traditional norms rather than representing a distinct break with them. In addition to these examples from Weber's own theory of charisma, there are important philosophical reasons why charisma must be understood as a particular interpretation of existing social frameworks rather than a creation of radically new world-views (Turner, 1974: 25-26).

Both Weber and Turner are wrong here, because the Koran regularly challenges both the organisations of current and historic nations. There have been false prophets and absurd religions throughout history that have mocked the messenger of God, and God says that: 'at length I seized them, and how (awful) was my punishment' (Koran, 13: 32). It cannot, therefore, be claimed that the Prophets based their missions on an idealised retrogression.

4- Turner (1974: 33) contends that:

Yet, the miraculous nature of the Qur'an did not rest, even for the Prophet, on a claim of specific originality.

Islam, *contra* Turner, considers itself as the heir to a lengthy chain of Prophets, from Adam to Muhammad. According to Nasr (2007: 37, 40), Islam belongs to all of the 124,000 prophets, although Islam does not admit that it has formulated and inherited its doctrines and teachings from their historical resources, because a prophet owes nothing to anybody except to God, as he receives everything from divine sovereignty. Islam contends that it has received all God's messages, and that Muhammad was the world's final prophet. However, as well as being closely related to the monotheistic religions, including Christianity and Judaism, Islam is also internally related to other religions, such as Hinduism, Pythagoreanism, Zoroastrianism and Confucianism.

For Muslims, the Glorious Koran perfected the previous Holy Scriptures, but the Koran has never *depreciated* other Scriptures. In its various verses, the Koran introduces itself as a testifier of previous Holy Scriptures, in particular the Old and New testaments, and maintains their immutable principles. However, it cancels their mutable branches in order to adapt changes that have occurred in human positions and needs over the course of time. On this basis, the Koran can be claimed to have a specific originality, and it is the miracle of Muhammad as the most eloquent text.

5- Turner believes that:

The Shi'a preserved the belief that: God might one day speak to His community through prophets (1974: 88).

Muslims hold the world will never experience any other revelation after Islam, as this is clearly stated in the Koran. In other words, 'there will be no other prophet after Muhammad because the message or the revelation given to him – the Qur'an – is Divine guidance completed' (Hamid, 1989: 18). Interestingly, no other preceding holy scriptures claimed this. Moreover, all Muslims, whether Shiites or Sunnites, accept the termination of prophecy. Therefore, Turner has mistakenly attributed this belief to the Shi'a.

6- Turner says that:

In Weber's view, this Jewish idea was the model by which Islam developed the idea of the holy war as a religious duty; it was the peculiar combination of an Arab warrior group, the idea of a universal god, the holy war and faith as submission which gave Islam all the features of a warrior religion (1974: 95).

Also, in his article 'Politics and Culture in Islamic Globalism', Turner (2003: 91) points out that *jihad* involves a struggle against unbelief.

In the modern period, no Islamic terminology has been distorted and misunderstood more than *jihad* has. To put it another way, 'Islam is perhaps the most misunderstood religion to the West, and many stereotypes still hinder clarity about its tenets and practices' (Firestone, 1999: 13):

The term "holy war" is a European invention and derives from the study of war in its European context. It does not define types of warfare, such as "primitive" or "modern", nor does it define whether a specific engagement is defensive preemptive, or initiatory. Rather, in its most broad definition, the term defines a form of justification for engaging in war by providing religious legitimization ... The semantic meaning of the Arabic term *jihad* has no relation to holy war or even war in general. It derives, rather from the root *j.h.d.,* the meaning of which is to strive, exert oneself, or take extraordinary pains ... such an object is often categorized in the literature as deriving from one of three sources: a visible enemy, the devil, and aspects of one's own self. There are, therefore, many kinds of jihad, and most have nothing to do with warfare. "Jihad of the heart," for example, denotes struggle against one's own sinful inclinations, while "jihad of the tongue" requires speaking on behalf of the good and forbidding evil (Firestone, 1999: 15-17).

In the Arabic language, *jihad* is derived from the root jhd, whose meaning is 'to strive hard', and refers to the practice of unceasing effort. Within Islam, there are two types of *Jihad*: A- The greater or inner *jihad*, and B- The lesser *Jihad*. Let us start by looking at the first. The greater or inner *jihad* is the struggle to cleanse the soul of deficiencies and impurities, and the struggle to remove negligence and ignorance in order to embrace God's commandment.

From Rumi's (1207-1273) point of view, this struggle involves three layers of the self: *1- Nafs-e-Ammara:* Nafs, or the ego, is the mother of all idols, which forces mankind to be obsessed with lust, greed, and power. *2- Nafs-e-Lavvama:* This is a higher layer of being, in which the person is consciously involved in a conflict against the lower layer of his Nafs. The person begins to analyse himself, and to purify and control his desires through reason. *3- Nafs-e-Motmaenna:* In this stage, the lover is totally immersed in the ocean of divine love. The lover and beloved are never without each other, and they act and react through each other (Bahram, 2011: 78-82). This stage must be experienced to be understood. As Rumi notes:

This is what is signified by the words Anal-Haqq 'I am God'. People imagine that it is a presumptuous claim, whereas it is really a presumptuous claim to say Anal-abd 'I am the slave of God's; and Anal-Haqq 'I am God' is an expression of great humility. The man who says Anal-abd 'I am the slave of God' affirms two existences, his own and God's, but he that says Anal-Haqq 'I am God' has made himself non-existent and has given himself up and says 'I am God', e.g. 'I am nought, He is all: there is no being but God's'. This is the extreme of humility and self-abasement (Ovanessian, 1991: 411).

Love is an experience that is situated beyond reason and that cannot be described in words. Indeed, 'the pen breaks when it is to describe Love' (Schimmel, 1982: 101). To sum up, Rumi's account of his spiritual journey is simple: 'Three short phrases tell the story of my life: I was raw, I got cooked, and I burned' (Lewis, 2000: 404).

From Kierkegaard's (1813-1855) point of view, this struggle also has three stages: *1-The Aesthetic Stage:* Life is defined as a search for beauty and joy, and the person who lives in this stage is like non-human animals. *2- The Moral Stage:* In this stage, the person is pure and honest in character and behaviour. *3- The Religious Stage:* The individual achieves faith, which is an enthusiastic and energetic movement towards eternal happiness – a movement that is strengthened by the will. The truth of faith can never be 'objective' – it is always personal, internal, and, as a result, 'subjective' – that is, it can never be described (Bahram, 2011: 77-81).

Kierkegaard believes that man must first reject the objectivity of the aesthetic life where in he is a slave to things. Next he must develop the responsible inwardness of duty and self-fulfilment, but a still greater subjectivity is found in the life in which exists a passionate tension of concern for eternal blessedness (Arbaugh, 1968: 211).

From the spiritual point of view, 'all the "pillars" of Islam can be seen as being related to *jihad*. The fundamental witnesses (shahadah), "there is no divinity but Allah" and "Muhammad is the messenger of Allah", the daily prayers (*salat* or *namaz*), which constitute the heart of the Islamic rites, the fast of Ramadan, *hajj* and *Zakat* or religious tax' (Nasr, 1990: 31-32).

The lesser *jihad*: 'The Twelver Shiites hold *jihad* can only be waged under the leadership of the rightful Imam. After the absence of the last one in 873[A.D.], no lawful *jihad* can be fought' (Peters, 1996: 4). Indeed, all Shiite theologians, and a majority of Sunnite ones, hold that *jihad* can only be used for defence, and cannot be the grounds for initiating a verdict for Muslims to go to war. Thus, it is a defensive, not an offensive or aggressive act: 'The word "defence" in its general meaning means resistance against an existing Zulm or injustice and oppression. Islam never gives permission to be humiliated, while at the same time it strongly advocates peace' (Mutahhari, 1985: 24, 27). It is necessary to emphasise that no *jihad* is ever waged in the non-Islamic nations, and that those who are performing acts of terror in the West in the name of *jihad* have abused this holy term. The Koran (5: 32) declares that 'if anyone slew a person ... it would be as if he slew the whole people. And if anyone saved a life, it would be as if he saved the life of the whole people'. However:

It must be remembered, ... that even in cases where the idea of *jihad* has been evoked in certain parts of the Islamic world, it has not usually been a question of religion simply sanctioning war but rather of the attempt of a society in which religion remains of central concern to protect itself from being conquered either by military and economic forces or by ideas of an alien nature. This does not mean, however, that in some cases, especially in recent times, religious sentiments have not been used or misused to intensify or legitimize a conflict. But to say the least, the Islamic world does not have a monopoly on this abuse, as the history of other civilizations, including even that of the secularized West, demonstrates so amply (Nasr, 1990: 30).

Indeed, 'any attempt to ground upon religious faith a particular political claim as absolute or unalterable is invalid as a misuse of religious language. It is misuse because it does not respect the way religious language is created and functions' (Davis, 1994: 114).

The Glorious Koran warns Muslims to be careful not to wage defensive *jihad* as a result of anger, abhorrence, vengeance, or intolerance. The enemy must be treated with kindness and justice. The Koran (5: 8) emphasises that 'let not the hatred of others to you make you swerve to wrong and depart from Justice'.

Once more worth observing is that 'the holy war has ten parts: one is fighting the enemy of Islam, nine are fighting the self' (Netton, 2008: 332).

7- In his discussion of Islamic law, Weber brought into focus ... the inflexible content of the Shari'a (Holy Law) ... (Turner, 1974: 110).

In his introduction to *Weber and Islam*, Turner (1974: 110) points out that 'Weber's own observations on Islam refer almost exclusively to the traditional Arabic location of Islamic culture'. It is natural, therefore, that Weber is ignorant of Islam. He is unable to comprehend the fact that the inflexible content of the Shari'a is adhered to by an isolated few in the Islamic world, whereas most Muslims believe in a dynamic *ijtihad,* or the right to exercise independent judgement to derive new laws. According to Muslims, an intelligible understanding of Shari'a depends on the juridical-prophetic power of legal interpretation (*ijtihad*), and this is not possible unless qualified jurists care and accommodate for the issues and exigencies of particular times and places. Thus, the passage of time brings new issues, which are not explicitly addressed in the available Shari'a, and the function of a qualified religious jurist is to extract any related commandment within the framework of Shari'a. Indeed, reason is the best and the most decisive means of finding the right way to lead both a material and spiritual life.

The rejection of imitation [*taqlid*] is closely associated with the re-opening of 'the gate to ijtihad' (independent reasoning) in the field of law, but it also entailed for al-Afghani an appreciation of rational merits of the Qur'an. In the Qur'an, Muslims find a philosophical content which anticipated many of the discoveries of modern science and technology ... Indeed, 'Abduh went so far as to argue that the real rejection of Islam, the real *kafir*, was the refusal to accept the proof of rational argument. The hallmark of the perfect Muslim community was both law and reason. Muslims could happily accept the results of science and rational inquiry. In any case, Rifa'a al-Tahtawi (1801-73) pointed out that the European sciences were originally Arabic and that the progress of Europe was heavily dependent on the achievements of Islamic Spain (Turner, 1974: 146-147).

Interestingly, Muslims rank reason as being as important as the *Koran* (the divine revelation), *Sunna* (the Prophet's traditions) and *ijma* (the consensus of scholars). Islam is a religion that has centred its theology and beliefs on human reason and intelligence, with The Glorious Koran repeatedly emphasising the importance of one's consciousness, meditation, intuition, deliberation and proofs. Islam prefers an hour of thinking to a yearlong worship, and therefore, contrary to Pope Benedict XVI claims in a lecture that he delivered at the University of Regensburg in Germany on 12th September 2006, these features of Islam allow Muslims to exercise a close relationship between reason and Islam, and show that rationality is compatible with and deeply valued by Islam. Muhammad Reza Hakimi (2002: 2-3) remarks that *ijtihad* is more than sociology; *Ijtihad* builds society. The religion of Islam is a "divine-social" phenomenon and whenever you add the adjective of "social" you point to a triangle: individual, society and sovereignty. Islam, as a "divine-social" phenomenon, must express its expectation from these three units. Islam supports a system that acts as a just administrator, a society where an equity and equanimity prevails, and individuals are honest and faithful. *Ijtihad*, in the age of absenteeism of the Shi'ite's twelfth Imam, can act as an operative power to lead this triangle.

Islam's flexibility lies in the fact that it is not only easy to carry out its requirements, but it also gives Muslims many ways to facilitate acting as it requires, such as blessing, forgiveness, repentance, and attributing other people's actions to veracity.

He [God] has chosen you, and has imposed no difficulties on you in religion; it is the cult of your father Abraham. It is He who has named you Muslims, both before and in this (Revelation); that the Messenger may be a witness for you, and ye be witnesses for mankind. So establish regular prayer, give regular charity, and hold fast to Allah. He is your Protector – the best to protect and the best to help (Koran, 22: 78).

It is interesting to note that, according to the Shi'ite tradition, the findings of religious jurisprudence do not necessarily correspond to real divine laws, because errors may slip into these findings. Thus, the Shi'ite tradition accepts possible criticism, and puts its findings into question. This feature not only accounts for an open, lively, and dynamic *ijtihad*, but also demonstrates the permanent presence of qualified religious jurists in their society.

So far in this chapter, I have considered Marx's and Weber's thought on religion, because their explanations of religion had a great influence on Habermas's early works. For instance, like Marx and Weber, Habermas believed that religion is a pure illusion with harmful individual and societal consequences, being the most extreme example of an ideology that paralyses and imprisons human beings. Thus, religion should not just be dismissed, but dismissed with scorn. In this regard, I have noted significant problems with Weber's interpretation of Islam in particular as an example of some reductive and negative assumptions about religion, which have exercised an influence on the intellectual traditions out of which Habermas's work emerges. As I shall examine in more detail in the next chapter, however, Habermas's recent work displays a significant break away from Marx's and Weber's thought, towards a more positive and optimistic view of religion. Before examining that in detail, it is important, I suggest, to clarify how, despite the influence of Marx and Weber in other respects, this break is made possible by Habermas's arguments concerning universal pragmatics, the ideal speech situation, communicative action, and lifeworld. In what follows, I shall consider how Habermas develops his arguments in this respect.

3.2. Habermas and The Frankfurt School's Critical Theory

Habermas was born in Dusseldorf in 1929 and grew up in Gummersbach. 'He studied philosophy, history, psychology and German literature at the University of Gottingen, and then in Zurich and Bonn, where he obtained his doctorate in 1954 with a rather traditional dissertation on Schelling' (Outhwaite, 1994: 2). He was Adorno's assistant at the Institute for Social Research in the Frankfurt School in 1954. Habermas is considered as one of the outstanding figures in contemporary German intellectualism, thought by many to be the most important sociologist since Weber. He is perceived as a leader of the second generation of the Frankfurt School, and retired from his post there in 1994. He 'lives and writes in Starnberg and teaches part-time in the United States. He still regularly appears in print, and is as active a political and cultural commentator as he ever was' (Finlayson, 2005: xi).

The Frankfurt School, the most prominent institute for Marxist studies in the Western world, 'developed in Germany in the 1920s and 1930s before going into exile during the Nazi era' (Shilling and Mellor, 2001: 109). Its prominent founding members, including Max Horkheimer, Theodor Adorno and Herbert Marcuse, were popularised as messengers of critical theory, which was designed for critiquing and changing society, rather than just understanding and explaining it.

Outhwaite (1994: 5) holds that the term 'critical theory' had two original forms: firstly, it referred to a tradition beginning with Simmel and Lukacs; second, it referred to the works of some of the authors who established firm links with the Frankfurt School. In other words, the term 'Frankfurt School', which is used synonymously with 'critical theory' in the English-speaking world, was employed in West Germany to refer to the Frankfurt Social Research Institute after its re-establishment in 1950. Horkheimer mentions the following characteristics of critical theory:

A critical theory should be critical. This requirement comprised several distinct claims. Generally it meant that the task of theory was practical, not just theoretical: that is, it should aim not just to bring about correct understanding, but to create social and political conditions more conductive to human flourishing than the present ones. More specifically, it meant that the theory had two different kinds of normative aim, diagnostic and remedial. The goal of the theory was not just to determine what was wrong with contemporary society at present, but by identifying progressive aspects and tendencies within it, to help transform society for the better (Finlayson, 2005: 3-4).

To put it another way, critical theory is designed to characterise how the focus on instrumental rationality can hinder agents from achieving their autonomies. A critical theory, then, 'is a reflective theory which gives agents a kind of knowledge inherently productive of enlightenment and emancipation' (Geuss, 1981: 2).

The problems with instrumental rationality, combined with the unfulfilled promises made by Marx, persuaded the Frankfurt School to check and revise Marx's Materialistic Dialectics.

Reviewing Marx's philosophical dialectics, they considered an infrastructural role for reflection, value, culture, and policy. Also, unlike Marx, they became convinced that the history of the human community cannot be constructed from an economically determined progress through primitive communism, the Asiatic mode of production, the feudal system, capitalism and communism. That is, the economy cannot be the infrastructure of culture and policy. The Frankfurt School extended its criticism and research to modernity and positivism by taking the concept of reification from Lukacs, and that of instrumental rationality from Weber. Hence, they showed a pessimistic attitude to the whole project of enlightenment, instrumental rationality, and positivism. Indeed:

In Weber's view, the more society becomes functionally organized and removed from tradition, the less freedom and meaningfulness are available to the individual. Similarly, the Frankfurt School was concerned that rationalization entailed an ultimately senseless proliferation of bureaucratic offices, each issuing in further constraints on the individual. This absurd pursuit of perfect control leads, in the end, only to barbarism. "Enlightenment destroys itself" (Braaten, 1991: 11).

The entire negation of modernity and positivism can be seen clearly in *Dialectic of Enlightenment,* written by Horkheimer and Adorno.

Habermas (1984: 366-399) proposes the term 'critical theory' in *The Theory of Communicative Action,* and claims that Horkheimer and Adorno do not understand "the mastery of nature" as a metaphor. Rather, they reduce the control of external nature, the command over human beings, and the repression of one's own internal nature to a common denominator under the name of "domination": 'domination of nature involves domination of man' (Habermas, 1984: 379).

Challenging this pessimistic diagnosis, McCarthy, in the introduction of *The Theory of Communicative Action* (Habermas, 1984: xxi), suggests that 'it could, at best, disclose the unreason at the heart of what passes for reason, without offering any positive account of its own'.

Although Habermas is an inheritor of the Frankfurt School, he revises their fundamental ideas. While the critical theory of the Frankfurt School was confined to philosophical and materialistic domains, Habermas extended it to other jurisdictions of the social sciences, such as sociology, politics, psychology, ethics, and communication. In fact, he has reconstructed ideas introduced by Kant, Hegel, Marx, Weber, Lukacs, Freud, Parsons, Dilthey, Mead and Durkheim rather than those of the Frankfurt School. Habermas holds that critical theory 'has two sorts of tasks: philosophical and social-scientific ... The former task is that of developing "a theory of rationality" ... The later task investigates the pathologies, disequilibria and new forms of oppositional movements in advanced capitalism' (White, 1988: 128). Habermas describes himself as a Marxist, but his theories and approaches linking the social sciences with the concepts of rational consensus and human emancipation are far removed from Marxist approaches. Indeed, 'while Marx's theory of conflict has been interpreted as a theory of how to change society, Habermas's analysis of positive social change rests on the concept of rational consensus' (Shilling and Mellor, 2001: 122).

Habermas considers both orthodox and neo-orthodox (Frankfurtian) hermeneutics to be imperfect, and introduces humanistic hermeneutics to replace them. To put it another way, after Marx, Marxism was divided into three main branches: orthodox, neo-orthodox, and humanistic.

Habermas's reconstructions of Marx clearly belong to the third stream [humanistic]. In his eyes the other two variants [orthodox and neo-orthodox] are seen as 'scientistic' because they rely on a positivist history or a positivist economic theory, or both. Habermas's Marxism is cautions, tentative, and self-critical. He is far removed from workers and working classes, but for all this is still certainly a man driven, above all, by an intellectual anticipation of a world in which production, labour, and social organization are geared rationally to human needs rather than, as now in the West, irrationally to capital accumulation (profit) (Pusey, 1987: 27).

Habermas is certainly not as optimistic about the progress of science as Marx was. He is also less pessimistic than Horkheimer or Adorno were concerning positivism, modernity, and rationalisation. In his challenge to Materialism, he argues that by taking a non-critical approach to technological hegemony, Marx, along with the positivists, contributed to the suppression of any criticism of the Marxist regime. Indeed, Marxism, like positivism, is a philosophy that does not make room for self-criticism. Habermas also considered metaphysical realism as a pre-critical philosophy that makes itself immune from critique. In addition,

The degeneration of the Russian revolution into Stalinism and technocratic social management; the failure hitherto of mass revolution in the West; the absence of mass proletarian revolutionary class consciousness; the frequent collapse of Marxist theory into either a deterministic, objectivistic science or a pessimistic culture critique: all, he holds, are important features of recent times ... Habermas contends that in light of these events, doubt can be cast on the validity of Marx's work, the general Marxian framework and on many other well known theories of society. He finds it necessary, therefore, to assess, and in fact reformulate, the major traditions of social thought (Held, 1990: 250).

However, like Marx, Habermas contends that human beings must work to live, and they become familiar with their nature by doing so, which then enables them to dominate and govern it.

Likewise, Habermas challenges Weber and the Frankfurt School claiming that they cannot distinguish between instrumental rationality and communicative rationality. He argues that they entirely deny rationality and modernity, but that rationality cannot be equated with what Weber called instrumental rationality. As Calhoun notes (1992: 292), 'in contrast with Horkheimer and Adorno, he [Habermas] upheld the Enlightenment's progressive tradition'. Habermas believes that the project of modernity has not yet been fulfilled, and that this has caused contemporary social crises. However, if it could be developed and completed, it would emancipate human beings from Weber's iron cage. Hence, 'Habermas's latest work, in particular, provides a new and potentially fruitful approach to social rationalisation and modernity which allows for a distinction between the advance represented by modern forms of life and their deformations or pathologies' (Roderick, 1986: 166-167). While Habermas believes in the utilitarian aspects of instrumental rationality's achievements in dominating nature, he asserts that this positivism encroaches on the public sphere and the everyday social lives of human beings. Its consequences are the colonisation of the lifeworld, reification, commodity fetishism, and the suppression of individuality. In other words, not only does positivism degenerate humanity into an object that is controlled, monitored, and manipulated, it also causes the decline of hermeneutics and the critical social sciences. On the other hand, the critical social sciences, 'notably psychoanalysis and the critique of ideology, are governed, like philosophy, by an emancipatory cognitive interest which operates through self-reflection' (Outhwaite, 1987: 81). In order to transform society so that the good, happy and rational life can be realised:

Habermas has been concerned systematically to develop its philosophical underpinnings. This involved a reconstruction of some of the central theses of classical Greek and German philosophy: the inseparability of truth and virtue, of facts and values, of theory and practice. The project is defined as a 'struggle for the critical soul of science' and 'the scientific soul of criticism' (Held, 1990: 250).

Having developed the new concepts of critical theory; universal pragmatics and the ideal speech situation; instrumental rationality and communicative action; the uncoupling of lifeworld and system; Habermas tries to reconstruct, and complete the critical theory.

Habermas's solution is to expand the public sphere or communicative action: an action that can bring union without preventing others from being different. In summary:

The single purpose of the [Habermas's] work is to anticipate and to justify a better world society – one that affords greater opportunities for happiness, peace, and community. Since Habermas is also a rationalist the better society is the more rational society, in short, a society that is geared to collective needs rather than to arbitrary power (Pusey, 1987: 14).

As McCarthy explains in his introduction to *Communication and the Evolution of Society* (Habermas, 1979: vii): 'Habermas introduced his idea of a critical social theory that would be empirical and scientific without being reducible to empirical-analytic science, philosophical in the sense of critique but not of presuppositionless "first philosophy," historical without being historicist, and practical in the sense of being oriented to an emancipatory political practice but not to technological-administrative control'.

3.3. Universal Pragmatics and the Ideal Speech Situation

In order to break new ground and to avoid sabotaging his own project, Habermas must, on one side, avoid all regressions into the philosophy of consciousness. On the other hand, his model of social action must guard against all tendencies to scientize society into a thing-like entity that would again subsume all action under a false empiricism of cause and behaviour. And the whole project has to be carried off in a way that will rescue Weber and Marx (and also Durkheim, Parsons, and Mead) from their own 'mistakes', as it explains, more clearly than before, how late capitalist society has developed 'one-sidedly' and in a way that selectively favours the institutionalization of only instrumental and rational purposive-structures of action (Pusey, 1987: 75).

Therefore, the three major thrusts of this transposition into the paradigm of communication are universal pragmatics and the ideal speech situation; instrumental rationality and communicative action; and lifeworld and system.

Habermas utilises the linguistic traditions of Chomsky, Wittgenstein, Austin, and Searle to define universal pragmatics, and calls it a reconstructive science that seeks to discover the rule of human communication. Universal pragmatics, or what Habermas later called 'formal pragmatics', is closely intertwined with the idea of democracy because it contains actions based on dialogue and intersubjective understanding. Although the philosophy of history, the evolution of reason and subjectivity are important for Hegel, Habermas endeavours to substitute them with the concept of reconstructive science. Universal pragmatics is opposed to the "philosophy of the subject", which is philosophy of monologue. In *Habermas: A Critical introduction,* Outhwaite (1994: 39) elucidates that:

The philosophy of the subject does not offer an adequate account of communicative experience: in Richard Bernstein's phrase, it "obscures and even blocks the way to grasping the intrinsic intersubjective and dialogical character of communicative action". Habermas therefore began to pursue a strategy of generalizing some relatively new analyses of communication into a more holistic and historical theory.

In addition to this (and in opposition to Marx who sought to found a society wherein no work has been distorted), Habermas uses universal pragmatics to try to show how there could be a society in which human communication is not distorted. Indeed, under the modernist view, only an individual can perceive the world and distinguish between truth and falsehood. Contrastingly, postmodernists deny that an individual is like the axis of society. Habermas, however, develops an intermediate view on this. According to him, all human beings can act as subjects, and for that reason he uses the term "collective subject". This collective subject is crystallised into the public sphere by way of discourse, mutual understanding and, finally, consensus. Thus, the public sphere is able to discover true natural laws. The consensus theory of truth is an essential concept in Habermas's work, and in *The theory of Communicative Action*, he contends that 'no one would enter into moral argumentation if he did not start from the strong presupposition that a grounded consensus could in principle be achieved among those involved' (Habermas, 1984: 19).

In his article 'What Is Universal Pragmatics?', Habermas (1979: 26) defines the fundamental goal of universal pragmatics as follows:

The basic universal-pragmatic intention of speech-act theory is expressed in the fact that it thematizes the elementary units of speech (utterances) in an attitude similar to that in which linguistics does the units of language (sentences). The goal of reconstructive language analysis is an explicit description of the rules that a competent speaker must master in order to form grammatical sentences and to utter them in an acceptable way. The theory of speech acts shares this task with linguistics. Whereas the latter starts from the assumption that every adult speaker possesses an implicit, reconstructible knowledge, in which is expressed his linguistic rule competence (to produce sentences), speech-act theory postulates a corresponding communicative rule competence, namely the competence to employ sentences in speech acts. It is further assumed that communicative competence has just as universal a core as linguistic competence. A general theory of speech actions would thus describe exactly that fundamental system of rules that adult subjects master to the extent that they can fulfil the conditions for a happy employment of sentences in utterances, no matter to which particular language the sentences may belong and in which accidental contexts the utterances may be embedded.

Habermas then examines the universal presuppositions of communicative action. It is this project that produced the two substantial books of *The Communicative Action* in later years, as the concept of universal pragmatics is fundamental for the theory of communicative action. In this article, Habermas (1979: 2) argues that whenever any speech act is performed, the speaker must raise a series of universal validity claims, and must believe that these validity claims can be vindicated by the listener. Thus, whoever seeks to participate in a process aimed at reaching an understanding claims to be:

1. Uttering something understandably;

2. Giving [the listener] something to understand;

3. Thereby making himself understandable; and

4. Coming to an understanding with another person.

Habermas (1979: 2-3) holds that the function of universal pragmatics is to diagnose and reconstruct the universal presuppositions of communication. As a result, anyone who wants to be involved in the process of reaching understanding must raise four different types of claims:

The speaker must choose a comprehensible [verstandlich] expression so that speaker and hearer can understand one another. The speaker must have the intention of communicating a true [wabr] proposition (or a propositional content, the existential presuppositions of which are satisfied) so that the hearer can share the knowledge of the speaker. The speaker must want to express his intentions truthfully [wabrbaftig] so that the hearer can believe the utterance of the speaker (can trust him). Finally, the speaker must choose an utterance that is right [richtig] so that the hearer can accept the utterance and speaker and hearer can agree with one another in the utterance with respect to a recognized normative background. Moreover, communicative action can continue undisturbed only as long as participants suppose that the validity claims they reciprocally raise are justified.

Habermas (1990b: 313) explains further that:

Each elementary speech act as a whole can be contested under three different aspects of validity. The hearer can reject the utterance of a speaker *in toto* by either disputing the *truth* of the proposition asserted in it (or of the existential presuppositions of its propositional content), or the *rightness* of the speech act in view of the normative context of the utterance (or the legitimacy of the presupposed context itself), or the *truthfulness* of the intention expressed by the speaker (that is, the agreement of what is meant with what is stated).

McCarthy (1978: 280) suggests that, out of these four validity claims, the claim of comprehensibility is the only one that is "language-immanent". The others are raised from extralinguistic orders of reality. That is why some of Habermas's commentators reduce his validity claims to three, namely: truth, truthfulness and rightness. Thus, 'the pragmatic infrastructure of speech situations consists of general rules for arranging the elements to speech situations within a coordinate system formed by "the" world, one's "own" world, and "our" shared life-world' (McCarthy, ibid.).

Habermas (1979: 4) contends that participants in communicative action presuppose that they are aware of this process. Wherever the participants can rely on their common definition of the situation, and take actions consensually, then their implicit agreement and consensus will include the following items:

1.   Speaker and hearer know implicitly that each of them has to raise the aforementioned validity claims if there is to be communication at all (in the sense of action oriented to reaching understanding).

2.   Both suppose that they actually do satisfy these presuppositions of communication – that is, that they could justify their validity claims.

3.   Thus, there is a common conviction that any validity claims that are raised are either already vindicated (which is the case with respect to the comprehensibility of the sentences uttered) or could be vindicated because the sentences, propositions, expressed intentions, and utterances satisfy corresponding adequacy conditions (which is the case with respect to truth, truthfulness, and rightness).

Therefore, Habermas (1979: 3) argues that:

The goal of coming to an understanding is to bring about an agreement that terminates in the intersubjective mutuality of reciprocal understanding, shared knowledge, mutual trust, and accord with one another. Agreement is based on recognition of the corresponding validity claims of comprehensibility, truth, truthfulness, and rightness. In other words, although the details of a programme of universal pragmatics remain in an unfinished form, the over-all aim is clear: to investigate the general competencies required for the successful performance of speech-acts and thereby to reconstruct the universal validity basis of speech (Thompson and Held, 1982: 116).

Habermas (1979: 68) constructs the following table at the end of "What Is Universal Pragmatics?"

Domains of Reality	Modes of Communication: Basic Attitudes	Validity Claims	General Functions of Speech
"The" World of External Nature	Cognitive: Objectivating Attitude	Truth	Representation of Facts
"Our" World of Society	Interactive: Conformative Attitude	Rightness	Establishment of Legitimate Interpersonal Relations
"My" World of Internal Nature	Expressive: Expressive Attitude	Truthfulness	Disclosure of Speaker's Subjectivity
Language	-	Comprehensibility	-

Table 1: Habermas - What is universal pragmatics?

Habermas divides the domains of reality into four parts: external nature, society, internal nature, and language. The mode of communication that governs the external nature is cognitive, its validity claim is truth, and its general function of speech is the representation of facts. The communicative approach to our social world is interactive, its validity claim is rightness, and the main function of speech is to establish legitimate interpersonal relations. The dominant approach to internal nature is expressive, its validity claim is truthfulness and the basic application of speech is the disclosure of the speaker's subjectivity. Finally, language evolves in speech, and speech is a medium where verbal instruments are reflected. Its validity claim is comprehensibility. Indeed, language serves as a means to establish relationships among external, social, and internal worlds.

Edgar (2006: 121) claims that 'in his later work, Peirce's image of an ideal community of scientists becomes an inspiration to Habermas's account of the ideal speech situation, which is to say the counterfactual presupposition of open and truthful dialogue that people bring with them to any conversation or social interaction'. Habermas believes that if the four validity claims of speech are present in one speaker, it will have to be counted as the ideal speech situation. This ideal speech situation is neither characterised as an objective nor a subjective phenomenon. Rather, it is a hypothetical construct that can be presumed in all speech actions, and that can be used as a yardstick for measuring the degree of proximity and remoteness of a dialogue in comparison with the best possible speech-act situation. What is more, the ideal speech situation puts a critical criterion at the disposal of participants in order to help them to find better arguments, thus providing a transcendental criterion for truth, freedom, and rationality. Habermas holds that a discourse must be based on the framework of the ideal speech situation. As McCarthy puts it in the introduction of *Legitimation Crisis* (Habermas, 1976: xvii-xviii), from Habermas's point of view:

The ideal speech situation is neither an empirical phenomenon nor simply a construct, but a reciprocal supposition [Unterstellung] unavoidable in discourse. This supposition can, but need not be, counterfactual; but even when counterfactual it is a fiction that is operatively effective in communication. I would therefore prefer to speak of an anticipation of an ideal speech situation ... This anticipation alone is the warrant that permits us to join to an actually attained consensus the claim of a rational consensus. At the same time it is a critical standard against which every actually realized consensus can be called into question and tested.

The ideal speech situation ensures that equal rights and power are distributed among all participants in a discourse, namely:

There is a symmetrical distribution of chances to select and employ speech acts, when there is an effective equality of chances to assume dialogue roles. In particular, all participants must have the same chance to initiate and perpetuate discourse, to put forward, call into question, and give reasons for or against statements, explanations, interpretations, and justifications. Furthermore, they must have the same chance to express attitudes, feelings, intentions and the like, and to command, to oppose, to permit, and to forbid, etc (Habermas, 1976: xvii).

Moreover, the ideal speech situation ensures that participants interact with one another equally, free from all the internal and external constraints of domination in the public sphere. Under these circumstances, disputes and conflicts are therefore resolved in a rational and logical way, and the outcome of the discussion will be the acceptance of the conclusion of the better argument. Thus, there will be mutual understanding and consensus. Habermas also adduces that, if this discourse runs on for a sufficient period of time, the participants will ascertain freedom and justice because truth (unconstrained consensus) cannot be analysed independently of freedom (unimpaired self-representation) and justice (universal norms). To put it another way:

Discourse presupposed the ideal speech situation, because it presupposed that an uncoerced agreement was possible. An ideal speech situation was one free from domination, where the only force was the forceless force of the better argument. In its turn the ideal speech situation anticipated an ideal form of social life, where freedom and responsibility were possible (Davis, 1994: 197).

Habermas holds that truth has not been discovered completely because the past history was based on a distorted and imperfect communicative action. He provides the model of the ideal speech situation as a way of enabling persons to be released from these verbal damages. Following Habermas's analysis, Alexy has suggested that the following rules hold in the ideal speech situation:

1.   Each subject who is capable of speech and action is allowed to participate in discourse.

2.   a) Each is allowed to call into question any proposal.

b) Each is allowed to introduce any proposal into the discourse.

c) Each is allowed to express his attitudes, wishes, and needs.

3.   No speaker ought to be hindered by compulsion – whether arising from inside the discourse or outside of it – from making use of the rights secured under [1 and 2] (White, 1988: 56).

Nevertheless, in *Moral Consciousness and Communicative Action,* Habermas (1990a: 104) tries to limit the scope of application of deontological ethics, and claims that 'it covers only practical questions that can be debated rationally, i.e., those that hold out the prospect of consensus. It deals not with value preferences but with the normative validity of norms of action'. In fact, Habermas distinguishes between 'value preferences' and 'norms of action', but this seems to be a mistaken distinction, as it is usually impossible to separate values from norms in the ideal speech situation.

Lyotard (1984: 61, 66) says that 'consensus is a horizon that is never reached and has become an outmoded and suspect value'. Those who have criticised Habermas claim that no ideal speech situation is ever entirely developed, and neither can it ever be actualised.

Of course, Habermas knows that it is impossible to achieve an ideal speech situation within a capitalist system, where it is impossible for instrumental rationality to be dominated. Nevertheless, he holds that the ideal speech situation would provide the perfect conditions for debate, and that it provides a critical criterion that helps all relevant parties to offer better arguments, free from coercion and other distortions that could interfere with the conclusions reached.

3.4. Instrumental Rationality, Communicative Action and Shura in Islam

Habermas began discussing instrumental rationality and the theory of communicative action in various books, including *Knowledge and Human Interest,* and then he expanded the discussion of these two subjects by publishing his two- volume book *The Theory of Communicative Action*. These theories show the influence of Hegel and Heidegger. Indeed, it is:

Not that Habermas suddenly discovered the theme of communication. As we have seen, it was a substantive preoccupation in the *Structural Transformation of the Public Sphere* and in his essays on theory and practice and science and technology, and a central theoretical element in his critical appropriation of Marxism and hermeneutics. He was already claiming in 1965 that in the structure of language, autonomy and responsibility are posited for us. Our first sentence expresses unequivocally the intention of universal and unconstrained consensus (Outhwaite, 1994: 38).

The change in paradigm from goal-directedness to communicative action encouraged Habermas to re-examine and re-criticise the counter-discourse that accompanied modernity from the beginning, and this communicative action 'is not a metatheory but the beginning of a social theory concerned to validate its own critical standards' (Habermas, 1984: xii). On this basis, Habermas began to criticise Marx, Weber, Horkheimer and Adorno for ignoring communicative action through their focus on instrumental rationality:

For Marx, the evolving use of human rationality in improving our means of controlling nature contained an emancipatory potential, leading toward an efficient as well as liberated mode of production in the future communist society. The Frankfurt School, on the other hand, shared Weber's ambivalence toward the emancipatory potential of rationalization. In Weber's view, the more society becomes functionally organized and removed from tradition, the less freedom and meaningfulness are available to the individual (Braaten, 1991: 11).

Thus, Habermas (1984: 145) holds that the 'action concepts' that Marx, Weber, Horkheimer and Adorno held to be basic are not comprehensive enough, and are unable to cover all those aspects of social actions that come into being in societal rationalisation.

Marx believes that a man turns into a human if he actively exercises changes in nature through production, using its resources and increasingly dominating day after day. According to Marx, history is an action and reaction between both human beings and nature in order to reach economic equality and freedom. He reduces the function of human beings to sheer work in such a way that he assumes the method of producing material necessities to be a model of politics, art and philosophy. Habermas postulates this view as adopting an instrumental rationality that ignores communicative action. This instrumental rationality differentiates subject from object. Having argued that the subject is within lifeworld, Habermas has given some hints regarding the inseparability of subject and object. Furthermore, in *Knowledge and Human Interest,* Habermas (1972: 282) suggests that 'Marx was not able to see that power and ideology are distorted communication, because he made the assumption that men distinguished themselves from animals when they began to produce their means of subsistence'.

Weber is a major source for Habermas's reflection on instrumental rationality. Although Weber criticises instrumental rationality, and expresses despair at the fact that bureaucratisation and modernism will lead to a reification of social relationships, he nevertheless considers instrumental rationality as the only solution. Weber holds that an analysis of the recent history of Western civilisation shows that it adopts two versions of rationalisation: rationalising the practice and rationalising the thought. These are associated with purposive or goal-directed rationality, bureaucratisation, modern technology, and capitalism. While these rationalisations have invigorated knowledge, Weber's analysis of their effects contains fundamentally pessimistic ideas. In these rationalisations, there is no ethics, objective value, individual freedom, or autonomy. As Weber points out, 'rationalization as the loss of meaning + rationalization as the loss of freedom = reification = the increasing penetration of exchange values and power into society, culture, and the lifeworld' (Pusey, 1987: 35). In designing the theory of communicative action, Habermas (1990b: 315-316) challenges Weber's theory, and claims that:

Its underlying assumption is that the disenchantment of religious-metaphysical world views robs rationality, along with the contents of tradition, of all substantive connotations and thereby strips it of its power to have a structure-forming influence on the lifeworld beyond the purposive-rational organization of means. As opposed to this, I would like to insist that, despite its purely procedural character as disburdened of all religious and metaphysical mortgages, communicative reason is directly implicated in social life-processes insofar as acts of mutual understanding take on the role of a mechanism for coordinating action. The network of communicative actions is nourished by resources of the lifeworld and is at the same time the medium by which concrete forms of life are reproduced.

Horkheimer, Adorno, and Marcuse – the Frankfurt School theorists – adapted Weber's pessimistic analysis, and integrated it with the Enlightenment in the 18th century. Habermas (1984: 144) explains that 'Horkheimer and Adorno, and later Marcuse, interpret Marx in this Weberian perspective ... The Dialectic of

Enlightenment removes the ambivalence that Weber still entertained in relation to rationalization processes, and it abruptly reverses Marx's positive assessment. Science and technology – for Marx an unambiguously emancipatory potential – themselves become the medium of social repression'.

3.4.1. Instrumental Rationality

The model of purposive-rational action takes as its point of departure the view that the actor is primarily oriented to attaining an end (which has been rendered sufficiently precise in terms of purpose), that he selects means that seem to him appropriate in the given situation, and that he calculates other foreseeable consequences of action as secondary conditions of success. Success is defined as the appearance in the world of a desired state, which can, in a given situation, be causally produced through goal-oriented action or mission. The effects of action comprise the results of action (which the actor foresaw and intended, or made allowance for) and the side effects (which the actor did not foresee). We call an action oriented to success instrumental when we consider it under the aspect of following technical rules of action and assess the efficiency of an intervention into a complex of circumstances and events (Habermas, 1984: 285).

Instrumental rationality has a non-social dimension and depends largely on success. This action is directly associated with nature and has been designed to manipulate and control the natural world by the empirical-analytic approach. In particular, 'instrumental action is contrasted to both social action, which is performed between persons in the social world, and strategic action, which is a specific form of social action in which one person takes an instrumental attitude to other people (but not to natural objects)' (Edgar, 2006: 73). In other words, Habermas (1984: 285) categorises three types of action as follows:

Action Orientation Action Situation	Oriented to Success	Oriented to Reaching Understanding
Nonsocial	Instrumental action	------------
Social	Strategic action	Communicative action

Table 2: Habermas - Types of action

Based on this analysis of action types, Habermas holds that all participants pursue only illocutionary aims in order to reach an agreement in communicative action:

Agreement rests on common *convictions*. The speech act of one person succeeds only if the other accepts the offer contained in it by taking (however implicitly) a "yes" or "no" position on a validity claim that is in principle criticizable. Both ego, who raises a validity claim with his utterance, and alter, who recognizes or rejects it, base their decisions on potential grounds or reasons (Habermas, 1984: 287).

But strategic action, according to Habermas (1984: 295), comprises 'those interactions in which at least one of the participants wants with his speech acts to produce perlocutionary effects on his opposite number'. It is, therefore, impossible to have mutual understanding through instrumental and strategic actions. When an empirical-analytic approach is applied inappropriately in the social world, human beings are degraded into nonsensical objects. In capitalism, human beings have turned themselves into tools for production, and this instrumentalism has spread into all areas of human life. Through instrumentalism, language has degenerated into an inanimate thing, and this has destroyed the communicative action. This prevents human beings from feeling a robust sense of freedom and, thus, according to Habermas, it is necessary for philosophy and the social sciences to solve these problems. In *The Communicative Action,* Habermas (1984: 379) claims that: 'identifying thought, first expanded into instrumental reason, is now further expanded into a logic of domination over things and human beings. Left to itself, instrumental reason makes "the domination of nature, without and within, into the absolute aim of life"; it is the motor force behind a "self-assertion gone wild"'.

3.4.2. Communicative Action

The "pursuit of happiness" might one day mean something different - for example, not accumulating material objects of which one disposes privately, but bringing about social relations in which mutuality predominates and satisfaction does not mean the triumph of one over the repressed needs of the other (Habermas, 1979: 199).

The original conception of the theory of communicative action is based on the fact that the human species preserves itself through the socially coordinated activities of its members. This coordination can only be made possible through communication and consensus, with language at its foundation. Thus, Habermas utilises language as the basis for social theory, and argues that human action must be harmonised in a social way. Our ability to establish communication and interaction centres on a common core that consists of a validity claim. Although a validity claim is almost implicit, it is in our every word and action. In Habermas's theory, communicative action is a proper type of social action and reaction. In this interaction, participants expect one another to coordinate their different purposes and actions through consensus that is produced by communication and mutual understanding. Moreover, human attempts to attain a consensus or agreement are founded on the use of language. A common language is a medium that allows participants to reach an understanding, as well as to assess their beliefs and common objectives. When a speaker begins to make an assertion, he hopes that his words will be understood and that the content of his claim will be agreed to. In *The Theory of Communicative Action*, Habermas (1984: 86) explains that:

Finally the concept of communicative action refers to the interaction of at least two subjects capable of speech and action who establish interpersonal relations (whether by verbal or by extra-verbal means). The actors seek to reach an understanding about the action situation and their plans of action in order to coordinate their actions by way of agreement.

When a dispute emerges between speakers and hearers, they should adduce reason and appropriate evidence in order to maintain interaction. In fact:

In contexts of communicative action, we call someone rational not only if he is able to put forward an assertion and, when criticized, to provide grounds for it by pointing to appropriate evidence, but also if he is following an established norm and is able, when criticized, to justify his action by explicating the given situation in the light of legitimate expectations (Habermas, 1984: 15).

Because language can have an influence in solving disputes, rational discourse provides security to all of our everyday relationships. In this way, democracy, from Habermas's point of view, requires the participation of citizens in an equal and public debate. The main objective of democracy is to substitute enemies with the conflict of ideas. In the process of inimical conflicts, many people are killed without reason. However, during the conflict of ideas, people are made aware and take cognizance of many things. Hence, this approach lends itself to establishing a just and emancipated society:

If the object of hope is a just and emancipated society, a social and political life of freedom, reciprocity and shared responsibility, then an orientation towards that goal is, according to Habermas's analysis, indelibly written into the very structure of communicative action. We are inevitably as social subjects engaged in communicative action. As participants in communicative action we cannot but affirm, in performance if not in words, the norms and values of communicative rationality. Because of that, we are justified in seeing our hope for an emancipated society, not as a figment of wishful thinking, but as an intrinsic possibility of our actual situation (Davis, 1994: 202).

In his 1967 address, 'Epistemology without a Knowing Subject', Popper makes an unexpected proposal: we may distinguish the following three worlds or universes: firstly the world of physical objects or physical states; secondly, the world of states of consciousness, or of mental states, or of behavioural dispositions to act; and thirdly, the world of *objective contents of thought*, especially of scientific and poetic thoughts and of works of art (Habermas, 1984: 76).

Holub (1991: 13) holds that Habermas employs Popper's three-world theory to implement his rational reconstruction. Like Popper, Habermas assumes that we simultaneously live in three worlds: 1- an external world of objects; 2- an internal world of ideas, thoughts, and emotions, and; 3- a normative world of intersubjectively determined norms and values. Habermas believes that every statement associates with these three worlds because 1- all statements are connected to an external world of affairs; 2- all utterances involve an internal motivation or intention; 3- every statement is related to a normative reality. These connections, in turn, contain validity claims that are not found in the abstract world of conventional linguistic analysis, but are revealed only under pragmatic conditions. These validity claims are comprehensibility, truth, truthfulness and rightness.

Habermas utilises Popper's three-world theory creatively in order to explain his own theory of communicative action. He divides communicative action into these three dimensions of ontic, normative and expressive; each of which has its own measuring standard. The ontic consists of propositional measurement, the normative of rightness, and the expressive of truthfulness. In a similar way, our orientation towards the world belongs to one of the categories of ontic, normative or expressive. The first dimension is related to science, the second to ethics, and the third to art. As Habermas holds, the separation of these domains from one another is the key for illustrating how the West has become rationalised. These three areas were intermixed in pre-modern periods and within traditional cultures, and their separation has resulted from the rationalisation process of religious worldviews. It is notable that, in recent writings such as 'Modernity versus Post-Modernity' (1981) and *Postmetaphysical Thinking: Philosophical Essays* (1992), Habermas has amended his views regarding religion, and now believes in the need for interaction between these three dimensions.

According to Habermas, our current community is a sick one, and this sickness has been caused by distorted communication and a lack of mutual understanding based on common language. In his critical science, Habermas (in *Knowledge and Human Interest)* embraces Freud's psychoanalysis as an effective approach for treating this pathology: 'Psychoanalysis is taken as the model of a critical science because it attempts to reveal to the patient the unconscious processes which determine her action and bring them under some conscious control in what should eventually become a relationship of equality with the analyst' (Craib, 1992: 234). In Habermas's model of dialogue, every actor is a social critic, and his role can be made analogous to that of the psychiatrist, with his aim of bringing self-awareness through self-reflection. The psychiatrist or the actor not only wants to help his patient to reach self-awareness, but also tries to enable his patient to recover her self-awareness. Indeed, 'self-reflection is no longer the act of an absolute ego but takes place under the conditions of communication between physician and patient forced into being by pathology' (Habermas, 1972: 287). The psychiatrist or actor endeavours to encourage the patient in order to receive the power of communication through language and speech. Given this, it is clear that a communication between the patient's external and internal worlds can be established. As Habermas comments, the psychiatrist or actor extracts systematic distortions of the patient's life. However, in

'Habermas and Marxism', Heller (1982: 21-22) interprets Habermas's ideas as follows:

The lack of the sensuous experiences of hope and despair, of venture and humiliation, is discernible in the structure of his theory: the creature-like aspects of human beings are missing. Habermas has always rejected the philosophy of hope and of despair ... The sensuous, the needing, the feeling human being never ceased to be one of his main concerns. Habermasian man has, however, no body, no feeling; the 'structure of personality' is identified with cognition language and interaction. Although Habermas accepts the Aristotelian differentiation between 'life' and 'the good life', one gets the impression that the good life consists solely of rational communication and that needs can be argued for without being felt.

Although Habermas makes a mistake in not pursuing a religious understanding of the universe and of human existence in terms of faith, hope and charity, theologians need to utilise and embrace part of Habermas's theories in order to re-examine their religious attitudes. Indeed, religious people should not cease to be rational in becoming believers, and faith, hope, and charity cannot establish a transcendent relationship beyond the range of reason and communicative action.

3.4.3. Communicative Action and Shura in Islam

There are three types of ruling in the minds of Muslims:

1.   God's absolute sovereignty on the order of the universe, which encompasses all the creations of mankind and existence based on truth because God is truth. Support for this comes from numerous verses of the Glorious Koran, including verse 57 of chapter "Al-Anam": '... The command rests with none

but Allah [God]: He declares the truth, and He is the best of judges'.

2. The rule of God over man and his actions, namely, Divine Law, which is manifested in Divine legislation and religious legal obligations.

3. The substantial rule of man over his own doing and fate, which is based on the fact that Almighty God has created human beings to be free and allowed him to govern his destiny through his own choice. That is why man is the 'caliph of God', instructed to rule on the earth.

Chapter "Fatir", verse 39 proclaims: 'He it is that has made you inheritors in the earth ...' In addition, human beings are free to choose their own ways of living and religions. Thus, in (Chapter 2, verse 256) the Koran says that:

There be no compulsion in religion: Truth stands out clear from error: whoever rejects evil and believes in Allah hath grasped the most trustworthy handhold that never breaks. And Allah heareth, and knoweth all things.

On these grounds, Islam holds that it is imperative to win the satisfaction of people, and people have the right to express their opinions and exchange their views with one another in a free and unlimited process of dialogue. Shura (consultation) involve political participation by the public that is aimed at providing popular solutions for different social problems. All the participants need to exchange their views freely and defend their preferences rationally in order to reach a unanimous agreement. It is worth pointing out that the sphere of Shura is more extensive than that of liberal democracy, as it encompasses different aspects of the individual – the social and political lives of human beings – and is not considered the only method of aligning a political life based on a majority of votes. Islam emphasises that logic and reason must govern all, considering them the most important tools for making or accepting decisions. Chapter "Shura", verse 38, advises people to exchange their views with one another as follows:

Those who harken to their Lord, and establish regular prayer; who (conduct) their affairs by mutual consultation; who spend out of what we bestow on them for sustenance...

Moreover, in chapter "Al-Imran", verse 159, God orders Muhammad to consult people as follows:

... So pass over (their faults), and ask for (Allah's) forgiveness for them; and consult them in affairs...

As the Koran clarifies (Verses 38 in chapter "Shura", and 159 of "Al-Imran"), the principle of consultation (Shura) is the characteristic aspect of the believer's community. In all the excellent behaviours shown by the Prophet of Islam, consultation occupies an especially valued position, with the Prophet holding consultations with his disciples, as God strongly advised him to.

During the previous two centuries – when the model of democracy was introduced to the modern world and developed all over the Islamic world – many have tried to homogenise it with the concept of Shura in Islam (Behroozlak, 2007: 326). For instance, amongst the contemporary reformist theologians, an Egyptian (Towfiq Muhammad Al-Shavi) introduced the theory of Shura. According to Al-Shavi (1995: 31), the combination of Islamic modernism and Shura Laws provide a strong case for embracing a religious reform in the areas of ethics, society and politics. Al-Shavi holds that Shura enables people to participate in the process of free dialogue and consultation prior to any decision-making and arrangement. Shura, like communicative action, ensures that rights for free interactions and disputes are resolved on the basis of the evidence and arguments provided by all participants in a free dialogue. This dialogue is not focused on the wills of the majority, as in a liberal democracy, but on the value of every opinion with respect to truth and justice. In Shavi's view, Shura is an Islamic interpretation of freedom and democracy, and gains its legitimacy from religious sources. Shura is not a political philosophy or religion, but a social principle and a methodology for ensuring mutual understanding. Shura is based on freedom, and this freedom is more important than the state. Thus, Islamic states, with all its power and authority, should nonetheless obey Shura. This is the only fulcrum that cannot be dispensed with, or ignored, by a government.

It can be concluded that, unlike liberal democracy, both Islamic consultation (Shura) and communicative action are founded on the concepts of deliberative reason, deliberative democracy, an association between liberty and equality, the balance between an individual's rights and those of society, the necessity of reaching a mutual understanding and consensus, and a critical account of the use of power and money that holds that its use needs to be supervised.

3.5. Lifeworld and System

In *The Theory of Communicative Action* vol. 2, Habermas not only introduces the key concepts of lifeworld and system, but also reviews the theories of Mead, Durkheim, Parsons, Luhmann, Weber, and Marx. In this book, Habermas (1987: 119) seeks to take up the question of 'how the lifeworld – as the horizon within which communicative actions are "always already" moving – is in turn limited and changed by the structural transformation of society as a whole'. From Habermas's point of view, both the paradigms of system and lifeworld are significant and he, like Mead, strives to demonstrate their interaction. To do so, Habermas (1987: 120) says, 'takes us to the limit of theoretical approaches that identify society with the lifeworld. I shall therefore propose that we conceive of society simultaneously as a system and as a lifeworld'. In other words:

There are internal relations between the capacity for decentered perception and manipulation of things and events on the one hand, and the capacity for reaching intersubjective understanding about things and events on the other. For this reason, Piaget chooses the model of *social cooperation*, in which several subjects coordinate their interventions in the objective world through communicative action (Habermas, 1984: 14).

Describing the terms of lifeworld and system, Habermas utilises the views of Husserl, Wittgenstein, Schutz and Luckmann. However, he also challenges Schutz, Luckmann, and Husserl.

Schutz and Luckmann hold on to the model of the philosophy of consciousness. Like Husserl, they begin with the ego-logical consciousness for which the general structures of the lifeworld are given as necessary subjective conditions of the experience of a concretely shaped, historically stamped, social lifeworld ... Although Schutz and Luckmann, operating on the premises of the philosophy of consciousness, play down the importance of language, particularly of the linguistic mediation of social interaction, they stress the intersubjectivity of the lifeworld (Habermas, 1987: 129, 131).

On the one hand, Habermas provides an historical analysis of the rationalisation of the lifeworld and, on the other, he gives a detailed hint to the uncoupling of system and lifeworld. He holds that social evolution has not merely accounted for a rationalisation of the lifeworld, but also for a differentiation between lifeworld and system. He defines these two processes as follows:

I shall be guided by the hypothesis that the socially integrative and expressive functions that were at first fulfilled by ritual practice pass over to communicative action; the authority of the holy is gradually replaced by the authority of an achieved consensus. This means a freeing of communicative action from sacrally protected normative contexts ... On this plane of analysis, the uncoupling of system and lifeworld is depicted in such a way that the lifeworld, which is at first coextensive with a scarcely differentiated social system, gets cut down more and more to one subsystem among others. In the process, system mechanisms get further and further detached from the social structures through which social integration takes place (Habermas, 1987: 77, 154).

3.5.1. Lifeworld

The structural components of the lifeworld are culture, society and person. In this respect, Habermas (1987: 138) says:

I use the term *culture* for the stock of knowledge from which participants in communication supply themselves with interpretations as they come to an understanding about something in the world. I use the term *society* for the legitimate orders through which participants regulate their memberships in social groups and thereby secure solidarity. By *personality* I understand the competences that make a subject capable of speaking and acting that put him in a position to take part in processes of reaching understanding and thereby to assert his own identity. The dimensions in which communicative action extends comprise the semantic field of symbolic contents, social space, and historical time. The interactions woven into the fabric of everyday communicative practice constitute the medium through which culture, society, and person get reproduced.

These three components construct a series of common and undoubted convictions on the world, community, etc. They also have a set of agreed upon interpretations that make intersubjective understanding and consensus possible. Lifeworld always remains in the background, and is the unquestionable frame for everything in life, because its elements do not have the status of facts or norms or experiences that speakers and hearers could come to some understanding of. Indeed, it is a 'background consensus of everyday life', and a 'storehouse of knowledge' that is at the same time 'intuitively present' and passed on to different generations. Lifeworld shapes a context that, 'itself boundless, draws boundaries'. In other words, 'the lifeworld appears as a reservoir of taken-for-granteds, of unshaken convictions that participants in communication draw upon in cooperative processes of interpretation ... We can think of the lifeworld as represented by a culturally transmitted and linguistically organized stock of interpretive patterns' (Habermas, 1987: 124). In fact, 'every explication within the life-world goes on within the milieu of affairs which have already been explicated, within a reality that is fundamentally and typically familiar' (Schutz and Luckmann, 1974: 7). In *The Philosophical*

Discourse of Modernity: Twelve Lectures, Habermas (1990b: 298) indicates this idea as follows:

Insofar as speakers and hearers straightforwardly achieve a mutual understanding about something in the world, they move within the horizon of their common lifeworld; this remains in the background of the participants-as an intuitively known, unproblematic, and unanalyzable, holistic background. The speech situation is the segment of a lifeworld tailored to the relevant theme; it both forms a context and furnishes resources for the process of mutual understanding. The lifeworld forms a horizon and at the same time offers a store of things taken for granted in the given culture from which communicative participants draw consensual interpretive patterns in their efforts at interpretation. The solidarities of groups integrated by values and the competences of socialized individuals belong, as do culturally ingrained background assumptions, to the components of the lifeworld.

For Habermas (1987: 125-126), language and culture are thus constitutive of the lifeworld. The storehouse of knowledge provides unproblematic and common beliefs, as well as a framework for the members of community that is assumed to be guaranteed. This can create a background for reaching mutual understanding and, indeed:

Every life is, above all, life with and by means of the language I share with my fellowmen, an understanding of language is thus essential for any understanding of the reality of everyday life ... My interaction with others in everyday life is, therefore, constantly affected by our common participation in the available social stock of knowledge. The social stock of knowledge includes knowledge of my situation and its limits (Berger and Luckmann, 1967: 51-52, 56).

The lifeworld can thus be seen as the transcendental site in which speaker and hearer meet each other and make claims about anything in the realm of the objective, social, or subjective world. Within this lifeworld, validity claims can be criticised and confirmed, disputes solved, and agreements arrived at. Habermas, like Durkheim, believes that if a community is to be prevented from disintegrating from within, we need to maintain a certain proportion of our share of creeds and individual norms. Thus, according to Schutz and Luckmann (1974: 4), 'my life-world is not my private world but, rather, is intersubjective; the fundamental structure of its reality is that it is shared by us'.

Lifeworld has three functions: cultural reproduction, or the propagation of cultural traditions; social integration, or the integration of groups by norms and values; and socialisation, or the socialisation of succeeding generations. It is proper to point out that the lifeworld is defined as containing the background notions of shared meaning, the reaching of understanding, consensus, and communicative action. Communicative action is the principal medium for reproducing the lifeworld because 'under the functional aspect of mutual understanding, communicative action serves to transmit and renew cultural knowledge; under the aspect of coordinating action, it serves social integration and the establishment of solidarity; finally, under the aspect of socialization, communicative action serves the formation of personal identities' (Habermas, 1987: 137).

3.5.2. System

System is the process of instrumental rationality that produces economic and bureaucratic spheres in which social relations are controlled through money and power alone. To put it another way, 'system refers to those vast tracts of modern society that are "uncoupled" from communicatively shared experience in ordinary language and coordinated, instead, through the media of money and power' (Pusey, 1987: 107). Berger (1969: 22-23) holds that under such conditions, the individual loses emotionally satisfying ties, an orientation to his experiences, and his sense of reality and identity. The ultimate danger is that the individual is submerged in a world of disorder, senselessness, and madness.

According to Habermas, although system contributes to advancements in human life, its consequences are juridification, alienation, and reification of the lifeworld. This involves the loss of meaning or unity in a fully disenchanted world, and the loss of freedom within the increasingly bureaucratised social-cultural impoverishment of the lifeworld. Habermas (1987: 143) categorises some of these crises in thed following table.

White (1988: 99-100) observes that:

We can see that, as a consequence of the structural differentiation of the lifeworld into culture, society and personality, we must also think in terms of differentiated processes of reproduction. These processes are identified by Habermas as, respectively, "cultural reproduction, social integration, and socialization." The first process is evaluated by the degree to which there is "a continuation of valid knowledge"; the second by the degree to which there is "a stabilization of group solidarity"; and the third by the degree to which there is "a formation of responsible actors"

Structural Components / Disturbances In the domain of	Culture	Society	Person	Dimension of evaluation
Cultural Reproduction	Loss of meaning	Withdrawal of legitimation	Crisis in orientation and education	Rationality of knowledge
Social Integration	Unsettling of collective identity	Anomie	Alienation	Solidarity of members
Socialization	Rupture of tradition	Withdrawal of motivation	Psychopathologies	Personal responsibility

Table 3: Manifestations of crisis when reproduction processes are disturbed (Pathologies)

Habermas (1987: 140-141) explains that the cultural reproduction of the lifeworld secures a *continuity* of tradition and a *coherence* of knowledge sufficient for daily practice. The social integration of the lifeworld also coordinates actions by legitimately regulating interpersonal relations and stabilising the identity of groups to an extent that is sufficient for everyday practice. Finally, the socialisation of the members of a lifeworld secures the acquisition of *generalised competences for action* for succeeding generations, and ensures that *individual life histories are in harmony with collective forms of life.*

Habermas stipulates that the economy and the state have been two central systems in the modern community, and their coordinated mechanisms have been money and power respectively. Money and power not only direct the mass media, but also regulate actions for all participants. According to Habermas, the main problems in the public sphere arise when these mass media escape from their statutory domains and launch an attack on the lifeworld in order to seize its main jurisdictions. It is within this state that individuals and cohorts of people are prevented from living their independent collective lives. Hence, money and political power push aside communicative action, and instrumental actions govern social life:

The transfer of action coordination from language over to steering media means an uncoupling of interaction from lifeworld contexts. Media such as money and power attach to empirical ties; they encode a purposive-rational attitude toward calculable amounts of value and make it possible to exert generalized, strategic influence on the decisions of other participants while *bypassing* processes of consensus-oriented communication. Inasmuch as they do not merely simplify linguistic communication, but *replace* it with a symbolic generalization of rewards and punishments, the lifeworld contexts in which processes of reaching understanding are always embedded are devalued in favor of media-steered interactions; the lifeworld is no longer needed for the coordination of action (Habermas, 1987: 183).

This phenomenon not only prevents democratic agreement, but also hurts the structure of mutual understanding in the lifeworld, which constitutes the foundation of democracy. These conditions also segregate validity claims from one another and from daily orientation. As a result, human beings lose their sense of meaning and identity, and their freedom, and the lifeworld is then distorted. In fact, Habermas, like Weber, sees system growth with suspicion and uncertainty. That is to say, Habermas claims that although system has brought some benefits, it is itself a threat to the integrity of the lifeworld and communicative action. He refers to this threat as the colonisation of the lifeworld, and adds:

In the end, systemic mechanisms suppress forms of social integration even in those areas where a consensus-dependent coordination of action cannot be replaced, that is, where the symbolic reproduction of the lifeworld is at stake. In these areas, the *mediatization* of the lifeworld assumes the form of colonization (Habermas, 1987: 196).

Habermas (1987: 293-294) provides examples of social pathology and the misuse of money and power, including the destruction of urban environments as a result of uncontrolled capitalist growth, and the over bureaucratization of the educational system. He adds that this misuse originates from the misguided perception that the 'rational management of steering is possible only by way of calculated operations with money and power' (Habermas, ibid.).

In this chapter, I have sought to achieve two things. Firstly, I have introduced Marx's and Weber's work on religion, which has been a strong influence on Habermas's work, particularly his earlier writing, and led him to take an instrumental approach to religion. Nevertheless, the second section elucidated some of the new and distinctive themes and directions that Habermas's work began to take in the 1970's. These included the ideas of universal pragmatics and the ideal speech situation, the theory of communicative action, and lifeworld and system, which have led him to consider religion as an inseparable part of lifeworld.

Habermas argues that the project of modernity needs to be reconstructed, and proposes to do so by applying the critical theory to it. This means releasing the project of modernity from the control of instrumental rationality by extending the jurisdiction of communicative action and the lifeworld. It is under these conditions that system is placed in its right position; and in a dialectic process, system and lifeworld become correlations, enabling mutual understanding and deliberative democracy to emerge. Although Habermas has provided a positive means for reconstructing modernity in a potentially liberating manner, this chapter has shown that there are still problems and ambiguities within his analysis of religion. In particular, there is a tension between his confrontation with instrumentalisation (in broad terms), and his apparent acceptance of modern instrumentalised views of religion. It is to this tension and ambiguity that I now turn.

Chapter 4: Habermas's Early and Recent Thought on the Role of Religion in Public Life

Habermas's intellectual concerns are broad, embracing philosophy, sociology, theology, politics, ethics, law, psychology, linguistics, hermeneutics and communication. However, his account of religion has been relatively neglected within the large body of literature that explores Habermas's work. Broadly understood, Habermas's work on the exchange of views and the intersubjectivity of mutual understanding between secular and religious groups and orientations, as well as his work on dialogues between religions and civilisations in the modern world, reflects his commitment to the importance of communication, dialogue and the need to prevent violence and war. The limited attention that his work on religion has received has not always fully grasped this fact. This may be due to the often abstract and technical nature of much of his writing, but may also be a reflection of the significant changes that have occurred in his views about religion.

In his paper, 'On Social Identity' (1974a), Habermas discusses religion as a social phenomenon, repeatedly referring to Hegel's philosophy in order to explain religion. He begins by analysing different stages of social evolution with regard to ego and group identity by looking at human identity in archaic communities through their mythical world images, symbols and practices (which are, ironically, incorporated in later monotheistic religions). For example, pagan practices relating to mythical or magic origin are incorporated in a universal rationality of social life. In this article, Habermas (1974a: 91) considers the individual's identity in archaic society to be the natural identity of the child, who establishes new forms of religious action and interaction with the gods through prayer, sacrifice and worship. He (1974a: 95) concludes that 'once it was confronted with the rival claims of science and profane morality, Christianity could no longer satisfy this demand. Here, then, philosophy must step in its place'. Put differently, in the modern age, religion has no position in human beings' private or social lives, and must be replaced by philosophy, which provides a vigorous form of rationality as a substitute for religion. Modernity 'has no tradition to fall back upon, no myth to rely upon, no religion for which it may exist as a rational counterpart. Philosophy suddenly finds itself alone, perhaps even at an end' (Rasmussen, 1990: 8). According to Habermas, all that remains from religion is universalistic ethical systems. He (1974a: 94) asserts that:

These trends characterize a development in which what is left of universal religions is but the core of universalistic moral systems, and this in greater proportion, the more transparent the infrastructure of monotheistic belief systems has become.

However, it is noteworthy that Habermas's essays and lectures on religion in recent years represent some notable changes in his views. He now takes a more positive view about religion and holds that religion is the main source of the good life.

4.1. The Role of Religion in Habermas's Early Thought and the Three Stages of the World

Habermas divides his account of the evolution of 'worldviews' (or what he also calls 'social evolution') into three stages: the mythical, the religious-metaphysical and the modern. These three phases of social evolution correspond to the differentiation of the cognitive capacities that Piaget indentifies. Habermas develops his theory of modernity against the mythical and religious-metaphysical worldviews. He sees religious thought as mythical and metaphysical in contrast to the rational and post-metaphysical nature of modern thought. He believes that public life is an arena for rational-critical discourse rather than for religious goals and individual interests. In arguing for this, Habermas appeals to Evans-Pritchard's investigations on belief in witchcraft among the African Azande, as well as to Peter Winch's philosophical analysis of traditional cultures. He claims that: 'we would have to assume that the scientist who belongs to a modern society could not seriously understand the Azande belief in witches, or even the crucifixion of Jesus' (Habermas, 1984: 67).

4.1.1. The Mythical Worldview

In *Legitimation Crisis* (1976: 18) and *Communication and the Evolution of Society* (1979: 157), Habermas claims that the first phase of social formation is that of "Neolithic" or "Primitive". This age is substantially founded on a kinship system, and its organisational maxim is grounded primarily in the age and gender of the members of the community. At this stage, the kinship system represents a total institution, with family structure that there is no social communication outside the family unit. The family structure maintains both social and system integration. In the "primitive" social formation, there is rarely a notable difference between worldviews and norms, which are stabilised by rituals and taboos that require no independent sanctions. Such an organisational principle can only be in accord with familial and tribal morals. In these communities, it was impossible to have vertical or horizontal social relationships that transgressed the bounds of the kinship system. In other words:

Apparently the magical-animistic representational world of paleolithic societies was very particularistic and not very coherent. The ordering representations of mythology first made possible the construction of a complex of analogies in which all natural and social phenomena were interwoven and could be transformed into one another. In the egocentric world conception of the child at the preoperational level of thought, these phenomena are made relative to the centre of child's ego; similarly, in sociomorphic worldviews they are made relative to the centre of the tribal group (Habermas, 1979: 104).

In this regard, 'the mythical world comprehends all its entities as analogues; men are substances in the same way as are stones, plants, animals, and gods. Thus, the tribe is not a reality which stands out in contrast to its individual members or to nature' (Habermas, 1974a: 91).

According to Habermas, the primitive man was unable to reasonably explain and illustrate social and natural phenomena, and unable to discover the interconnections between the events occurring in the world. Therefore, he located the causes of these events as occurring outside the world, and resorted to appealing to gods and goddesses as explanations for such phenomena. Nonetheless, myths had their own communicative values and benefit:

In archaic societies myths fulfil the unifying of worldviews in an exemplary way – they permeate life-practice. At the same time, within the cultural traditions accessible to us, they present the sharpest contrast to the understanding of the world dominant in modern societies. Mythical worldviews are far from making possible rational orientations of action in our sense. With respect to the conditions for a rational conduct of life in this sense, they present an antithesis to the modern understanding of the world ... As Levi-Strauss has put it, the world of myths is both round and hollow. Analogical thought weaves all appearances into a single network of correspondence, but its interpretations do not penetrate the surface of what can be grasped perceptually (Habermas, 1984: 44, 46).

As we have seen, Habermas (1984: 99-100) posits the existence of three separate worlds:

1.   The objective world (the totality of all entities about which true statements are possible);

2.   The social world (the totality of all legitimately regulated interpersonal relations);

3.   The subjective world (the totality of the experiences of the speaker to which he has privileged access).

At another level, Habermas divides human knowledge and practice into the three categories of science, morality, and art; or relations with the material world, with others, and with the expressive realm of aesthetics. The standards of evaluation within these categories are understood to be truth, rightness and truthfulness respectively. Thus, the speaker claims truth for statements, rightness for legitimately regulated actions, and truthfulness for subjective experiences.

According to Habermas, these dimensions are not separated from one another in mythical imagery, and it is precisely the undifferentiated form of these domains that shapes a mythical image of the world.

In a nutshell, a mythical worldview is like a starting-point in a long-term process of rationalisation, and it does not have any differentiation. Nevertheless, 'separation', in Habermas's thought, is the natural disposition of rationality; that is, the differentiation of science, morality, and art implies a general evolution towards an expansion of rationality. Therefore, a mythical worldview cannot be rational, because in the mythical worldview, 'the concept of the world is dogmatically invested with a specific content that is withdrawn from rational discussion and thus from criticism' (Habermas, 1984: 51). The only way to rationalise it is to find a substitution for a myth, and it is this substitution that shows flexibility towards criticism. As Habermas contends, there is no way to rationalise a mythical worldview whilst maintaining its identity. Thus, he suggests, it is impossible to have communicative action in a mythical world.

Utilising the "closed society" introduced by Popper and the "authority of the holy" by Durkheim, Habermas concludes that the lifeworld of the primitive community is founded on a mythical thought that is irrational and, in these conditions, the background beliefs that conduct communication come into practice in a highly reified and nature-like way. Indeed:

These worldviews establish an analogical nexus between man, nature, and society which is represented as a totality in the basic concepts of mythical powers. Because these worldviews project a totality in which everything corresponds with everything else, they subjectively attach the collective identity of the group or the tribe to the cosmic order and integrate it with the system of social institutions. In the limit case, worldviews function as a kind of drive belt that transforms the basic religious consensus into the energy of social solidarity and passes it on to social institutions, thus giving them a moral authority (Habermas, 1987: 56).

Therefore, Neolithic or primitive society has a constitutive significance rather than a subsequent legitimating significance, and is unable to understand the distinction between nature and culture, language and the world, validity claims, and culture and internal nature. Thus, mythical thought is imperfect in these aspects:

• Confusion between Nature (or the Objective World) and Culture

In his terminological definition of nature or the objective world, Habermas (1984: 52) considers nature as the totality of facts in which a statement about the existence of a corresponding state of affairs can count as true. Discussing the structural components of the lifeworld, he also says that 'I use the term *Culture* for the stock of knowledge from which participants in communication supply themselves with interpretations as they come to an understanding about something in the world'(Habermas, 1987: 138).

Braaten (1991: 82) notes that 'this discussion draws heavily on Levi-Strauss's structuralist analysis of the mythical – and for Levi-Strauss, largely analogical – understanding of the world'. Utilising the work of Levi-Strauss and Durkheim, Habermas explains that the mythical worldview is derived from the model of the kinship system. This model seeks the peculiar levelling of the various areas of reality, such as nature and culture. On the one hand, this reciprocal assimilation of nature to culture and culture to nature turns out a nature that contains anthropomorphic features that have been drawn into the communicative network of social subjects, and has thus been humanised. On the other hand, it suggests a culture that has been naturalised, reified and absorbed into the objective network of the operation of unknown forces:

Such an interpretation of the world, in which each appearance is in correspondence with every other appearance through the influence of mythical powers, makes possible not only a theory that explains the world narratively and renders it plausible, but also a practice through which the world can be controlled in an imaginary way. The technique of magically influencing the world is a logical inference from the mythical interrelation of perspectives between man and world, between culture and nature (Habermas, 1984: 47-48).

By the term "confusion between nature and culture", Habermas means that the mythic worldview assimilates nature to culture and, conversely, culture to nature. Thus, while human beings had a 'mythical image' paradigm of the world, they were unable to understand the fact that myths, which are based on their culture, are not really objective facts of nature. Indeed, 'the development of techniques for magical influence is a natural, even logical, choice given a world-view structured by analogies between human relationships and natural events' (Braaten, 1991: 82). Thus, for Habermas, the mythically imbued way of thinking, or the confusion of nature and culture, results in a reification of worldview. Habermas (1984: 48) argues that:

What irritates us members of a modern lifeworld is that in a mythically interpreted world we cannot, or cannot with sufficient precision, make certain differentiations that are fundamental to our understanding of the world. From Durkheim to Lévi-Strauss, anthropologists have repeatedly pointed out the peculiar *confusion between nature and culture*. We can understand this phenomenon to begin with as a mixing of two object domains, physical nature and the sociocultural environment. Myths do not permit a clear, basic, conceptual differentiation between things and persons, between objects that can be manipulated and agents-subject capable of speaking and acting to whom we attribute linguistic utterances. Thus it is only consistent when magical practices do not recognize the distinction between teleological and communicative action ... The demythologization of worldviews means the desocialization of nature and the denaturalization of society.

Finally, Habermas (1984: 49) argues that:

As soon as we are to specify explicitly wherein things are distinct from persons, causes from motives, happenings from actions, and so forth, we have to go beyond differentiating object domains to differentiating between a basic attitude toward the objective world of what is the case and a basic attitude toward the social world of what can legitimately be expected, what is commanded or ought to be.

• The Deficient Differentiation between Language and the World

The confusion between language and the world is the confusion between speech as a tool for establishing a relationship and the world that can be comprehended by linguistic communication; namely, a confusion between communication and what the communication is about. As Habermas (1984: 49) points out in *The Theory of Communicative Action*, this deficient differentiation is 'between speech as the medium of communication and that about which understanding can be reached in linguistic communication'. He then explains that:

In the totalizing mode of thought of mythical worldview, it is apparently difficult to draw with sufficient precision the familiar (to us) semiotic distinctions between the sign-substratum of a linguistic expression, its semantic content, and the referent to which a speaker can refer with its help. The magical relation between names and designated object, the concretistic relation between the meaning of expressions and the states-of-affairs represented give evidence of systematic confusion between *internal connections of meaning and external connections of objects*. Internal relations obtain between symbolic expressions, external relations between entities that appear in the world (Habermas, 1984: 49).

According to the evolutionary interpretation of history that Habermas provides, the further humanity advances in rationalisation, the more the different features of the world are made distinct and the mythical worldview is disenchanted.

- The Deficient Clear Separation between Validity Claims

The concept of validity claims plays a significant role in *The Theory of Communicative Action*. As Habermas has put it, anyone who produces an utterance with propositional content thereby raises a validity claim. Participants in discourse must be committed to defending their utterances with reasons. This means that 'they must not only adduce empirical evidence for their claims; they must also give reasons why the features invoked should be accounted evidence for the claims' (Harrington, 2001: 125). Habermas (1984: 99) mentions that different speech acts or utterances raise different types of validity claims, which consist of:

1.   Truth: this is closely associated with an objective world. Indeed, it means that the statement made by the speaker is true and the content is satisfactory.

2.   Rightness: this is related to the social world, and imperative premises are bound to elucidate it. It means that the speech act is right with respect to the existing normative context.

3.   Truthfulness: this is concerned with human internal world and, in relation to this, the manifest intention of the speaker is meant as it is expressed.

Another way of saying this is that:

He [the participant] claims truth for a stated propositional content or for the existential presuppositions of a mentioned propositional content. He claims rightness (or appropriateness) for norms (or values), which in a given context, justify an interpersonal relation that is to be performatively established. Finally, he claims truthfulness for the intentions expressed (Habermas, 1979: 65-66).

The basic characteristic of mythical thought is that different validity claims (such as propositional truth, normative rightness, and expressive truthfulness or theoretical, practical, and aesthetic-expressive) have not yet been separated from one another. Habermas (1984: 50-51) points out that even the diffuse meanings of validity have not been liberated from empirical admixtures. Concepts of validity, like those of morality and truth, have been intermixed with empirical ordering concepts such as causality and health. Therefore, a linguistically constituted worldview may be equated with the world. Consequently, this interpretation of the world is not exposed to rational discussion and criticism. As Outhwaite (1994: 93) says: 'Habermas suggests, these religious systems (or the validity-claims they raise) are too undifferentiated to be accessible to rational critique; the ideological message, in other words, is wrapped up in a mishmash of sacred and profane beliefs'. Habermas attributes this stage of mythical worldview to the low-level thinking of humankind in the primitive period of history:

In "primitive" or "mythical" worldviews, there is a characteristic levelling of the distinctions between worlds, attitudes and validity claims, a lack of clear separation between nature, society and personality, as well as a reification of the worldview as the "world order". Habermas relates this worldview to the "systems problem" of an overwhelming natural environment and low level of productive forces, representing unresolved constraints to autonomy (Rothberg, 1986: 223).

• Confusion between Culture and Internal Nature (or the Subjective World)

According to Habermas (1984: 52), the definition of the internal nature or the subjective world (in distinction to that of the objective and social worlds) is as follows:

The subjective world counts as the totality of experiences to which, in each instance, only one individual has privileged access. The expression "subjective world" is justified inasmuch as here too we are dealing with an abstract concept which, in the form of common presuppositions, delimits from the objective and social worlds a domain for each member of what is not common.

As far as an individual bases his conception of the world and his actions on a mythical worldview, he does not yet have any conceptual instruments to distinguish between a culturally closed system of doctrines and valuations imposed by society and his own personal beliefs or inner values. Habermas elucidates that it is only when the glass of the mythical worldview is cracked that 'the concept of the *internal world* or of subjectivity arise, that is, a world to which the individual has privileged access and to which everything is attributed that cannot be incorporated in the external world' (Habermas, 1984: 51).

Habermas holds that, to the degree that mythical worldviews govern cognition and act-orientations, it is not obviously possible to demarcate a domain of subjectivity. Intentions and motives are only partly detached from actions, and the feelings that result are only slightly separated from their normatively fixed, stereotyped expressions. As a result of this, members of archaic communities strongly linked their identities to the details of the collective knowledge established in myths, as well as to those of the formal features of ritual prescriptions. These communities were not well inculcated with a formal concept of the world that 'could secure the identity of natural and social reality in the face of the changing interpretations of temporalized cultural traditions; nor can the individual rely on a formal concept of the ego that could secure his own identity in the face of a subjectivity that has become independent and fluid' (Habermas, 1984: 51-52).

There is no solid documentation to support Habermas's view on the mythical worldview, and Habermas is unable to prove that myth is the first stage of human evolution to be functionally incorporated within traditional societies and a religious-metaphysical worldview. Habermas might be correct about some primitive religions or polytheism, but there are no historical documents to validate Habermas's interpretation about monotheism. In addition, it is clearly erroneous to generalise the mythical characteristics of some Neolithic tribes to all primitive communities, as Habermas has. If, as Habermas believes, the levelling of the different domains of reality, superstitions and magic are inseparable from the mythical worldview, why do many of them still abound in the modern world, in scientific and intelligible cultures? This suggests that not only is Habermas's meditative system on the mythical worldview disputable, but also illogical.

Furthermore, Habermas makes a mistake when he construes religions as products of human feeling and reflection and then seeks to determine their evolutionary processes. History, prophets, scriptures and traditions reveal that monotheistic religions have originated from God and not from human sources. All divine religions substantially aim for human happiness and, notably, they have always fought superstition, magic and myth, as is mentioned in the holy books. Nor is religion the result of the evolutionary process of the human mind, as Tylor and Frazer suppose; the worship and product of society, as Durkheim thinks; or of repressed sexual instincts and moral disorders, as Freud believes. Neither is it an ideology and an opium of the masses, as Marx says; a childish way of thinking, as Piaget contends; a pre-logical feature, as Bruhl mentions; or, finally, a response to natural problems, i.e. an output of fear and horror in response to natural phenomena and inborn human needs, and a sheer product of backwardness and lack of civilisation, as Habermas held.

Indeed, the religious tendency in all communities and historical periods is undoubtedly the most fundamental interior human appetite. Human being always feels a need to be intellectually, emotionally and morally supported by a superior power, and thus, human beings always search for God because Almighty God has created human beings with this inner inclination.

4.1.2. The Religious-Metaphysical Worldview

According to Pusey (1987: 41-42), Habermas believes that the second phase of social evolution began somewhere between the eighth and fourth century BC with the transition from ancient civilisations (such as those of Egypt) to developed civilisations (like those of ancient Greece, China, and Rome). In *Legitimation Crisis*, Habermas (1976: 18-19) calls this stage a *traditional social formation,* and holds that the principle of organisation in traditional society is a class hegemony in its political form. Production and distribution of social wealth are transformed from familial configuration of organisation into ownership of the tools of production. The kinship system is no longer considered the institutional nucleus of the whole system, and surrenders the main functions of authority and control to the government. At this stage of development, the family loses all of its economic functions, as well as some of its socialising ones. Next, legal order comes into existence, which, in turn, needs legitimation: 'To the differentiation between the authority apparatus and the legal order on the one side, and the counterfactual justifications and moral systems on the other, there corresponds the institutional separation of secular and sacred powers' (Habermas, 1976: 19). In the introduction to

Religion and Rationality: Essays on Reason, God, and Modernity (Habermas, 2002b: 15), Mendieta alleges that:

Habermas distinguishes among archaic, primitive, traditional and modern or post-conventional societies. Traditional societies differ from archaic or primitive societies in that traditional societies: (1) have developed centralized ruling powers, (2) have divided vertically into socio-economic casts or groups, (3) have developed centralized world-views to legitimate centralized powers and the distribution of social goods. But what is true about the distinction between archaic and traditional societies is also true of the distinction between traditional and modern societies. Their differences can be gauged by the asymmetry between the harnessing of productive forces, and the dictates and goals of legitimation strategies of force and coercion, and how the latter are overtaken by the former.

Pusey (1987: 42-43) goes on to say that, whilst Habermas holds that mythical narration was sufficient to justify the power of sovereigns in the early phase of social formation, he holds that with the development of the early imperial civilisations belonging to the middle dynasties (such as China, Rome, and Greece), we witness more internal complexity and social separation, as well as a more elaborate structure of domination, and hence an additional need for legitimation. It is a need that is assessed today with ethics based on cosmology, higher religions and philosophies that are rationalised. We are still in the early stages of what Habermas and Weber term as traditional communities, where authority is legitimated through tradition. These traditions have been increasingly rationalised; that is to say, they are internally focused on unifying principles, and training is provided by priests and teachers. This is an important change because 'the law is no longer Caesar's will but a rationalized body of principles against which Caesar may be judged' (Pusey, 1987: 43). Nevertheless, this rationalisation of culture is still locked within the framework of ontology and a metaphysics that attributes ultimate reality to God, Being or Nature. Therefore, it sets a limit to the range of rational action and individual autonomy. In *Communication and the Evolution of Society*, Habermas (1979: 183-184) elaborates these phases as follows:

In early civilizations the ruling families justified themselves with the hope of myths of origin. Thus the pharaohs represented themselves first as gods – for example, as the god Horus, son of Osiris. On this level narrative grounds are sufficient, Viz-mythiological stories. With the imperial development of the ancient civilizations the need for legitimation grew; now not only the person of the ruler had to be justified, but a political order (against which the ruler could transgress). This end was served by cosmologically grounded ethics, higher religions, and philosophies, which go back to the great founders: Confucius, Buddha, Socrates, the prophets of Israel, and Jesus. These rationalized world views had the form of dogmatizable Knowledge. Arguments took the place of narrative. There were to be sure ultimate grounds, unifying principles, which explained the world as a whole (the natural and human world). The ontological tradition of thought was also on this level.

Focusing on the social performance of religion, Habermas attributes three functions to religion:

1. Providing a worldview for religious people and consequently providing a profound meaning for life by presenting an image of the world as a coordinated whole. In *The Recent Work of Jurgen Habermas: Reason, Justice and*

Modernity, White (1988: 93) states that Habermas considers Weber's analysis of rationalisation appealing because the magical-mythical thought of the world breaks down under the influence of what he called "world religions" (Christianity, Judaism, Hinduism, Buddhism and Islam). Religious-metaphysical worldviews introduce the universe 'as a coherent meaningful whole, within which an explanation for suffering is given as well as directions for the sort of life conduct which is necessary to earn salvation from that suffering' (ibid.).

2. Introducing ethical criteria and a motivation for embracing these criteria.

3. Improving human responses to unexpected and abnormal accidents of life, such as disasters, catastrophes, pains and so on. In other words, as Habermas (1976: 118-119) explains in *Legitimation Crisis*, religious systems related the ethical-practical function of constituting ego and group-identities (differentiating between the ego and the social-reference group on the one hand, and between the collective and natural-social environment on the other) to the cognitive interpretation of the world (to settling problems of survival that evolve at a time when individual faces an outer nature). They do so 'in such a way that the contingencies of an imperfectly controlled environment could be processed simultaneously with the fundamental risks of human existence' (Habermas, 1976: 119). The 'crises' arise through the life-cycle and the dangers that result from socialisation, as well as through injuries to ethical and physical health (guilt and loneliness, sickness and death):

The "meaning" promised by religion has always been ambivalent. On the one hand, by promising meaning, it preserved the claim – until now constitutive for the socio-cultural form of life – that men ought not to be satisfied with fictions but only with "truths" when they wish to know why something happens in the way it does, how it happens, and how what they do and ought to do can be justified. On the other hand, promise of meaning has always implied a promise of consolation as well, for proffered interpretations do not simply bring the unsettling contingencies to consciousness but make them bearable as well – even when, and precisely when, they cannot be removed as contingencies (Habermas, ibid.).

Habermas not only considers the first function as common between religious-metaphysical and mythical worldviews, but also defends the substitution of modern rationality for such worldviews. Although Habermas believes that the second function (which is the determination of ethical criteria) can and necessarily will be replaced at some point by the ethical human mind, such an ethical mind still fails to provide the stimulus for a moral functioning, and also fails to respond to the elementary question of why we should live ethically and morally. As Adams (2006: 19-20) says:

Habermas associates religious thinking with metaphysical thinking. Metaphysical thinking, for Habermas, is the kind of philosophy that strives to acquire the God's-eye view. Habermas also associates religious thinking with mythic thinking. Mythic thinking is the kind that confuses natural and human, personal and impersonal, world and worldview. Finally, Habermas associates religious thinking with a language of hope and redemption, indispensable for modern life, which has not as yet been overcome by philosophical categories. It is only this last aspect of religion that Habermas thinks can contribute positively to modern social life.

With regard to the third function of religion, in *Postmetaphysical Thinking: Philosophical Essays,* Habermas

(1992: 51) comments that although religion, from an external point of view, has been deprived of its efficiencies in relation to worldviews, it is still irreplaceable in its role of dealing with unexpected accidents of life and, for that reason, the post-metaphysical meditation still walks hand in hand with peaceful existence under the cover of religious customs and rites. Furthermore, 'the public impact of philosophy could not keep pace with world religions that promised salvation for the masses. Thus, as of late Classical Antiquity, Greek philosophy entered into a close symbiosis with institutional Christianity' (Habermas, 2003b: 278). Therefore, Habermas (1992: 51) states that:

Philosophy, even in its Postmetaphysical form, will be able neither to replace nor to repress religion as long as religious language is the bearer of a semantic content that is inspiring and even indispensable, for this content eludes (for the time being?) the explanatory force of philosophical language and continues to resist translation into reasoning discourses.

Habermas (1984: 201-204), along with Weber, considers the function of the religious worldview to be that of justifying the unequal distribution of life's goods. The fundamental moral dilemma that broke the limits of myth and resulted in the appearance of religion has originated from a need to justify pain and suffering that is interpreted as unjust. The theocentric worldview tries to accommodate the intellectual interest in ideal and material equalisation, taking into consideration the obvious unequal distribution of earthly goods, and 'they do so by way of offering explanations for this inequality. Behind them always lies a stand towards something in the actual world which is experienced as specifically senseless' (Habermas, 1984: 202). These religions claim that the entire world system is, could, or should be a meaningful cosmos. Habermas holds that religion, in its attempt to justify social injustices, uses all the possible means at its disposal to do so (such as theological, cosmological and metaphysical viewpoints) rather than using only ethical arguments. In this world order, ontic and normative questions are merged together. According to Habermas, within the framework of the religious-metaphysical worldview about world order, Weber considers that the "God of Action" is developed in the form of Jahweh. In this condition, believers see themselves as instruments of God and make every effort to win God's mercy in order to be saved. In other words:

Another new idea comes into the world with emissary prophecy that is with Judaism, because now men had to understand themselves as God's instruments working in the world. And it was again a new idea when Protestantism added predestination to this (Habermas, 1984: 196).

Habermas (1984: 204) agrees with Weber's claim about social contrast and the appearance of prophets: 'Emissary prophecies, as in the Judaeo-Christian tradition, promoted a particularly radical split between the here and the hereafter and correspondingly consistent forms of world rejection'.

Furthermore, Habermas contends that although the phenomena related to the objective, social and subjective worlds have been discussed separately in certain religious-metaphysical discourses, they are still fused when it comes to their fundamental concepts, and magical thought has not thus been radically overcome. As Habermas (1984: 214) puts it, the unity of the rationalised worldview is supported by concepts such as "God", "being" or "nature", or by ultimate principles and "beginnings", and while all proofs can be restored to such beginnings, these beginnings are not exposed to argumentative uncertainty. In these fundamental concepts, descriptive, normative and expressive features are still intermixed. Thus, it is in these beginnings that an element of mythical meditation continues. Put differently:

In Habermas's analysis, religious worldviews (both those of "primitive" and those of "world" religions) reveal a framework in which one finds either an absence or a low level of development. As a consequence, rational knowledge and action are not possible. Although the "religious-metaphysical" worldview represents a major advance according to developmental-logical criteria, it too still blends the different value spheres together in an undifferentiated manner, merging the ontic, normative and expressive dimensions (Rothberg, 1986: 223).

Thus, Habermas argues that religion is the product of the human mind and responds to his needs. Man seeks help from religion in his encounters with the three worlds of the objective, social and subjective. Some scholars believe that Habermas has put religion to rest, pronouncing its theoretical and social-developmental death. Habermas held that the validity of social norms is grounded only in the intersubjectivity of mutual understanding of intentions and secured by the general recognition of obligations.

In his *Critique of Practical Reason* (morality), Kant believes that religion must be founded not on theoretical logic or pure reason (epistemology), but on practical reason and ethical sense. If the formalities and rites in a religion prevail over its ethical spirit, that religion should be rejected. Thus, in this meditation, metaphysics is considered to be an irrational thing, which can only be attained through faith because it is embedded in the heart not in the head; namely, the religious worldview must be criticised as irrational, as not making rational knowledge and action possible, and such a worldview has no validity in modernity. Habermas (2003a, 110) in *The Future of Human* Nature stipulates that:

He [Kant] enlarged subjective freedom ... to autonomy (or free will), thus giving the first great example – after metaphysic – of a secularizing, but at the same time salvaging, deconstruction of religious truths. With Kant, the authority of divine commands is unmistakably echoed in the unconditional validity of moral duties. With his concept of autonomy, to be sure, he destroys the traditional image of men as children of God. But the preempts the trivial consequences of such a deflation by a critical assimilation of religious contents.

In *An Introduction to Modern European Philosophy*, Graham White (2008: 211-212) also expounds the idea that, for Kant, historical traditions, institutionalised religions, and cultural superstitions removed the possibility of establishing permanent peace between human beings. Enlightenment brought with it an achievement for the critical theory, which was a free association of wise human beings that could act to criticise historical and ideological events. Therefore, for Habermas, any support and praise for the authority of tradition will wipe out modern plans.

However, there are two points that can be raised against this picture. Firstly, although Habermas denies metaphysics, being partial to Kant's ideas, he reduces religion to a form of social ethics. Indeed, Habermas's perspective on religion, like Freud's, Durkheim's, Marx's and Frazer's, is a totally reductionist one. This reductionism is a gross mistake because it places religion within the limitations of certain dimensions and social functions. For instance, Habermas reduces the function of religion to one of its marginal features; namely, its tranquillising property. It is proper to point out that Habermas's ideas regarding ethical doctrine differs from those of Kant. While Kant contended that there is fundamental ethical doctrine whose universality can be recognised by everybody, Habermas holds that an individual can achieve ethical norms by agreeing with other participants in a discourse. Habermas considers morality, like reality, to be a phenomenon that occurs in a process of dialogue, and to be grounded in the intersubjectivity of action-orienting mutual understanding.

Secondly, it is also dubious to suggest that religious knowledge and metaphysics are contrary to rational argument. For example, Islamic thought is grounded in rational argumentation, and also many Iranian Muslim philosophers, such as Farabi, Ibn Sina (Avicenna), Sadr-e-din Shirazi and Allameh Tabatabai understand their theological task to be the reconciliation of religion with reason (Bahram, 2003: 39).

Like Tylor and Frazer, Habermas considers religion to be a set of ideas that people develop to illustrate what they find in their objective, social and subjective worlds. This means that religion is a product of the human mind and an interim response to human needs. Therefore, according to Habermas, myth and animism represent the earliest forms of religion, and polytheism and monotheism are later morphologies of religion that are doomed to destruction. Of course, the most rational phase is that of the modern, which implies desisting from any religion.

Two points can be made against Habermas's claims here. Firstly, the historical grounds for Habermas's view are weak. According to Pals (1996: 47), 'scholars such as Lang and Schmidt have pointed out the uncomfortable fact that monotheism, supposedly the "higher" form of religion, was more common in the simpler cultures of people who hunted and gathered food than in the later, advanced communities of those who farmed and kept herds of domestic animals'.

Secondly, Habermas had not personally studied religions when he put forward these claims, but contented himself with making judgments based on other scientists' presuppositions. As Eliade has argued, however, religion can only be comprehended if we try to see it from the standpoint of the believer. Hence, religion must sometimes be understood at its own level and studied *as* a religious doctrine, rather than being understood and explained by appealing to the doctrines of Freud, Durkheim and Marx, and Kantian philosophical assumptions, as Habermas does. Habermas's attitude to religion was unfair, and this accounts for his incorrect beliefs about and understanding of religion.

Like Marx, Habermas considers religion to be an instrument that is used to justify oppression by the authorities, priests and the owners of the tools of production. As far as Habermas is concerned, religion is the opium of the people in that it allows them to be negligent of their real pains and sufferings by providing purely imaginary ideas.

A further two points can be made in response to Habermas's reasoning here. Firstly, even if one accepts Habermas's claim that Divine religions have often been used as an instrument of oppression by dominant social classes in the West and the East, and that their doctrines have been distorted theoretically and practically (or just practically), this social reality does not harm the truth, nature and principles of religions, because monotheistic religions contest tyrants, oppression and indecent deeds because they undermine peace and justice. For instance,

The Glorious Koran has repeatedly criticised and opposed oppressors:

-If any do transgress the limits ordained by Allah, such persons wrong. (2: 299)

-But Allah loveth not those who do wrong. (3:57)

-The curse of Allah is on those who do wrong. (11: 18)

Because of his ignorance concerning the real doctrines of monotheistic religions, Habermas seems unable to separate social reality from religious truths.

Secondly, Habermas is not aware of the fact that even though heavenly religions have the same origin, these religions – as their holy scriptures have highlighted – have different elements, features and functions in addition to their similarities. Therefore, it is not appropriate for Habermas to issue a universal judgement on all religions, and his opinions on religion suggest that he is unfamiliar with monotheistic religions, especially Islam.

Nonetheless, even if we acknowledge these potential problems in some of Habermas's key philosophical and historical assumptions, his account of the effect of modernity upon religion is worth considering in some detail, since it offers a more complex account of the influence of religion upon society and vice-versa than most, albeit one which is also ultimately reductive.

4.1.3. Habermas's Understanding of Religion in Modernity

Habermas claims that, in the modern period especially since the rise of modern science, we have learned to distinguish more accurately between theoretical and practical argumentation. Classical natural law was reconstructed, and the nascent theories of natural law that legitimated the emerging new government claimed that they enjoyed creditable positions as opposed to systems of cosmologies, religions or ontologies, and acted independently.

With Rousseau and Kant this development led to the conclusion that the formal principle of reason replaced material principles like Nature or God in practical questions, questions concerning the justification of norms and actions ... In contract theories, from Hobbes and Locke to John Rawls, the fiction of a state of nature or of an original position also has the meaning of specifying the conditions under which an agreement will express the common interest of all involved – and to this extent can count as rational. In transcendentally oriented theories, from Kant to Karl-Otto Apel, these conditions, as universal and unavoidable presuppositions of rational will-formation, are transposed either into the subject as such or into the ideal communication community. In both traditions, it is the formal conditions of possible consensus formation, rather than ultimate grounds, which possess legitimating force ... The idea of an agreement that comes to pass among all parties, as free and equal, determines the procedural type of legitimacy of modern times (Habermas, 1979: 184-185).

Pusey (1987: 60) explains this stage by suggesting that in modern developed societies, the rationalisation of the base (economy, state and etc) has accounted for a greater rationalisation of the lifeworld. It is evident that the present cultural tradition contains formal concepts that provide rather stable separations of the objective, social and subjective dimensions of our world. In this regard, we witness specialised languages that first allow and then deepen evaluative criticism in the cognitive, moral and aesthetic dimensions of the cultural tradition. Above all, with the advancement of the rationalisation of the lifeworld, an 'increasingly *reflective* and *critical* processes of evaluation gradually dissolve those elements of the cultural tradition that were once dogmatically ascribed' (ibid.). According to Habermas, this process will lead us to extend the possibilities for learning. The point that must be taken into account is that rationalisation is not the outcome of the contents of the cultural tradition, but ensues from the new possibilities that permit us to criticise the contents that have become more deeply institutionalised in the rationalised lifeworld.

Habermas (1987: 146-147) holds that the promise of the enlightenment was that traditions would become reflective and then submit themselves to successive revision. In the end, we will reach a lifeworld in which there is nothing sacred except wisdom and consensus that rests on the authority of the best argument.

Pusey (1987: 47) notes that, illustrations from the process of modernisation are embedded within the discipline of sociology, and within every major social theory. Tonnies considers that dislocation from traditional to modern society as a shift from community to society. According to Durkheim, it is a transformation from mechanical to organic solidarity. In Marx's thought, it is construed as a shift in the mode of production. Although Habermas includes all these purports into his own theory, his reconstruction of Weber's theory of rationalisation is certainly one basic constituent of his theory.

Like Weber, Habermas defines the development of human community as a process of differentiation between the 'cultural value spheres (science, morality, art) governed by distinct claims to validity (truth, rightness, authenticity) and the embodiment of different rationality structures (cognitive-instrumental, moral-practical, aesthetic-expressive), which gradually undercut the ability of religion to provide the integration of society' (D'Entreves and Benhabib, 1996: 3). For Habermas:

Religion has become obsolete in the process of modernity. The modern dichotomy between the transcendent and immanent, the sacred and the profane, has led to the antagonism between individual and collective in modern action systems (Siebert, 1985: 83).

Elaborating on this, Habermas describes rationalisation as having characteristics such as the 'decentration', 'disenchantment' and 'linguistification' of the sacred.

• Decentration of the Religious-Metaphysical Worldview

Habermas attributes the notion of 'decentration' to Weber, and claims that the decentration of our understanding of the world proved to be the most important dimension in the development of modern worldviews. This idea is grounded in Piaget's theory of the cognitive growth of a child, which has been extended and applied to the history of human thinking.

Habermas considers the concept of egocentrism as decentration, and assumes that egocentrism is renewed at each stage. Accordingly, the egocentrism of a child is closely associated with his inability to differentiate himself from the group that he is a part of, as well as his failure to separate himself from external objective phenomena. Moreover, at this stage of development, a child considers himself to be the centre of being. Overcoming this constraint requires a decentration of one's self. Adams (2006: 135) asserts that:

This is one of the concepts Habermas takes over from Piaget: its original context is the development of the child who learns to see things from other people's perspectives and not only his or her own. Habermas speculates that something like this is true of societies as they begin to see themselves from other societies' point of view.

Habermas compares the concept of God with the early concept of the self, and attributes religious thought to the childhood of mankind. He equates the eradication of such thought (in the process of rationalisation) with decentration. Moreover:

Extending Piaget's notion of 'decentration' from an individual to a social level, Habermas finds support for his concept of communicative rationality in terms of the growing rationalisation of worldviews. According to Habermas, Piaget himself suggests such an extension by; (i) regarding the development of intelligence as only one dimension of the process of decentration; (ii) understanding all traditions as progressive steps in decentration; and (iii) viewing the egocentric perspective of the child as a model for mythical thought (Roderick, 1986: 119).

Habermas (1984: 70) also argues that:

The more the worldview that furnishes the cultural stock of knowledge is decentred, the less the need for understanding is covered *in advance* by an interpreted lifeworld immune from critique, and the more this need has to be met by the interpretive accomplishments of the participants themselves, that is, by way of risky (because rationally motivated) agreement, the more frequently we can expect rational action orientations.

Habermas (1984: 45) explains that he invokes Piaget's concept of decentration to show that we must accept the evolutionary perspective if we want (along with Weber) to appreciate the world-historical processes relevant to the rationalisation of the lifeworld. This process drives an understanding of the world that opens the way for a rationalisation of the lifeworld. Habermas (1984: 71) holds that mythical worldviews show an instructive limiting case: to the degree that the lifeworld of a social group is construed through a mythical worldview, the task of interpretation is taken away from the individual member. As a result, there is less chance for an individual to reach an agreement that is open to criticism: 'To the extent that the worldview remains sociocentric in Piaget's sense, it does not permit differentiation between the world of existing states of affairs, valid norms and expressible subjective experiences' (Habermas, ibid.). Within this system of orientation, actions do not reach the critical range where communicatively achieved agreement depends upon independent yes/no responses to criticisable validity claims. Thus, cultural traditions must display the following formal characteristics 'if rational action orientations are to be possible in a lifeworld interpreted correspondingly, [and] if they are to be able to consolidate into a rational conduct of life' (Habermas, ibid.):

1. The cultural tradition must provide formal concepts for the objective, social and subjective world. It must allow separated validity claims (propositional truth, normative rightness and subjective truthfulness) and provoke a corresponding differentiation of fundamental attitudes (objectivating, norm-conformative and expressive). Under such circumstances, symbolic expressions can be presented 'on a formal level at which they are systematically connected with reasons and accessible to objective assessment' (Habermas, ibid.). In other words:

The basic criterion used by Habermas, following Weber and Durkheim, as well as later writers on religion and "modernization" such as Parsons, Bellah, and Dobert, is differentiation: the separation out of what Weber calls the three cultural "value spheres" of science, morality, and art from their relatively undifferentiated unity in religious worldviews; each of these spheres is thus freed to follow its own inner logic. This process is simultaneously a differentiation of three "worlds" ("objective", "social" and "subjective"), three "attitudes" (Einstellungen) by which to approach these worlds ("objectivating," "norm-conformative," and "expressive"), and, very crucially, three types of "validity claims" (truth, rightness, and truthfulness) (Rothberg, 1986: 222).

2. The cultural tradition must provide a reflective relation to itself. It must be so far free of its dogmatism that it can let the reserved interpretations in tradition be put to question and subjected to critical revision. To put it another way, 'reflexivity involves, for Habermas, the ability to thematize as problematic any explicit or implicit claim, and to investigate the validity of such a claim free of coercive, dogmatic, or unconscious constraints' (Rothberg, 1986: 222-223).

3. In its cognitive, ethical and evaluative dimensions, the cultural tradition must facilitate a feedback-relation with specialised forms of argumentation. Like Beyer (1994: 67, 80), Habermas argues that this is how cultural subsystems can evolve for science, law, morality, music, art and literature, and how they can provide traditions 'that are supported by arguments rendered fluid through permanent criticism but at the same time professionally secured' (Habermas, 1984: 72).

4. Finally, 'the cultural tradition must interpret the lifeworld in such a way that action oriented to success can be freed from the imperatives of an understanding that is to be communicatively renewed over and over again and can be at least partially uncoupled from action oriented to reaching understanding' (Habermas, 1984: 72).

Habermas (1984: 72) continues to explain that, if we regard the concept of decentration that Piaget introduced as a guideline for explaining the internal connection between the structure of a worldview, the lifeworld as an area of understanding processes, and the feasibilities of a rational life, then we again confront the concept of communicative rationality, and 'this concept relates a decentered understanding of the world to the possibility of discursively redeeming criticizable validity claims'.

- Disenchantment of the Religious-Metaphysical Worldview

Habermas adopts the concept of disenchantment from Weber, but reconstructs it within his own system. He explores, through the work of Mead and Durkheim, the fundamental areas within Weber's theory of rationalisation that can be accepted and delivered from the difficulties and contradictions of the philosophy of consciousness (Habermas, 1984: 399). Habermas

(1984: 186-215) discusses the issue of the disenchantment of religious-metaphysical worldviews and the emergence of modern structures of consciousness. In an early part of his discussion on disenchantment, Habermas (1984: 186) points out that Weber construes the separation between cultural value spheres to be key for highlighting Western rationalism, and that Weber understood this separation as an outcome of an internal history of the rationalisation of religious worldviews. As Outhwaite (1996: 337) puts it:

He [Weber] described as "rational" the process of disenchantment which led in Europe to a disintegration of religious world-views that issued in a secular culture. With the modern empirical sciences, autonomous arts, and theories of morality and law grounded on principles, cultural spheres of value took shape which mode possible learning process in accord with the respective inner logics of theoretical, aesthetic, and moral-practical problems.

Pusey defines the disenchantment process in such a way that the passage from traditional communities to our current one is seen as a deliverance from magic, witchcraft and sorcery, as well as from many types of 'holy horror' that 'produced the Inquisition, poor Galileo's unhappy end, and the witches of Salem. This progress, together with the development of science, learning, technology and art is a rational progress' (Pusey, 1987: 48). Weber considers this rational progress as disenchantment. Pusey claims that the main point that Weber emphasised was that, Protestantism embraced disenchantment in the face of modern capitalism; that is, it submitted itself to mundane necessities and to instrumental rationality.

In the introduction of *The Theory of Communicative Action* (Habermas, 1984: xxiv-xxv), McCarthy also explains that:

Taking Durkheim's analysis of the shift from mechanical to organic solidarity as his point of departure, Habermas examines the process whereby social functions originally fulfilled by ritual practice and religious symbolism gradually shift to the domain of communicative action. This disenchantment means a growing sublimation of the spellbinding and terrifying power of the sacred ... into the rationally binding/bonding force of criticizable claims to validity ... The authority of tradition is increasingly open to discursive questioning; the range of applicability of norms expands while the latitude for interpretation and the need for reasoned justification increases; the differentiation of individual identities grows, as does the sphere of personal autonomy.

Like Weber, Habermas stipulates that, unable to perceive the connections between different phenomena, people construed them as the actions of a creator. God was a new idea, and with the birth of this idea came the idea that human destiny, both in this world and the next, depends on obeying ethical commandments. However, as empirical science has usurped God within modernity, there is no longer any need for this theory. Consequently, 'the fate of our times is characterized by rationalization and intellectualization and, above all, by the disenchantment of the world' (Weber, 1948: 155).

- The Rational Structure of the Linguistification of the Sacred

In the second volume of *The Theory of the Communicative Action*, Habermas (1987: 77-111) elaborates on the rational structure of the linguistification of the sacred. In this discussion, he attempts to recognise social interaction by utilising and adhering to Mead's and Durkheim's views regarding the hypothetical starting point of sociocultural development. Indeed, linguistification of the sacred serves as a suitable rational course for practising disenchantment. Accordingly, Habermas states that he enlists, from this hypothesis, the idea that the socially integrative and expressive functions were transformed into communicative action from their ritual practice. The authority of the holy is progressively supplanted by the authority of an achieved consensus. This consensus arises from a liberated communicative action that has been released from sacredly protected normative contexts:

The disenchantment and disempowering of the domain of the sacred takes place by way of a linguistification of the ritually secured, basic normative agreement; going along with this is a release of the rationality potential in communicative action. The aura of rapture and terror that emanates from the sacred, the spellbinding power of the holy, is sublimated into the binding/bonding force of criticizable validity claims and at the same time turned into an everyday occurrence (Habermas, 1987: 77).

Outhwaite (1994: 84) writes that Habermas's argument here is a combination of Durkheim's and Weber's visions on the development of law, religion and ethics 'with a thought-experiment involving the differentiation of a hypothetical limit case of a totally integrated society'. Habermas (1987: 78-81) holds that Durkheim, like Weber, analysed legal development as a disenchantment process. Archaic law is basically a penal one, whereas Durkheim counts civil law as the model of modern law. Modern law focuses on the balancing of private interests, putting aside the holy character of law. Durkheim claims that ownership originates from human beings' relationships with their gods. Taxes were ritual presents, paid primarily to the gods, and then to the priests and the state authorities. As a result of this holy origin, ownership has a magical quality, while the appearance of the contract of mutual consensus that accompanied the growth of human compassion has led to the idea that the contract is moral and lawful (when it is not a tool for exploiting one of the contracting parties). Habermas (1987: 82) explains that 'the development of the contract from a ritual formalism into the most important instrument of bourgeois private law suggests the idea of a 'linguistification'' of a basic religious consensus that has been set communicatively a flow'.

Habermas (1987: 87-89) also makes use of Wittgenstein's work on language when he talks about language "going on holiday" in religious communities. What this means is that language does not have a special place in religious communities. Habermas (1987: 88-89) alleges that 'only when the structures of action oriented to reaching understanding become effective does a linguistification of the sacred arise, determining the logic of the changing forms of social integration as described by Durkheim'. Therefore, the validity basis of tradition is transferred from ritual action to communicative action. Creeds owe their validity less and less to the magic and the aura of the holy, and more and more to agreement:

We can make clear what it means when institutions grounded in the sacred not only act effectively in and through processes of reaching understanding –by steering, performing, prejudging – but themselves become dependent upon the binding effect of consensus formation in language. Then social integration no longer takes place directly *via* institutionalized values but by way of intersubjective recognition of validity claims raised in speech acts. Communicative actions also remain embedded in existing normative contexts, but speakers can explicitly refer to the latter in speech acts and take up different stances toward them (Habermas, 1987: 89).

It is proper to point out that Habermas seeks to replace religion with communicative action and morality. However, morality has the power to hold together a modern society and to be a substitute for traditional community only if society's norms could be reflectively embraced by everyone. Mead's theory can be used as a model for Habermas because Mead, through accepting Kant's idea that morality involves universality, illustrates his idealistic projection of a communicatively rationalised society. In other words,

The more communicative action takes over from religion the burdens of social integration, the more the ideal of an unlimited and undistorted communication community gains empirical influence in the real communication community. Mead supports this contention, as did Durkheim, by pointing to the spread of democratic ideas, the transformation of the foundations of legitimation in the modern state (Habermas, 1987: 96).

In brief, for Habermas, the linguistification of the sacred means a rationalisation of the lifeworld; that is, 'social realities are no longer shaped by rituals, symbols or emotional energies, but through communicative discourse ... The power of the sacred in modernity is translated into the authority of an achieved consensus established on the basis of criticisable validity claims' (Mellor, 2004: 140). In this regard, the authority of the holy is replaced by a fundamental normative agreement or communicative action and is thus no longer sacred.

4.2. The Role of Religion in Habermas's Current Thought

Despite the foregoing discussion, Habermas has exhibited a far more constructive engagement with religion and its role in public life in his more recent work than he did in his earlier work. Surprisingly, he has even insisted that religion is the principal source of the passions and motivations underpinning cultural life in modern secular societies, and that communicative action cannot simply take over the role of religion in the public sphere. He elucidates that 'religion provides orienting pictures of unspoilt forms of life that offer an at once limiting and disclosing horizon, images that inspire and encourage us in our repeated efforts at cooperatively bringing about the good, and thus offer regenerative power for a dwindling normative consciousness' (Harrington, 2007: 47). This reflects an acknowledgement that religion has not become marginal to social and cultural life in the way he expected it to, but also a desire to reassess certain aspects of his own philosophy of modernity.

4.2.1. Religiousness in a Secular Context: Secularisation in Postsecular Society

In a lecture on 'religiousness in a secular context' that Habermas (2002c: 18) delivered at Tehran University on 14th May 2002, he asserts that the term "secularisation" primarily had a juridical meaning. In Europe, we regarded this word as an historical outcome of an obligatory devolution of church properties to the secular state or laic sovereignty. In a cultural conflict in the 19th century, the meaning of this term was subsumed as a symbol for the victorious flow of modernity. Since then, some contrasting evaluations have linked modern periods of time with a secular meaning. One side that declared itself as liberal welcomed the surrender of church power through the means of mundane ruling and the successful taming of clerical authority. The other side, who were priests, objected to what they saw as the illegal dispossession or unlawful appropriation of church authority. Based on the first reading, religious forms were substituted with rational equivalents. Now, if we construe the function of the dispossession of ecclesiastical property as a symbol for the entirety of modernisation, then the first reading – that is, the picture of an abandoned religion that has been pushed aside by science and enlightenment – drives us to an optimistic interpretation of progressive disenchantment. In contrast, the second reading – that is to say, that the church had its authority illegally dispossessed or stolen – drives us to a digressive interpretation of the unsheltered modernity. Under this reading, modern ways of thinking and modern forms of life are discredited as illegitimately appropriated goods. Habermas holds that both of these readings commit the same mistake. They both perceive secularisation as a kind of zero-sum game between capitalism and the church forces. In the game, gains on one side can only be achieved at the expense of losses on the other side. Both liberals and theologians contended that the rules of this game acted in favour of the driving forces of modernity, which led to the spokesmen for scientific enlightenment and the religious jurists of the 19th and 20th centuries confronting one another in an irreconcilable clash. In the meantime, it has been found that the game between religion and enlightenment does not correspond to Western postsecular societies.

Habermas (2002c: 18) explains that breaking with traditional forms of life naturally brings with it pain and suffering. Reckless modernisation ruins the old solidarities without compensation. What we mean by 'rationalisation of the lifeworld', with regard to the three categories of individuals, traditions and institutions, is that the areas of science and technique, law and ethics, art, and the art of critique, are originated from the renewed hermeneutics born of fallible knowledge.

Habermas (2002c: 18) notes that there are three models of 'secularism': the 'replacement', the 'expropriation' and the 'disruptive secularisation' model, and he declares that all three are wrong. 'Replacement', refers to the way in which religious approaches to thinking and religious forms of life have been replaced by their rational equivalents. 'Expropriation', simply means 'robbery'. In *The Future of Human Nature*, Habermas (2003a: 104) describes how:

The replacement model suggests a progressivist interpretation in terms of disenchanted modernity, while the expropriation model leads to an interpretation in terms of a theory of decline, that is, unsheltered modernity. Both readings make the same mistake.

For Habermas, the process of the rationalisation of lifeworld involves individuals moving towards an "individual freedom", that is, individuals are increasingly expected to have independent social relations. In the course of the process, however, cultural traditions lose their power, and are no longer beyond criticism.

According to Habermas (2002c: 18-19), the third model, 'disruptive secularisation', includes social institutions. In the process of rationalisation, these institutions lose their constancy and are identified as products of humankind. Thus, the relation between state and religion ruptures and religious society is distinguished from secular society. This differentiation has been drawn by Weber.

Habermas believes that the transformation of traditional life and the intermediation of modernity are experienced as secularisation by those who have been impressed by it. This is due to the fact that, during the long process of the rationalisation of life, religions (as a whole) have had to desist from claiming to be the sole interpreters of entities, architects of the souls of individuals, and judges and educators of the polity and community.

4.2.2. The Legitimacy of a Secular State

In describing the legitimacy of a secular government and the liberal conception of democratic citizenship in the Holberg Prize Seminar, Habermas (2005b: 5-6) explains that 'the self-understanding of the constitutional state has developed from a contractualist tradition that relies solely on public arguments to which all persons are supposed to have equal access'. The assumption that there is a common human wisdom became the epistemic basis for the justification of a secular government, which no longer depended on religious legitimation. This is the essential move that provided the background for a separation between the government and the church at a fundamental level. Of course, this liberal attitude took shape within an historical background that consisted of religious wars and confessional disputes in the new era. The shaping of the freedom of religion was the suitable political response to the challenges of religious pluralism. Nevertheless, the peculiarity of secular government is a necessary, but not a sufficient condition for ensuring an equal religious freedom for all individuals. Relying merely on the goodwill of a secularised authority is not enough, as the 'conflicting parties themselves must reach agreement on the precarious delimitations between a positive freedom to practice one's own religion and the negative freedom to remain spared of the religious practices of the others' (Habermas, 2005b: 5-6). Thus, these parties must adduce strong arguments for the definition of what can be tolerated and what cannot, and these must be acceptable to all parties. Equitable practices can only be found at a time when the concerned parties learn to look at the problems as the other parties do. The practice that best serves this purpose consists of the deliberative mode of democratic will-formation.

According to those who believe that governments should be secular, the democratic procedure is able to create a secular legitimation through two elements:

1. The equal political participation of all citizens, which ensures that the clients of the law can consider themselves as the authors of these laws.

2. The epistemic dimension of deliberation, which grounds the presumption of rationally acceptable outcomes.

Habermas holds that political decisions are legitimate only if they can be justified in the light of generally accessible reasons – vis-à-vis, reasons that can be accepted by– religious and non-religious citizens, and by citizens of different religious confessions. Furthermore, 'the principle of separation of state and church obliges politicians and officials within political institutions to formulate and justify laws, court rulings, decrees and measures only in a language which is equally accessible to all citizens' (Habermas, 2005b: 6).

4.2.3. The Duties of Citizens in the Political Public Sphere

In the continuation of his discussion regarding the legitimacy of a secular state, Habermas (2005b: 6-8) raises the question of what duties citizens have in the political public sphere. He notes that Rawls' position is the following:

The first is that reasonable comprehensive doctrines, religious or non-religious, may be introduced in public political discussion at any time, provided that in due course proper political reasons – and not reasons given solely by comprehensive doctrines – are presented that are sufficient to support whatever the comprehensive doctrines are said to support (Habermas, 2005b: 6-7).

Yet, in a recent discussion on citizens and the public use of rational reasons, this limitation regarding the proviso of secular justification is faced with many objections. The most serious is that many religious citizens do not have, in their own minds, good reasons to accept an artificial division between secular and religious issues, because they are not able to do this without upsetting the stability of their lifestyles as religious people. This objection is based on the idea that religion plays an integral role in the life of a religious person. In fact:

A devout person pursues her daily rounds by drawing on her belief. True belief is not only a doctrine, believed content, but a source of energy that the faithful person taps performatively. Faith nurtures an entire life. This totalizing trait of a mode of believing that infuses the very pores of daily life runs counter to any flimsy switchover of religiously rooted political convictions onto a different cognitive basis (Habermas, 2005b: 7).

Habermas (ibid.) continues by noting that Nicolas Wolterstorff claims that it belongs to the religious convictions of a good many religious people in our society that they ought to base their decisions concerning fundamental issues of justice on their religious convictions. They do not view this as optional, and are thus not only unwilling, but also incapable of discerning any pull from secular reasons.

Habermas believes that if we accept this rather rigorous protest, the liberal system of government (which supports religious lifestyles) cannot at the same time require all individual citizens to provide their political opinions independently of their credence and worldview. Thus:

We cannot derive from the secular character of the state an obligation for all citizens to supplement their public religious contributions by equivalents in a generally accessible language. The liberal state must not transform the requisite institutional separation of religion and politics into an undue mental and psychological burden for all those citizens who follow a faith (Habermas, 2005b: 7).

The state must expect citizens to recognise the fact that any legal, juridical or administrative decision should remain impartial with regard to rival worldviews. However, the liberal state 'must not expect them to split their identity in public and private components as long as they participate in public debates and contribute to the formation of public opinions' (Habermas, 2005b: 8).

4.2.4. Habermas and the End of Discrimination; the Beginning of Tolerance

In a talk delivered at the Iranian Philosophical Society, Habermas (2002d: 13-14) explains that the German term 'toleranz' was initially borrowed from Latin and French in the 16th century. As a result, the term has assumed the more particular sense of 'forbearance' vis-à-vis other religions for German people. In the 16th and 17th centuries, religious tolerance was adopted as a legal concept, and German governments formulated and approved laws involving the concept of tolerance, such as the moderation or tolerance of religious minorities, including Lutherans, Houghtons, and Papists. Once these tolerance laws were approved, people were expected to show tolerance towards religious adherents who had been suppressed, persecuted and prosecuted. In English, the term 'tolerance' means the ability to behave tolerantly, or the virtue of toleration as a lawful measure by which the government guarantees the right to the performance of religious actions, and this concept was thus extracted from the German use accurately.

During this talk, whose audience included Iranian Professors of philosophy, sociology and politics, Habermas went on to explain that, in German, the term 'toleranz' has two meanings. It denotes both a legal system assuring moderation, and a form of behaviour as a norm. Under the contemporary use of this term, we not only understand the general ability of the tolerant attitude with regard to outsiders, but also with regards to the citizens of other races. Religious tolerance also was later politically generalised, with religion being seen as portrayal of the world or, as Rawls puts it, as a doctrine of perception. Finally Habermas (2002d: 14) concludes that:

A. Rawls uses his approach to streamline the ethics of human rights in different religious worldviews. His approach has the advantage that it does not remove the claim of absolute truth from religions, whilst also making room for the notion of tolerance.

B. As Thomas Aquinas argues, eternal salvation has an absolute advantage over everything, and hence using violence in order to turn people back to an orthodox faith is not over at all. Thus, there are many alternatives to convert a dogmatic idea into tolerance. We must either deny some rudiments that inculcate all who differ are outside the realm of salvation, or argue that one cannot reach veracious faith through pressure.

C. Religious tolerance tries to hamper the social destruction that can ensue from an irreconcilable incompatibility between people. This incompatibility must not break the social communication that links a religious person to believers of other religions and to atheists. Tolerating other beliefs requires a differentiation of the roles in society. This separation should be undertaken between members of the religious community and the community of citizens, and must be justified by religion in such a way that religious believers may not conflict with one another. An ideal position would be one in which a cultural majority with a local, lingual and national minority not only live together without humiliating one another, but also live together with equal rights.

4.2.5. Habermas's Demarcation of Tolerance

At the Iranian Philosophical Society, Habermas (2002d: 13) stipulated that when some people negate or deny others for their skin colour, we must not invite or encourage the victims or the observers to act tolerantly towards this way of behaving, because in doing so we would accept their basis of pre-judgment as an ethical judgement: a judgment which is like a decline or rejection of someone else's religion. A "Racist" cannot accept tolerance and act tolerantly. As a first step, he must put aside the racist tendency and desist from it. In this regard, we prescribe that the prejudice is criticised, that discrimination is fought, and that equal rights are established, and hold that these, as opposed to additional tolerance, are the appropriate responses. Indeed, before we expect tolerance from each other, we must embrace the norm that all citizens have equal titles. Justice can provide ethical and lawful foundations for treating citizens with tolerance only when it has been accepted by all. These foundations can overcome those worldviews that reject tolerance. Thus, the permanent contrast between rival worldviews can be removed because of this normative agreement.

In avoiding a humiliating tolerance, Habermas (2002d: 13-14) asserts that we can remove the basic paradox based on mutual validation of rules of moderation. This is a paradox which made Goethe reject a scornful tolerance that degrades humankind. Any tolerance should be accompanied by descriptions of what is accepted and at the same time identify the limits of tolerance. Therefore, this paradox can find its solution in a democratic lawful government. Religious tolerance that has been demanded mutually by all must rely on an acceptable moderation. This demarcation can be developed only by discourse and consultation. Thus, religious tolerance is only ensured when religious freedom is legalized. The legitimate power of such a doctrine is generalized and continued at the time when democratic common sense or the contractualist tradition is developed. Habermas (2003a: 118) adds:

Of course, the contractualist tradition, too, has religious roots – roots in the very revolution of the ways of thinking that were brought about by the ascent of the great world religions. But this legitimation of law and politics in terms of modern natural law feeds on religious sources that have long since become secularized.

4.2.6. Habermas and the Revival of Religion in the West

In responding to the challenges of religious revival in the west, Habermas (2005b: 2) explained during the Holberg Prize Seminar that:

We can hardly fail to notice the fact that religious traditions and communities of faith have gained a new, hitherto unexpected political importance. The fact is at least unexpected for those of us who followed the conventional wisdom of mainstream social science and assumed that modernization inevitably goes hand in hand with secularization in the sense of a diminishing influence of religious beliefs and practices on politics and society at large.

Furthermore, Habermas (2005b: 4) declares that the political revitalisation of religion at the centre of the Western community is the most astonishing social occurrence of this era. Although statistical evidence supports the thesis that a secularisation wave has struck all European countries since the end of the World War II, all data in the United States indicates that a large majority of its national population is composed of pious and religiously energetic citizens, and that this has remained fairly constant over the past six decades:

It tends to intensify, at the cultural level, the political division of the West that was prompted by the Iraq war. With the abolition of the death penalty, with liberal regulations on abortion, with setting homosexual partnerships on a par with heterosexual marriages, with an unconditional rejection of torture, and generally with the privileging of individual rights versus collective goods, e.g. national security, the European states seem now to be moving forward alone down the path they had trodden side by side with the United States (Habermas, 2005b: 4).

The Western image of modernity has seemed, as sometimes happens in psychological experiments, to have undergone a drastic change: 'what has been the supposedly "normal" model for the future of all other cultures suddenly changes into a special-case scenario' (Habermas, 2005b: 4). Irrespective of how one evaluates the facts, the cultural wave in the United States has provided a background for academic discussion on the role of religion in the political public sphere. Habermas predicts that the development of religious beliefs will be reflected in the arena of internal politics. Religion is becoming involved in the international field in a variety of different roles, and 'world religions that to this very day shape the physiognomy of all major civilizations fuel the agenda of multiple modernities with requisite cultural self-esteem' (Habermas, 2005b: 3).

4.2.7. Recommendations for Religious and Secular Citizens

Habermas (2005b: 9-11) asserts that the liberal ethics of citizenship seems to impose an inappropriate pressure on the religious portion of a population. The need to translate religious reasons into secular ones, as a result of the priority given to secular reasoning, requires religious citizens to make more effort to learn and adapt themselves to the concepts that are understood by, and made available to, secular citizens.

Sociologists have described this modernisation of religious consciousness as a response to three challenges:

1. The reality of pluralism

2. The renaissance and the emergence of modern science

3. The spread of positive law and a profane ethics

Habermas offers recommendations to religious and secular citizens for meeting these challenges. Firstly, he argues that religious citizens should take an epistemic attitude toward other religions and worldviews. They succeed to the degree that they must describe their religious credence for rival theories and, consequently, their own claims to truth can be checked and amended: 'Every religious teaching today encounters the pluralism of different form of religious truth, as well as the scepticism of secular scientific knowledge which owes its social authority to its declared fallibility and learning process based on unceasing revision' (Habermas, 2006b: 152). Secondly, religious citizens should then develop an epistemic stance towards the independence of secular and sacred knowledge. Finally, religious citizens must develop an epistemic stance towards the priority that secular reasons enjoy in political and social arenas.

Habermas also makes the following recommendation to secular citizens: as long as secular citizens construe religious traditions and communities as obsolete rites of pre-modern societies that continue to exist in the present time, they fall prey to what he will call a "secularist" view: 'secularist in the sense that they can understand freedom of religion only as the natural preservation of an endangered species. From their viewpoint, religion lacks any intrinsic justification to exist. The principle of the separation of state and church can for them only have the Laic meaning of sparing indifference' (Habermas, 2005b: 11). Therefore, the liberal ethics of citizenship require complementary learning processes to be undertaken by both secular and religious citizens.

In summary, Habermas's earlier views of religion located it in a premodern stage of 'social evolution' – initially at a 'mythical' stage where subjective, objective and social phenomena were largely undifferentiated, then at a 'religious-metaphysical' stage determined by traditions that limit individual and collective rationality and autonomy. The evolution of societies into modern forms were understood to render religion philosophically irrelevant and socially obsolete, with its marginalisation in the West a preface to its complete obliteration from public life. In recent years, however, it has become clear that religion has become more, not less, important in public life, and it is Habermas's view of religion that has had to evolve. In the course of this chapter, I have mapped this evolution, but I have also suggested that what Habermas has now recognised is that religion is a far more important part of the lifeworld than he previously understood, and that while the social system has undoubtedly threatened religion, it has also proved far more resilient in the face of this than some other parts of the lifeworld.

4.3. An Analytical Assessment of Habermas's Current Approach Towards Religion

Like other secular theorists, Habermas negates any divine origin for religions, reducing them to human products. Even in the light of his revised understanding of religion, religious propositions are still unable to act as a basis for discourse in the communicative action: 'Habermas finally decides that theology cannot accommodate itself to Postmetaphysical thought lest it abandon the very thing which substantiates its claim to be the *logos* of the *theos*' (Lalonde, 2007: 53). More positively, nevertheless, Habermas claims that 'in short, post-metaphysical thought is prepared to learn from religion, but remains agnostic in the process' (Habermas, 2006a: 17).

Lalonde challenges Habermas, claiming that there is a shortage of positive ethical meaning in his critical theory, and holding that Habermas wants to compensate for this insufficiency through using religion to 'assist toward the growth of spontaneous empathy and caring relationships. To be sure, this gesture inevitably clashed with the emphatic modernity supporting the theory of communicative action and reason – one that presages, in turn, an instrumental analysis of religion in the face of certain postmodern pressures' (Lalonde, 1999: 102). Lalonde considers Habermas's position to involve an undue recourse or awkward appeal to religious issues that is necessarily in contrast to Habermas's theoretical suppositions. In fact, 'it is an appeal that originates from within his own critical reflections rather than being forced from without by extraneous theological ambitions. Habermas's religious interest, however, exhibits the breach of a split conviction' (Lalonde, 1999: 83). In other words, Habermas's appeal to religion originates from an attitude that religious issues can act as a vital support for compensating the ethical imperatives that arise from the contemporary social status. Lalonde (1999: 3) cannot accept Habermas's suggestion that theology might put aside its cognitive contents as belonging to extraordinary religious experiences in order to be critical. Rather, 'by doing so, theology not only loses its boundaries as an independent discipline, it ceases to be a discipline altogether' (Lalonde, 1999: 53).

However, a fair critique of Habermas must acknowledge how his more recent engagement with religion not only signals a welcome move on his part to modify his theoretical perspectives in the light of changing circumstances, and also that it attempts to meet the insufficiency of secular approaches to religion that have dominated much philosophical and sociological approaches in the modern era. He stipulates that:

Post-metaphysical thinking cannot understand itself if it does not include religious traditions side by side with metaphysics in its own genealogy. On this premise it would be mistaken to lay aside these strong traditions merely as archaic vestiges of the past, since religious inheritances articulate for us today a consciousness of something that is lacking to us (Harrington, 2007: 49).

The restoration of religions to the centre of public life, and the appearance of religious movements all over the world, is not a subject to be ignored. Secular states believed that history would advance in favour of political secularism, and they have tended, at best, to tolerate religion and adopt an impartial view of its costs and benefits as a social phenomenon. More recently, however, secular states have begun to abandon their impartial positions concerning the revival of religion to the public sphere, and have started to question and restrict their religious citizens.

On the basis of his early work, it could have been anticipated that Habermas might have endorsed such secularism, but he challenges a structural violence that exists in Western society, and contends that it contains unconscionable social inequality, contemptuous discrimination, pauperisation, and a marginalisation of various individuals. In other words, he holds that 'our social relations are permeated by violence, strategic action and manipulation' (Borradori, 2003: 35). Habermas says that there are two more relevant facts in Western society: the praxis of our daily life is based on a common background of creeds, axiomatic cultural realities and mutual expectations, which have more or less suitable validity in the public sphere, and for that reason, all contrasts within the West are derived from a distorted communication, misunderstanding and misinterpretation, hypocrisy and deception. According to Habermas, 'the spiral of violence begins as a spiral of distorted communication that leads through the spiral of uncontrolled reciprocal mistrust, to the breakdown of communication' (Borradori, 2003: 35). For Habermas, desirable changes in subjectivity take place through improving quality of life and removing fear and repression, and trust must be more widespread in communicative everyday practices.

Habermas wants the West to have a different form of normative self-representation vis-à-vis other cultures, and to change its politics if it wants to be construed as a shaping power with a civilising impact. To achieve this, the West must be able to politically tame unleashed capitalism (Borradori, 2003: 35-36). It must also, however, adopt a radically different view of the potential role for religion in public life. Thus, Habermas now talks of 'postsecular' societies, and rejects the logic of mainstream social science, where it has been assumed that religion has retreated as a consequence of the processes of modernisation and secularisation. Although these 'upsurges' in religion are inherently opposed to much that Habermas himself would like to see happen, he still emphasises that religious citizens should be 'allowed to express and justify their convictions in a religious language' (Habermas, 2006a: 10). As McLennan (2007: 867) puts it:

In Habermasian postsecularism, non-believers, just like believers, are required to undergo an equivalent, and intertwined, *learning process*. They too have to overcome cognitive dissonance, by accepting the continuing value of the religious consciousness and by genuinely appreciating not only the human *motivation* for, but also the possible *truth-content* of, religious worldviews.

What Habermas recognises is that, while secularism assumed the reduction of religion to a private and individual phenomenon, the 'self-building' function of religion should be grasped alongside its 'society-building'. Habermas's current approach to religion, while undoubtedly very different to that in his earlier thought, can be seen as emanating from the inner logic of his thought in a broader sense. He now advocates dialogue in the encounter between religion and modernity, since he has come to grant religion a special position and merit as a fundamental part of the lifeworld.

Chapter 5: Religious and Secular Worldviews in Iranian Thought

So far in this book, I have examined Habermas's arguments concerning religion and the public sphere within the context of his philosophical focus on democracy and freedom, and, more broadly, with respect to his views about the challenges and opportunities presented by modernity and its impact upon traditional modes of thought and practice. This chapter occupies a pivotal position in the overall structure of this book. It introduces the ideas of Iranian intellectuals concerning the role of religion in public life, which will then be compared to those of Habermas, with a particular focus on the arguments of Shariati.

5.1. The Iranian Intellectual Perspective on the Encounter of Tradition and Modernity

The revolution of subjectivity, the underlying ontological foundation of modernity, has left almost no part of the world untouched. Through colonization, economic exploitation, and cultural objectification, and through the introduction of new ideas, norms, and institutions, the modern West has reshaped the destiny of all societies on the globe. Third world countries have responded with denial, emulation, infatuation, confrontation, resentment or a combination of these. Iran has been no exception. Over the century and a half of its belated encounter with modernity, these responses have constituted the major elements of its history. What makes Iran unique, however, is its preoccupation with the metaphysical foundations of modernity – a preoccupation whose origins lie in a deeply entrenched tradition of monotheism going back to pre-Islamic religions and in an equally ancient sense of cultural identity, and one that has had important ramifications for Iran's institutions (Vahdat, 2002: 212).

Iranian intellectuals have taken three different approaches towards modernity over the last one hundred and fifty years – Westoxication, traditionalism, and reformism. This section of this chapter will look at these approaches in turn.

5.1.1. Westoxication

Both Mirza Fathali Akhundzadeh and Mirza Malkum Khan are partisans of the Westoxication view. This view is characterised by the following elements: an infatuation with the West and the achievements of modernity; a reproduction of Western thought and practice; an imitation of Western models of development; anti-traditionalism; the reformation of religion or Islamic Protestantism; the belief in a contrast between reason and religion; the belief in the separation of religion from politics; the defence of freedom of thought, equality and justice; the belief in law and its governance over society; and the reformation of the social and administrative system.

- Mirza Fathali Akhundzadeh (1812-1878)

Akhundzadeh, an intellectual of the constitutional movement, was deeply influenced by modernity and the scientific advances of the West. He claimed that religion should be rejected and Western civilisation embraced, as he saw religious doctrines as incompatible with reason and the ideas of development. He fought religion and divine orders, pursuing a typical Islamic Protestantism:

By which he meant a religion in which "God's rights [huququllah] and the worshipper's duties [takalif ibadullah] are annulled, and only human rights remain ... Needless to say, this means was provided by the modern European sciences, which had obviated the need for both beliefs and devotions" (Akhundzadeh, 1985: 222). In this way, Akhundzadeh delivered practical-ethical concerns, which he had just liberated from religion, into to the clutches of another type of determinism, science (Vahdat, 2002: 46).

He also showed his dissatisfaction of Islam's entry into Iran and his disgust at Arabs. He defended the establishment of a modern nation by working to build on and develop schools of thought such as nationalism, liberalism, socialism, and secularism. However, none of these schools of thought were made to be models for Iranian society.

- Mirza Malkum Khan (1833-1908)

Melkum Khan or Taghizadeh, who were directly influenced by the colonial British idea of modernity, offered a more rigid and totalistic vision of modernity for Iran ... It should not be surprising that some of the most prominent Constitutional reformers (or modernists as they called themselves) proposed "unconditional capitulation of Iran to European civilization." They not only voiced their desire for this, but some of them even volunteered to advance it. Fereydon Adamiy'at suggests that it was Malkum who proposed "Iran's capitulation to the Western values," and initiated the call for the "acquisition of

Western civilization without Iranian intervention." In fact, his political philosophy called for nothing less than an unconditional Iranian capitulation to European civilization (Mirsepassi, 2000: 61-62).

Malkum Khan, another famous intellectual of the constitutional movement, also engaged with Western culture and civilisation. He was 'one of the best known of the secular reformers. Malkam was in many ways typical of the newly emerging intellectuals, with his preference for Western ideas and values. His view of Islam suggests that he did not grasp the implications of its fundamental role in Persian society, nor its inherent tension with modernity' (Gheissari, 1998: 27). In fact, his social thought is founded on liberalism, and Al-e Ahmad considers intellectuals like Akhundzadeh and Malkum Khan as missionaries of Westoxication.

5.1.2. Traditionalism

The intellectuals that have had enormous effects on the Iranian people are Seyyed Fokhroddin Shadman (1907-1967), Ahmad Fardid (1912-1994), and Reza Davari-Ardakani (1933). They were critical of Western thought, lifestyles and goods, and attempted to repudiate and criticise all products of the modern world. According to Seyyed Fakhroddin Shadman, Ahmad Fardid, and Reza Davari-Ardakani, the discourse of traditionalism involves: negating the West and its achievements; the belief in the termination of modernity as a failed experience; the revival of traditional Islam; the belief in a contrast between Islam and modernity; the belief in a non-segregation of religion from politics; and the revival of religious and mystical ontology and anthropology.

- Seyyed Fokhroddin Shadman (1907-1967)

Shadman was a pioneer in publicising the discourse of *Gharbzadegi* (Westernisation). In his main work, *Taskhir-e Tamaddon-e Farangi* (The conquest of the Western civilisation) in 1948, he argued that Iran should absorb Western civilisation intelligently in order to liberate itself from Western domination. He considered the Persian language, which is a common asset of all Iranians, to be the only means for resisting the Western hegemony. In *Terazhedi-ye Farang* (The tragedy of the West), Shadman (1967: 113) criticises Europeans for holding double standards, arguing that whilst they repeatedly boast about the advantages of freedom and democracy, they do not admit freedom and democracy to non-Europeans. Although Shadman was a nationalist, he was not against Arabs and Islam. He powerfully opposed those who held Islam to be incompatible with science and development, declaring that: 'Islam cannot be contradictory to science. The heyday of Islamic civilisation, and the thousands of scientists, writers and philosophers who have dealt with the most subtle questions while under the inspiration of Islam, prove that this religion can live with science' (Boroujerdi, 1996: 58).

- Ahmad Fardid (1912-1994)

Fardid was one of the most influential philosophers and intellectuals in Iran, and has been nominated as the prime philosopher of Iranian modern history. From the 1950's onwards, he was responsible for familiarising Iranian intellectuals with German philosophers. A substantial cohort of Iranian intellectuals that were willing to recover their own identity sincerely embraced Fardid's ideas on 'Weststruckness' (or 'dysiplexia' in Greek). According to Fardid, 'from the moment human beings strove to place themselves in the position of God they become alienated from themselves. That desire to act like God belonged solely to the western civilization' (Ghamari-Tabrizi, 2008: 180). Boroujerdi (1996: 64-65) explains that:

For Fardid, then the West's inception occurs with Greek philosophy and its growth with Renaissance humanism ... This evolution, Fardid claims, has given rise to a technological, all-encompassing ethos that has deprived modern humans of morality. Thus, according to his ontological couplet, the Orient is the kingdom of benevolence and compassion while the Occident is the terrain of domination ... As such, Fardid reaches the conclusion that *Gharb* (the West) has to be abandoned both as an ontology and as a way of life.

Fardid held that metaphysics started with Socrates in Greece, as illustrated by Plato and Aristotle. Their metaphysics does not deal with the creator and ruler of the world, and Fardid criticises Plato and Aristotle, considering them to be a manifestation of Westoxication. He understands Westoxication as a position in which one is forced to embrace the Western civilisation and to follow it unquestionably. With the advent of Greek culture, the East lies down and the West rises up. However, the East has the religious reflections, and obligations to follow divine revelation and scriptures. In contrast, with the advent of metaphysics, the Greek meditation appeals to secularism. Even if Plato and Aristotle talk about God, this God is cosmos-centric in contrast to the God of the monotheistic religions. Therefore, he disagrees with Greek epistemology and modernity, and also opposes Western democracy and human rights (because they are not based on God's commandments).

Fardid firmly believes in Islamic mysticism, deeming it to be superior to philosophy. This mysticism pays attention to both this world and the next. He criticises Western philosophers for having an affinity with themselves and objects, but not with God and kingdom. That is why they avoid soaring beyond subject and object. He considers Heidegger to be a beacon – a shining ray of light in the darkness of the West. He says that the East can only talk to Heidegger, not to other Western philosophers. Heidegger is a thinker who caused humanism to tremble for the first time after a 2,500 year history in the West. He does not consider Heidegger to be an existentialist philosopher, as he holds that he goes beyond subjectivity and objectivity. According to Fardid, existentialism starts with Descartes and ends with humanism. In this school, it is human beings who have originality and validity, not God (Nasri, 2007: 207, 241).

However, in an interview that I had with Aavani on Monday 17th of January 2011, he claimed that although Heidegger has been impressed by some great theologians, he has transformed their ideas into secular ones, and hence he fails to reach the truth. Aavani also holds that Heidegger was influenced by modernity, and failed to step beyond it. Because he wants to omit God, Aavani claimed that Heidegger's *Dasein* was not absolute, but secular.

- Reza Davari-Ardakani (1933)

It [the West] is a way of thinking and a historical practice which started in Europe more than four hundred years ago, and has since expanded more or less universally. The West portrays the demise of the holy truth and the rise of a humanity which views itself as the sole possessor and focus of the universe. Its accomplishment is to possess everything in the celestial cosmos. Even if it were to prove the existence of God, it will be done not with the intention of obedience and submission but in order to prove itself (Davari, 1984: 18).

Davari is one of the most important current Iranian traditional intellectuals. Davari (2000: 13-14) contends that although the roots of Westoxication can be found in Greek philosophy, and date back 2,500 years, its current form has evolved from the renaissance. With the advent of Westoxication, the old form of history was annulled, and a nascent mankind came into existence. This new mankind is no longer amenable to the Haq (Truth or God). He forgets the Haq, replacing it with himself. Davari considers Descartes, Kant, Hegel, and the philosophers of the renaissance to be humanists, and holds that existentialism, the social sciences, freemasonry, and Marxism are also humanist. Even, religiosity is paraphrased on the basis of humanism, and humanism is Westoxication.

Davari believes that modern epistemology (in particular that of Kant) is responsible for this because it neglects God. Kant degenerates existence to the object of knowledge, and as a consequence, two types of knowledge have been made possible in modernity. One is the scientific knowledge of objects and the other the 'knowledge of the conditions of the possibility and realisation of such science', called critical philosophy. Davari finds even Hegel's philosophy inefficient in overcoming the ontological problems of modernity, because it grants a full explanation of the revolution of subjectivity that has been in the works from the time of the ancient Greeks (Vahdat, 2000: 188-191).

In his lecture at the University of Tehran on 22/02/2010 (which I took part in), Davari claimed that Western philosophy and modernity do not accept religions' participation in social affairs, and consider religions as sheer myths. However, the history of Islamic philosophy is an aggregation of philosophy, religion, and politics. Farabi (the founder of Islamic philosophy) holds that neither Plato nor Aristotle considered religion to be one of the guiding elements of philosophical thought, and neither of them believed in revelation and an omniscient God.

According to Davari, modern science is not perfect, and its research approach should not be applied for philosophy and religion. He postulates that postmodernity is not a period after modernity, but rather the termination of modernity – a period which focuses on and criticises the nature of modernity. Indeed, Davari's discourse on the West and modernity is the same as Fardid's, because he believes that human persons are subjected to the technological understanding of being. As Boroujerdi (1996: 161) puts it:

Far from making people into subjects, technology has led to their subjugation. In short, the agent of freedom has been turned into a medium of imprisonment. Based on the above set of pathological symptoms, Davari claimed that Western civilization has now reached its termination point and is struggling against alienation, solitude and solipsism. He cautioned Islamic intellectuals to recognize that the West must be viewed as a "totality," a "unified whole," and an "essence" from which the non-Western world cannot pick and choose. The only solution for the West, according to Davari, is to abandon its collective and individual egoism and humanism, to repudiate its skepticism, and to eradicate the rotten tree of modernity altogether.

5.1.3. Reformism

Jamal al-Din Assadabadi, Jalal Al-e Ahmad, and Ali Shariati are known as the most conspicuous religious reformists. Their aims concerning the encounter of tradition and modernity include: to reconcile Islam with the necessities of the age of modernity; to provide a critique of both tradition and modernity; to control and reform the consequences of modernity; and to incorporate the new. Additionally, they believe in the alienation and reification of the contemporary human; freedom, equality, and *erfan* (Gnostic knowledge); fighting exploitation, political despotism and colonisation; bazgasht beh khishtan or authenticity (which involves a return to the self or Iranian's Islamic roots); and the need to fight superstitions and anti-Islamic customs.

- Seyyed Jamal al-Din Assadabadi (1838-1897)

In this period, Jamal al-Din Assadabadi was the only theologian that considered the issues of the new world. He became known as the first Iranian religious reformist: 'He was a major political thinker and activist whose personal legend and discourse have had a lasting influence on the nativist anti-imperialist struggle, not only in Iran, but in countries and communities all across the Islamic world' (Vahdat, 2002: 54). Indeed, the 'Jamal al-Din effect' is felt not only in Iran, Afghanistan, the Arab world, Turkey, and India, but also in the European countries. According to Mortimer (1982: 116) 'he was a champion of Asian and African peoples confronted by European imperialism in its most dynamic age'. Jamal al-Din, better known as Afghani, claimed that no profound and permanent reform could be achieved until philosophy was revived. As Gheissari (1998: 13) notes, 'a similar argument would be put forward in the twentieth century by many Muslim intellectuals and Western Orientalists'. In the encounter between tradition and modernity, Jamal al-Din neither ignored tradition, nor gave any heedless to modernity. He criticised both tradition and the modern world – that is, he not only rejected the static-traditional views, but also the tendency of the religious intelligentsia to blindly follow Western thought. He separated the colonial dimensions of the West (Western encroachments on Muslim lands) from Western science. He wanted to make Islam compatible with modern Western science, arguing that: 'science in the West was the continuation of medieval Islamic science and therefore Muslims could adopt it while remaining Muslims and following their own traditions' (Jahanbegloo, 2004: 17). Jamal al-Din identified the concept of 'social solidarity' as the linchpin of collective subject – something that the West was trying to subvert. He believed that 'the "Neicheris" (materialists) – whether unorthodox or critical thinkers, socialists, communists, or nihilists – were bent on destroying the social solidarity of nations, both Islamic and non-Islamic alike (Afghani, 1968d: 140). What made social solidarity possible, in Afghani's analysis, was religious faith' (Vahdat, 2002: 59).

- Jalal Al-e Ahmad (1923-1969)

I Say that *Gharbzadegi* [Westernisation] is like cholera. If this seems distasteful, I could say it's like heatstroke or frostbite. But no. It's at least as bad as sawflies in the wheat fields. Have you ever seen how they infest wheat? From within. There's a healthy skin in place, but it's only a skin, just like the shell of a cicada on a tree. In any case, we're talking about a disease. A disease that comes from without, fostered in an environment made for breeding diseases (Jalal Al-e Ahmad, 2005: 4).

Al-e Ahmad engaged with politics more than Shadman and Fardid. His *Gharbzadegi* (Weststruckness or Westoxication) in 1962 challenged the principal bases of the social and intellectual history of Iran, the secular modernising programmes of the Pahlavi regime, and Western secularism. Reza Baraheni described the significance of this book as follows:

Al-e Ahmad's *Gharbzadegi* ... has the same significance in determining the duty of colonized nations vis-à-vis colonialist nations that the manifesto of Marx and Engels had in defining the responsibility of the proletariat vis-à-vis capitalism and the bourgeoisie, and that Franz Fanon's the *Wretched of the Earth* had in defining the role of African nations vis-a-vis foreign colonialists. Al-e Ahmad's *Gharbzadegi* is the first Eastern essay to make clear the situation of the East vis-à-vis the West – the colonialist West – and it may be the first Iranian essay to have social value on a world level (Boroujerdi, 1996: 67).

As a result of *Gharbzadegi*, Al-e Ahmad gained the reputation of being the most courageous critic of his time, and was a major influence on the work of Iranian scholars. Boroujerdi explains how *Gharbzadegi* performed a variety of important functions for Iranian intellectual society. First, Al-e Ahmad criticised the hundred-year record of enlightenment in Iran. Second, he raised a nativistic alternative to the universalism of the Iranian societies. Third, 'by providing a passionate eulogy for a passing era and its customs *Gharbzadegi* articulated a Third-Wordlist discourse very much skeptical of what the West had to offer' (Boroujerdi, 1996: 67-68). Fourth, 'it exhorted Iranian intellectuals to reassess their passive and servile embrace of Western ideas and culture and called for an awakening and resistance to the hegemony of an alien culture that increasingly dominated the intellectual, social, political, and economic landscape of Iranian society'(Boroujerdi, ibid.).

Al-e Ahmad traced the roots of *Gharbzadegi* to a 'contaminating social malady'; namely, the process of modernisation, which he considered a disease that degenerated Iranian cultural subjectivity and murdered its beauty, poetry, spirit, and humanity. His discussion is sometimes similar to the Marcusian criticism of positive science and, at other times, it is similar to the idea of authenticity and the nature of Western technology expressed by Heidegger. He reproached the non-religious intellectuals of the constitutional movement for going astray in their encounter with the West, and located the source of their deviation in the avoidance of their traditional heritage and their imitation of Western ways. In other words, 'he reserved his most caustic criticism for Iran's secular intelligentsia, whose greatest sin had been the rift and alienation from the social universal they had brought about by attacking the religious beliefs and traditions of the people' (Vahdat, 2002: 120). Al-e Ahmad concluded that in order to remedy this situation, the intellectuals needed to establish a union with the clerics, as they never succumbed to Western domination. He also called for a union between Shiite and Sunnite Muslims, arguing that such divisions between religious believers impeded the development of the Islamic civilisation.

However, unlike Shadman and Fardid, Al-e Ahmad did not oppose all aspects of modernity, believing that the best chance for liberation lay in the reconciliation of Islamic tradition with industrial and technological modernity.

Finally, we can turn to Shariati's work. The following discussion will provide a detailed account of his thought in order to compare his arguments with those of Habermas.

- Ali Shariati (1933-1977)

We are clearly standing on the frontier between two eras – one where both Western civilization and communist ideology have failed to liberate humanity, drawing it instead into disaster and causing the new spirit to recoil in disillusionment; and one where humanity in search of deliverance will try a new road and take a new direction, and will liberate its essential nature. Over this dark and dispirited world, it will set a holy lamp like a new sun; by its light, the man alienated from himself will perceive anew his primordial nature, rediscover himself, and see clearly the path of salvation. Islam will play a major role in this new life and movement. In the first place, with its pure *tauhid*, it offers a profound spiritual interpretation of the universe, one that is as noble and idealistic as it is logical and intelligible. In the second place, through the philosophy of the creation of Adam, Islam reveals in its humanism the conception of a free, independent, noble essence, but one that is as fully attuned to earthly reality as it is divine and idealistic (Shariati, 1980: 95).

Abrahamian (1982: 466) writes: 'The outstanding intellectual of the Liberation movement – if not of the whole of contemporary Iran – was a young Paris-educated sociologist named Ali Shariati ... Even though Shariati did not live to see the Shah's downfall, he is justly credited as the main intellectual, even the Fanon, of the Islamic Revolution'. Indeed, the Islamic liberation movement that developed in response to Westernisation commenced with the work of Seyyed Jamal al-Din Assadabadi during the 19th century and was taken up by Jalal Al-e Ahmad in the 1960s.

Whilst the intellectual panorama in Iran dominated by Jalal Al-e Ahmad's work during 1960s, the 1970's were dominated by Shariati. Shariati dedicated himself to finding both theoretical and practical solutions to Westernisation. Undoubtedly, his major concept of '*bazgasht beh khishtan* (return to the self) complemented Al-e Ahmad's discourse of gharbzadegi, of whom he had written' (Boroujerdi, 1996: 106). Shariati holds that notions such as 'returning to one's roots' or 'rediscovering one's Islamic roots' are often interpreted by intellectuals (religious or not) as suggesting that 'their societies must return to their roots and rediscover their history, culture, and popular language' (Mirsepassi, 2000: 114), and contends that:

"The return to ourselves" is not a superficial and imitative revival of certain local traditions, customs and rites. It is not the regurgitation of the past. It is a progressive movement for saving ourselves from "self-alienation" through the "elimination of the alien in our human condition and in our cultural and spiritual essence." It is a movement for finding lost truth and plundered values. It is a call for reliance upon our own roots. It is a movement to prevent talking with other people's tongues and people's feet (Shariati, 1986: 62-63).

Shariati (1979: 42) attempts to produce a type of sociology of religion based on Islam, utilising the terminology of the Koran and Islamic literature. By introducing a modern Islam, Shariati not only challenged Marxism, which had developed a strong following in intellectual circles, but also re-examined Islamic concepts and traditions. His aim was: 'the recovery of the ideal and unified Islamic society. Like Heidegger, he felt a pervading religious background had slipped away and left people atomized from the ontological bond to their community' (Mirsepassi, 2000: 118). He introduces true Islam as a liberation theology to the educated layers of people (in particular students) through his articles, classes and lectures.

Mortimer (1982: 341) notes that 'the students and young educated Iranians who attended his lectures were evidently spellbound. His influence on the revolution was enormous, perhaps second only to that of Khomeini'. The Iranian people welcomed Shariati's doctrine, and public protest against the arbitrary Pahlavi Regime followed. Then, during 1978-79, the Islamic revolution occurred in Iran. As Mirsepassi (2000: 114) notes:

While Al-e Ahmad concentrated on the critique of secularism and modernism in Iranian culture and politics, Shariati made every attempt to construct and popularize a modern Shi'i ideology as a more authentically grounded alternative to the existing secular ideologies ... He was by far the most influential Shi'i oppositional intellectual of the 1970s. Although Shariati died just before the Revolution in June of 1977 from a massive heart attack in London, he became one of its most celebrated figures.

Shariati's works uses different scientific methodologies to illustrate modern Islam in the light of the critical approach. He understands the Shiite faith as a religion of protest against oppressive rules and rulers. This critical vision attempts to subvert governors that have deviated religion from its divine course.

1. Materialistic and Religious worldview

Shariati (1981: 11-14) points out that our perception of existence directly affects our actions, beliefs, behaviours, and our social and individual lives. Thus, every person's life relates to his worldview, and to investigate these worldviews is to investigate human beings themselves. Indeed, studying the worldviews of any schools, groups or nations is the same as studying the qualities of the structure, nature, and other characteristics of that group and nation.

The materialistic worldview is based on the notion of 'originality of matter'; namely, there is a collection of elements, relations, and interactions that are all and only materialistic. Thus, according to materialism, the universe is not created by an intelligent and conscious will, and has no purpose or target: 'In Sartre's words, the world is the abode of an idiot; senseless, a heap of elements which are based upon material, physical, and chemical relations all busy making nothing' (Shariati, 1981: 12). According to Sartre, human beings are the only collection of elements that has attained self-consciousness in this void of futility. This represents the beginning of human distress, because persons live in a world that is inconsistent to them, incompatible with them, and inharmonious for them. From Shariati's perspective, the materialistic worldview reaches its logical conclusions in futility and nihilism. Shariati (1981: 14) challenges the Enlightenment, arguing that three hundred years after the renaissance and the victory of the material worldview over the religious, all the philosophies, schools of thought, and arts in the West have finally reached their logical conclusions regarding the futility of existence. Shariati (1979: 82) holds that 'the difference between my world-view and that of materialism or naturalism lies in this, that I regard the world as a living being, endowed with will and self-awareness, percipient, and having an ideal and a purpose'.

By contrast, the religious worldview, according to Shariati (1981: 15-16), endows the universe with an omnipotent God as its owner. Under this worldview, a human being is nothing but a plaything in the hands of a god or the gods.

Furthermore, in the religious world-vision it is believed that man must not depend upon his own will and consciousness to shape his fate, rather he should negate himself in front to God. We notice also that in the religious world-vision there is a fanaticism which leads to futility and unoriginality of man. In short, the religious world-vision, since its inception, culminates in the negation of man's true essence (Shariati, 1981: 16).

Thus, the universe is futile under the materialist worldview, and human beings are unimportant under the religious worldview. Shariati considers both worldviews to be wrong. We have adopted the religious worldview from two sources: from ancient history, through which we have inherited an anti-human and decadent religion – 'If we believe in it we are corrupt and superstitious, if we reject it we are anti-religious liberal thinkers' (Shariati: 1981: 16); and from the experiences of intelligentsia and scientists of the post renaissance that grappled with the religious Middle Ages.

Shariati holds that modern centuries grappled with religion, its opponents rejecting the religious worldview on behalf of science, superseding it with the materialistic worldview. In the past, the triad of powers (money, force and religion) that have governed through history have frequently deceived the common person. However, after the renaissance, and particularly during the 18th and 19th centuries, they deceived intellectuals as well by supplanting religion with materialism – an economic philosophy shrouded in the cloak of humanism: 'the modern materialistic and anti-religious world-vision, like polytheism, are the world-visions of the modern ruling class' (Shariati, 1981: 23). Shariati (1981: 25) emphasises that:

The spirit dominating the new culture and civilization is bourgeoisie; the spirit of money-making, business, power-seeking, tool-making, consumption and hedonism. What about its literature and art? They are comprised of futility, fun, propaganda and excitement! And the confusion lies in the fact that in rejecting the traditional culture, bourgeoisie just achieved a 'progressive crime!'

Shariati continues by observing that the bourgeoisie left behind the religious culture of the Middle ages – a degenerated spirituality. Feudalism, with its dependent clergies, was also put aside. However, this process also interred the most valuable parts of mankind's spirit, culture, and intellectual ethics under the debris of the Medieval period. We, the post-renaissance human beings, have admired the progressive revolution of the renaissance and its sensational slogans, perceiving them to be the vanguards of liberalism, democracy and science, and the repudiation of superstition, asceticism, and religious despotism. But we have never been able to feel the treason of this servant and see that, in this liberalism, mankind has lost the essential dimensions of his nature, love, idealism, values, and existential significance. In addition, 'this creature who has superiority over nature, and whom religion designates as vicegerent of God in the world ... has somehow become transformed to nature's most menacing beast. This is due to the fact that "man" of bourgeoisie is alienated (possessed) by the demon of money' (Shariati, 1981: 25-26). Mankind has been debased to a consuming beast, with obedience to a false cycle of "production for consumption and consumption for production". The human being has degenerated from being the only free and responsible being in the world into the being slave of machinism and bureaucracy. Shariati launches an assault on Europeans for attempting to impose their own type of enlightenment and thought on the rest of the world. The solution that Shariati proposes is that:

The peoples of the Third World could not fight imperialism unless they first regained their cultural identity, which, in some countries, was interwoven with popular religious traditions. They had to return to their religious roots before they could challenge the West (Abrahamian, 1982: 465).

According to Shariati (1981: 16), we need to know religion fully now, rather than just believing in it, because religion is not perceived as being valuable if it is left unknown. We need to become familiar with religion, science, society, history, and our own characters, rather than to blindly believe in them. A belief has no value and effect in itself if it is not backed up by intelligence.

2. Monotheism (*tauhid*) and Multitheism (*shirk*)

Shariati comments that monotheism and Multitheism are both religious worldview.

My world-view consists of *tauhid*. *Tauhid* in the sense of oneness of God is of course accepted by all monotheists. But *tauhid* as a world-view in the sense I intend in my theory means regarding the whole universe as a unity, instead of dividing it into this world and the hereafter, the natural and the supernatural, substance and meaning, spirit and body ... There are many people who believe in *tauhid*, but only as a religious-philosophical theory, meaning nothing but "God in one, not more than one." But I take *tauhid* in the sense of a world-view, and I am convinced that Islam also intends it in this sense ... So it is that I do not believe in pantheism, polytheism, trinitarianism, or dualism, but only in *tauhid*-monotheism. *Tauhid* represents a particular view of the world that demonstrates a universal unity in existence, a unity between three separate hypostases – God, nature, and man – because the origin of all three is the same. All have the same direction, the same will, the same spirit, the same motion, and the same life (Shariati, 1979: 82-83).

Therefore, monotheism comprises a worldview philosophy and cosmology that provides unity for the universe, mankind, and all elements of the world. It also aims to provide a background for uniting groups, races, and human classes. In fact, the unity of God brings about the unity of the world and the unity of the human being. In other words, 'nor can *tauhid* accept legal, class, social, political, racial, national, territorial, genetic or even economic contradictions, for it implies a mode of looking upon all being as a unity' (Shariati, 1979: 86). In Islamic doctrine, there is only one base – a single pillar, *tauhid*. All other principles – such as justice, prophecy, leadership and resurrection – are founded on *tauhid*. In other words, all ideas, all functions, and even all large and small economic, political, ethical, and social relationships are superstructure. They are all based on *tauhid*.

Monotheism is the worship of the One God, God in the Name of the Awake, Willed, Creator and Determiner of the universe. These are Qualities of God in all the Abrahamic religions ... The worship of this Absolute Power which is the great call of all of the Abrahamic Traditions, essentially, the goal of Abraham in announcing this well-known cry, consisted of the invitation to all human beings to worship the One Power in existence, to orient their attention to one direction in creation, to believe in one effective power in all of existence and one place of refuge throughout life (Shariati, 1988: 26).

Shariati, then, 'endowed the *movahhed* [monotheist] with those characteristics that would make an ideal Islamic revolutionary. The *movahhed* was an independent, fearless, selfless, dependable and wantless individual, who bowed to no other authority than to God' (Rahnema, 2005: 232). In Shariati's view, not even the Prophets had the purpose of promoting the worship of God, because all societies undoubtedly worshipped God before the rise of the Prophets. The Prophets only came to perform one single task – to replace *tauhid* with *shirk*.

Shirk is a world-view that regards the universe as a discordant assemblage full of disunity, contradiction, and heterogeneity, possessing a variety of independent and clashing poles, conflicting tendencies, variegated and unconnected desires, reckonings, customs, purposes and will. *Tauhid* sees the world as an empire; *shirk* as a feudal system (Shariati, 1979: 82).

Contrary to what we presume, multitheism is a religion, and multitheists are religious people: 'They have various deities. They believe in their servitude in relation to these deities and in the influence of these deities in the destiny of the world and their own fate. Thus, just as we look at God, a multitheist looks at his own gods' (Shariati, 1988: 24). The Prophets then came to replace one religion with another. However, the disbelief in God was a novel development that arose in Europe after the renaissance in the 16th and 17th centuries. Islam contends that all human beings follow monotheism according to their natures, but polytheism comes next. The ruling class, who has money, force and religion, has always tried to form multitheism. This multitheism is a religion of deceit that endows the justification for *shirk* and class discrimination in society, and enables the status quo to be maintained. Shariati (2005: 192) interprets Islam as the greatest, newest, and most universal religion to have created a great civilisation. It has also created the most beautiful spirits and the most sublime faces of humanity and personality. To sum up, Shariati's works thus have one clear message:

Islam - particularly Shi'ism – is not a conservative, fatalistic creed, as charged by many secular intellectuals, nor an apolitical personal faith, as claimed by some reactionary clerics; but rather a revolutionary ideology that permeates all spheres of life, especially politics, and inspires true believers to fight against all forms of oppression, exploitation, and social injustice. The Prophet had come to establish not just a community but a Muslim Ummat – a dynamic community in constant motion toward progress; and not just a monotheistic religion but a Nezam-i Towhid – a social order that would be completely united by virtue, striving toward justice, equity, human brotherhood, public ownership of wealth, and, most important of all, a classless society. Moreover, the Shi'i Imams, especially Hussein, had raised the banner of revolt because their contemporary rulers – the corrupt caliphs and the court elites – had betrayed the Ummat and given up the goals of a Nezam – i Towhid (Shariati, 1976: 27).

3.   Islam as an Ideology versus Islam as a Culture

Shariati distinguishes two types of Islam: Islam as an ideology and Islam as a culture.

Ideology is composed of two parts; "idea", which is thinking, imagination, motto, conception; and 'logy', which has a Latin root and means logic and recognition. So literally, ideology is "recognition of an idea," or in one word it is "idea", as we understand it in Persian. In the same vein, an ideologue is a person who possesses a particular idea or tenet. Therefore, ideology is the particular belief, opinion, or tenet of a group, class, nation or a race (Shariati, 1981: 82-83).

The ideology consists of a collection of beliefs and forms of worship that allow human beings to achieve spiritual perfection, self-esteem and ethical, intellectual, and social growth. As an ideology, Islam displays an image of the world, human beings, the truth of life, social order, standards of living, and self-building: 'Ideology includes both a belief and the knowing of it. It is to have a special attitude and consciousness which a person has in relation to himself, his class position, social base, national situation, world and historic destiny as well as the destiny of one's own society which one is dependent upon' (Shariati, 1989: 38).

In contrast, Islam as a culture (or a social custom) is constituted of a collection of sciences, such as philosophy, theology, mysticism, and religious jurisprudence. These sciences deal only with phenomenology or a survey of the objective realities, not with what is right or wrong. On the other hand, it is a series of inculcated social traditions, and fossilised forms. As Shariati (1981: 86) puts it:

Religion as a social custom is composed of [a] totality of inherited beliefs, inculcated sentiments, imitation of fashions, relationships, mottos, traditions, and unconscious practice[s] of particular precepts. In short, a customary religion is a relationship which makes the national continuation of a society possible throughout a few generations, centuries, and epochs ... Durkheim states, religion is the manifestation of the collective spirit ... I accept it only for customary religions rather religions of ideology.

Shariati maintained that Islam's transformation from an ideology to a culture caused it to become vulgarised and for common people to fall into reactionary thought. He believes that schools of thought such as Greek philosophy and Westoxication penetrated Islam and contributed to the conversion of ideological Islam into a culture. He introduces the majority of philosophers, theologians, and religious jurisprudents as religious cultural figures rather than intellectuals, because he believes that Islam is not as a culture, but rather a holy mission for salvation and justice. A theologian is an heir to Abraham, Moses, Jesus Christ, and Muhammad rather than to Plato and Aristotle (Nasri, 2007: 150-151).

According to Shariati (1989: 23), a school of thought or an ideology does not deal with technical details or information because this would turn it into a system of mutable rules that would be wiped out over the course of time. An ideology must be founded on a collection of general laws and immutable human ideals. It must be understood as a whole, and it is up to theologians and intellectuals to adapt its laws to the specifics of a culture and time. In *worldview and Ideology*, Shariati (1993: 61-62) compares science with ideology, and describes how science reveals a knowledge of realities through the systematic scrutiny of external facts and objects. However, an ideology goes further, seeking to evaluate realities. In an ideology, these facts are substantially abnormal, and the ideology involves finding out how they must be modified and ideally configured. Thus, Shariati (1981: 84) holds that an ideology is an idea which comprises: 1- A worldview or a typical interpretation of the world, life and human being; 2- A critical assessment of the status quo; and 3- Recommendations and solutions to problems in our social and intellectual situations and the presentation of ideal samples for changing the status quo to an ideal situation. Therefore, ideology comprises three stages: 'World-vision, critical evaluation of the problems and the environment, and finally suggestions and solutions in the form of ideals and aims. Each ideologue, then, is responsible to change the status quo relative to his ideals and convictions' (Shariati, 1981: 85).

To sum up, *tauhid* 'is to be interpreted in the sense of the unity of nature with metanature, of man with nature, of man with man, of God with the world and with man. It depicts all of these as constituting a total, harmonious, living and self-aware system' (Shariati, 1979: 85). Moreover, ideology is a conscious faith that deals with how the present condition must be changed, and it is a belief that is chosen, which can lead to awareness, commitment, and responsibility. Shariati concludes that *tauhid* and the ideology of Islam endow mankind with 'independence and dignity' (Shariati, 1979: 87). Furthermore: 'Submission to Him [God] alone – the supreme norm of all being – impels man to revolt against all lying powers, all the humiliating fetters of fear and of greed' (ibid.). At the same time, Shariati is not ignorant of the negative role that ideology plays. As he notes, some ideologies only justify the status quo, whereas some of them reform it.

4.   The Emancipatory Religion versus the Historical Religion

In my interview on Wednesday 29th of December 2010, Manoochehri explained that Shariati views the modern hostility towards religion as dating back to Greek mythologies on human strife with mythological gods, and later to the historical experiences of the Christian Middle Ages. Thus, this hostility is not directly connected to the monotheistic religions. Religion, in its original form, provided a basis for the gravest human emancipatory models, which have been regarded as an undeniable virtue of the monotheistic religions of the Abrahamic tradition. Shariati believes that without the Pope, the movement for human emancipation would have formulated its philosophy of history in association with religion rather than in opposition to it. It would have joined the religion whose Prophets have risen from the heart of the masses to invite human beings to emancipation, freedom, justice, piety and equality; and to condemn oppression, ignorance, and superstition. According to Shariati, while religion has a historical origin, its historical evolution resulted in the emergence of two different tendencies: human religion and historical religion. The human tendency is that which persists in being defined by its emancipatory goal for human beings and the criticism of the status quo. The mundane institutions of religion and their secular self-interest, however, have historically caused the suppression of the human tendency. These interests – which have their historical origins in the birth of private ownership – have been manifested in the historical trinity of *Zar* (the power of wealth), *Zoor* (physical force), and *Tazvir* (religious hypocrisy). It is this oppressive trinity that has been embodied in historical religion. Unlike the human trend, which has a revolutionary and critical attitude towards the status quo, the historical trend has been fundamentally apologetic and reactionary. In short, the history of religion can be characterized as 'Religion vs Religion'.

Shariati (1988: 20) claims that we know that religions have fought between themselves throughout history because history reports no society or epoch to be free of religion. Indeed, there is no recorded non-religious society. There has been no non-religious human being in any race, in any period of time, in any stage of social change, on any part of the earth.

That which today we define as atheism, non-religion or anti-religion, is a very new concept. That is, it relates to the last two or three centuries. It refers to that which took place after the Middle Ages. It is a definition which has been imported into the East in the form of a western intellectual product, that *Kufr* means a lack of belief of a human being in God, in the metaphysical and in another world. In Islam, in all ancient texts, in all histories, in all religions, when *Kufr* is spoken about, it is not in the sense of non-religion. Why? Because there was so such thing as non-religion (Shariati, 1988: 21-22).

According to Shariati (1988: 22), wherever a prophet or a religious revolution has appeared, they first emerged against the existing religion of their time. The first groups or forces that then arose against this new religious figure or movement were those of other established religions. For example, the forces that most hurt Moses' movement were the Samaritans and the Balaam. Moreover, 'those who confronted Jesus and his followers were believers, pursuers and preachers of the religion of multitheism ... The battle cry of the Quraysh, the battle cry of all of the Arabs who fought against Islam, throughout the lifetime of the Prophet, was the cry of religion vs religion' (Shariati, 1988: 29). Therefore, for Shariati, the history of human struggle is not based on the struggle between modern and traditional forces, or between the bourgeoisie and the proletariat, but between the forces of *tauhid* and *shirks*.

Shariati (1988: 31) considers emancipatory religion as a revolutionary religion in which an individual succeeds in obtaining a critical attitude to life in all its material, spiritual, and social aspects. It provides one with a mission and a duty to change, modify, and destroy what is invalid, and supplant it with the truth. The important characteristic of monotheistic religion is that it does not approve or justify the status quo, and take the form of rebellion against defilement – a rebellion that announces obedience to the creator. In other words, Shariati (1988: 39) mentions that the Abrahamic religions were responsible for uprooting the status quo and supplanting it with the scales of justice and equity, which are continuously emphasised in the Koran. Although Shariati repeatedly talks about revolutionary religion, this does not mean that all links with the past have to be cut off and destroyed. He insists that it is necessary to consider the Prophet Muhammad's method of opposing the conservative, revolutionary and reformative approaches. As Hussain notes (1985: 81): 'Shariati contended that Prophet Muhammad's method differed from all three in that the form was preserved while the meaning was changed. Many pre-Islamic forms were preserved while their meanings were changed. Though this did not cut the people from their roots but internalized new meanings into the minds of men'. However, the multitheistic religion or *shirk* always try to legitimate the status quo. 'That is, in the name of religion, people are made to believe, the situation which you have or which your society has is a situation which you and your society must have because this is the manifestation of God's Will. It is destiny and fate' (Shariati, 1988: 32). Put differently,

Religion legitimates social institutions by bestowing upon them an ultimately valid ontological status, that is, by locating them within a sacred and cosmic frame of reference ... The political structure simply extends into the human sphere the power of the divine cosmos. The political authority is conceived of as the agent of the gods, or ideally even as a divine incarnation. Human power, government, and punishment thus become sacramental phenomena, that is, channels by which divine forces are made to impinge upon the lives of men. The ruler speaks for the gods, or is a god, and to obey him is to be in a right relationship with the world of the gods (Berger, 1967: 33-34).

Shariati states that multitheism has economic roots. It is grounded in the ownership of a minority and the deprivation of a majority. It is the element of economics that needs a religion to maintain and legitimise itself. What is stronger than this religion, which makes an individual feel satisfied with his abjectness? Shariati argues that the religion of multitheism is born of the ignorance and fear of the people, because those who spread the religion of multitheism are afraid of the people awakening and becoming educated. The more knowledge advances, the sooner the religion of multitheism is destroyed, because the guard for this sort of religion is nothing but ignorance. In fact, the more the people become aware, the more a spirit of criticism and the quest for the divine ideal and justice are awakened, and this shakes the basis for multitheism. As Shariati (1988: 38) notes: 'This situation has existed throughout the history of humanity, from before the age of feudalism until the age of feudalism and afterwards in the East and in the West'. Shariati emphasises that it is not enough to say that we must return to 'Islam' – such an affirmation is nonsense. We have to specify *which* Islam. We want the dynamic Islam of the Ali family, not the static Islam of the Safavi dynasty.

If I speak about religion, I do not speak about a religion which had been realized in the past and which ruled society. Rather, I speak about a religion whose goals are to do away with a religion which ruled over society throughout history. I speak about a religion the prophets of which arose to destroy the various forms which the religion of multitheism had taken and which at no time in history was realized by the religion of monotheism in a complete form from the point of view of society and the social life of the people ... Thus, my reliance upon religion is not a return to the past but rather the continuation of the way of history (Shariati, 1988: 41-42).

Using Shariati's ideas, it can be concluded that Habermas's earlier analysis of the role of religion in the public sphere failed to distinguish between emancipatory or monotheistic religion, and historical or multitheistic religion. These two forms of religion not only bear no resemblance to each other, they are in fact contradictory, and locked in a war with one another. In other words, Habermas's early judgment on religion relates to historical religion, and to this degree it is correct. However, Habermas knew nothing of emancipatory religion, which was not realised at any time after the coming of the Prophets. Following on from Marx, Habermas was correct to say that 'religion is the opium of the people'. That is, religion is opium for the people because it inspires false hope after death in order for the masses to bear their misery and abasement; and because people hold the belief that what happens is already disposed to happen by God's Will, and that any effort to change the status quo is against God's Will.

This form of religion is the historical or cultural religion that has governed throughout history in the name of Moses, Jesus, and Muhammad. Therefore, Habermas is right to fight this religion. However, Habermas is mistaken when he attributes all the problems of historical religion to monotheistic religion. He wrongly passes the same judgment on the liberating religion as he does to the religion of history, failing to perceive the fact that there has always been more than one type of religion in human history.

Moreover, Shariati (1991: 230-231) declares that tradition and religion have been intermingled with each other throughout history, and constitute a series of creeds, tastes, behaviours, feelings, and socio-legal relations that are all conceived to be sacred by societies. However, tradition must be separated from religion, because religious laws and edicts are rules of nature – legislation that has been laid down by the Almighty creator of natural laws. The laws of nature never become old, but social traditions are generated by systems of production, consumption, and culture that change and become outdated, futile, degenerate, and reactionary. When religion, as a live and everlasting phenomenon, is embedded in a degenerated tradition, it will not be capable of playing an effective role in the lives of believers. Habermas was not able to sever the historical or cultural religion from the emancipatory one. Therefore, he fought the lofty values of the liberating religion at the same time as he contended the deviational tradition.

In an interview that I conducted on Tuesday 16th of February 2010, Qaramaleki declared that Shariati was determined to produce a newly thought-out understanding of religion and its system of knowledge, and that in order to achieve this goal, he followed a sociological and ideological pattern. He noted the efficiency and capability of religion as an ideology in comparison to Marxism, and constantly aimed to resuscitate religion. Shariati was also concerned about religion losing its dynamism and vivacity under a heavy load of laws, rituals, and readings, and how to address this problem.

5. Mysticism, Equality and Freedom

Shariati (1980: 97-122) perceives three basic currents of nature, humanity, and their interrelation: mysticism (*erfan*), equality (*barabary*), and freedom (*azady*). He holds that all other matters originate from these three principles of religion.

- Mysticism

Shariati believes that mysticism has always existed in both the East and the West.

The reason it is spoken of as having arisen in the East, and has acquired an Eastern mien, is not that only the Oriental has an aptitude for mysticism, but rather that, because civilization first arose in the East, the birthplace of thought, culture, and the great religions, mysticism must also, as a matter of course, have had its beginnings there ... But in general, mysticism is innate to human nature (Shariati, 1980: 97).

Thus, according to Shariati (1980: 99-100), mysticism is an intellectual current that originates from human nature. Mysticism is peoples' 'inner sense of apprehension' in the world of nature. This sense of agitation is generated by a deficiency in human beings' relationship with nature – namely that humans have some needs that nature is unable to satisfy. This causes human beings to have a sense of alienation and exile in this world, and to look to an invisible world for an escape from this loneliness. In short, mysticism is a manifestation of the human nature to impulse to enter and discover the unseen world. If sensible and obvious things were enough for human beings, they would remain static, but they are set in motion to ensure their perfection. This mystic emotion is the essence of every religion, and it is the mystical sense that grants human beings virtue and greatness.

According to Shariati (1980: 102), however, mysticism entered religion later, and slowly changed to an ecclesiastical establishment with a new ruling class. As a consequence, both mysticism and religion adopted superstitions and justifications for the existence of governing bodies to prevent the growth of human primordial nature:

And so it happened that the next major movement, in its pursuit of human freedom and scientific and intellectual growth, came to oppose religion as a matter of course. Likewise, religion, fallen into the paralytic hands of the custodians of the Middle Ages, and thus assuming a reactionary and inhuman role, opposed this new movement and therefore automatically followed the fateful course we have described, first in Europe, and, in time, throughout the world. Thus it was universally said: Human liberation entirely depends on the removal of the fetters that religion placed on people's hands and feet. Of course, by fetters, I mean the constraints that the religious establishment in Islam and Christianity, as well as in Judaism, Hinduism, and all the faiths, have imposed on human thought (Shariati, 1980: 102).

It is found that there is no real religion here, and the adoption of mysticism and spirituality is false because emancipatory religion cares substantially for independence, freedom, equality among classes, and justice. For instance, 'Islam is the religion of those who desire freedom and independence. It is the school of those who struggle against imperialism. But the servants of imperialism have presented Islam in a totally different light. They have created in men's minds a false notion of Islam' (Khomeini, 1981: 28).

- Equality

Shariati notes that the use of machines for production emerged during the 18th and 19th centuries. This intensified class polarisation and aggravated the levels of poverty, oppression and injustice. When religion was put aside from public life and the intellectual lives of the young, it was superseded by socialism. However, the goals of nineteenth century European socialists failed: they did not achieve equality and justice. In any case, European capitalism provided too much of a barrier for the socialist revolution. The liberals of the 19th century thought that if society adopted a socialist system, humanity would be released from the bonds of materialism, which would lead to class oppositions and conflicting interests being extinguished. As a result, wars would end, and all of the forces of humanity would be placed at the service of spiritual growth.

However, 'we have seen how that very socialist system that was to have freed people, as it was put into practice, wound up enslaving all to a single leader, and assumed the forms, first, of worship of personality and party, and then of worship of the state … and that worship of the state will replace worship of God' (Shariati, 1980: 107). Disillusionment with this system's affects on the thought of free spirits was manifested in a new school, existentialism. Existentialism opposes both religion and Marxism, which are seen as enslaving mankind to god and the state respectively.

- Freedom

According to Shariati, existentialism considers human freedom as a basis for solving humanity's problems and for rejecting Marxism and religion. Socialism has hindered all human initiative and passed it over to the state, which takes decisions instead of the people. It is socialism that plans for human production and consumption and that diminishes human beings within its organisational hierarchy by removing human freedom. Religion, on the other hand, expects everything to be given by God, and God is an entity external to the human essence. Therefore, religion contradicts freedom of choice. Let us return to humanity itself, however, and suppose that one is in this 'world of nature', alienated from nature, in which there is no God. If you stick to your own essential values and develop them, then 'you are nothing more than a thing among things, whence all your values originate. Choice and freedom are yours unconditionally. All values exist when this freedom exists; should this freedom be taken away from you, these values would cease to be; you would become as a slave to other powers: God or the state' (Shariati, 1980: 111).

- An Analytical Assessment of Mysticism, Equality, and Freedom

According to Shariati, these attempts to ground human wellbeing in mysticism, equality, and freedom are problematic, as none of them can accommodate the multi-dimensional, balanced, and harmonious growth that humanity requires. The weakness of present-day established religion is that it detaches human beings from their own humanity. It makes the person into a beggar and a slave to unseen forces, and alienates him from his own will. The weakness of socialism is that it commits itself to materialism and, in practice, leads to worship of the state, which has been transformed into the primacy of the head of state. The weakness of existentialism is that, in emphasising human freedom and choice, it negates the existence of God and social issues. Thus, 'it leaves man suspended in midair. When I am free to choose anything, because there is no other criterion, the question arises: on what basis am I to choose the good and reject the evil? ... Individual freedom without a specified direction will be debased' (Shariati, 1980: 111-112). With respect to the positive sides of these three currents of thought, Shariati elucidates that speech, thought, and consciousness are not signs of humanity. What distinguishes human beings from other creatures is their sense of apprehension before the unseen, and their escape from what is, or is not, through the pursuit of what ought to be. Therefore, mysticism pursues love of God as a non-physical entity, and religion is a manifestation of mysticism, whilst Marxism is based on equality and material justice between people, and existentialism also implies freedom and choice for human beings. In fact, each of these three currents comprises both human development and human aberration – by drawing attention to one direction and ignoring others, they each establish a defective type of guidance. For instance, mysticism brings human beings some intellectual and spiritual sensitivity, through which they are driven to achieve perfection. Nevertheless, mysticism blinds human beings to the tragic circumstances around them.

Outside the wall of his place of retreat, oppression, disaster, poverty, shameful acts, ignorance, corruption, and decadence are dishonoring all the spiritual values of man, but he never becomes aware of it; that is, his connection with the reality of his environment has been completely severed. That is how this mode of human deliverance is transformed into a kind of egotism (Shariati, 1980: 114).

According to Shariati, socialism is unable to respond to human needs. A human being that focuses solely on questions of socialism and economic relations between two classes with respect to determining the human good is limited to a narrow conception of humanity (his own included) due to his unilateral attention to class correspondence within society. As a result, all his values, human dimensions, and needs are entirely suspended. Indeed, socialism transforms humans into one-dimensional beings. Existentialism provides a type of deliverance from this, but it has no object or programme for this freedom it places such value in. If this freedom does not have any purpose, it merely leads to vagrancy and futility. Therefore, these three basic dimensions need to be assembled within a person or school for their negative respects to be extinguished, and Shariati (1980: 119) says:

In my opinion, we need look no further for an example than Islam. That is precisely its value – that it is harmoniously centered on all three dimensions. Its origin, spirit, and (as in the case of all religions, including Christianity) essence is mysticism. However, it emphasizes social justice and the fate of others, even of a single other, and it says, "If you keep one other person alive or revive him, it is as if you have revived all man, and if you kill another person, it is as if you have killed all other men".

Habermas also emphasises equality and freedom. However, the absence of God and religion from his view is a limitation. Since Habermas has no mystical apprehension in his ideas, he portrays human beings as 'frozen' or 'spiritually withered'. In fact, if love of God were taken away from humanity, they would become isolated beings, useful only to the system of production. In other words, by removing God from nature, everything becomes pointless and futile.

6. Modern Man and His Prisons

Shariati (1981: 46-62) alleges that human beings are incarcerated within four prisons, and that those who deliver themselves from these deterministic conditions tend to be true human beings. In analysing these four prisons, Shariati first provides a definition of 'human'. He holds that a human is a creature with a tendency towards God. This journey towards God is perpetual and eternal. Ensan (human) has three characteristics: 1- He is self-conscious; 2- He can make choices; 3- He can create, and all his other characteristics are derived from these three. Being an Ensan is being a conscious creature: 'perceiving one's quality and nature, perceiving the quality and the nature of the universe, and perceiving one's relationship with the universe. We are Ensan to the extent that we are conscious of these three principles' (Shariati, 1981: 50). A human is a chooser, in the sense that he is the only creature who can revolt against nature, and even against his own physical, psychological, and natural needs. He is free from all the causal associations that govern all phenomena, and this is the supreme aspect of humanity. Furthermore, a human can create, and creates not only the smallest technologies and artistic works, but the largest as well. Human beings have a manifestation of God's power in their nature – that is, they are able to become God's successors on the Earth.

In Islam man is not humbled before God, for he is the partner of God, His friend, the bearer of His trust upon earth. He enjoys affinity with God, has been instructed by Him, and seen all of God's angels fall prostrate before him. Two-dimensional man, bearing the burden of such responsibility, needs a religion that transcends exclusive orientation to this world or the next, and permits him to maintain a state of equilibrium. It is only such a religion that enables man to fulfill his great responsibility (Shariati, 1979: 81).

The four prisons that modern humans are incarcerated within are those that prohibit him from gaining self-consciousness, making choices, and creating. The four prisons are: 1- Naturalism; 2- Historicism; 3- Sociologism; and 4- One's self.

With respect to naturalism, Shariati holds that because human beings are physical and material creatures and live in nature, nature imposes its characteristics on them. Therefore, nature has made human intellectual tendencies, emotions, feelings and instincts: 'Naturalism is another victimizer of man which burgeoned from the eighteenth century to the beginning of the nineteenth century. Naturalism believes that originality belongs to a living being, though without consciousness, which is called nature, and man is one of its products. Thus, I am free, I can choose, and I can feel because of the nature's will' (Shariati, 1981: 52). Shariati claims that human beings can break out of the prison of nature by becoming familiar with nature's deterministic laws, as well as their effects upon them and technology; namely, that technology has placed the control of nature under the power of mankind, providing them with an ascendancy over it and an ability to shape it. Shariati describes technology and science 'as the liberator of humanity from the prisons of "nature" "heredity," and "history" – but this is possible only in a society which has achieved union with God ... Without being explicit about what the purpose behind technology will be, he codes the idea of technology in Islamic language, as if this alone will improve its moral character' (Mirsepassi, 2000: 123).

Historicism holds that human beings are the products of history, and that their characteristics are in the hand of history's will. Thus, our thought, language, creeds, and emotions, as well as what we raise and put forward, are all generated by our history. This means that human beings can be released from the determinism of history by knowing its determinism, movement, and deterministic laws.

Sociologism holds that social environment and order can control human beings:

It is believed that the social order which is composed of social relations, productive order, ownership order, the tools of production, and the bureaucracy of the ruler which all make up my society are all factors which shape my personality anyway they want. There is no individual or a chooser in sociologism; so, there is no Ensan, since the latter is capable of saying, "I," or, "I chose this for such and thus reason" (Shariati, 1981: 54).

Human beings can escape from this prison by studying sociology, and through comparative studies of the various social orders.

In my interview (on Tuesday 28th of December 2010), Susan Shariati (Shariati's daughter) described the last prison – one's self – to be the worst form of determinism – one that, makes human beings the most helpless prisoners. She holds that, in Shariati's view, when we feel that there is an intense instinct and tendency within us that governs us for the sake of our pleasures, we are in the captivity of our self's determinism: 'It [one's self] is a prison that I carry with myself. This is why becoming self-conscious and familiar with this one is the hardest task of all. Here, the prison and the prisoner are the same; that is, the disease and the patient have merged together. This is why getting rid of the malaise is so arduous' (Shariati, 1981: 58).

It is impossible to get out of one's self's prison through science, technology, the philosophy of history or sociology. One can only free oneself from this last prison through religion and the love of God. Only an almighty force within us can help us to rebel against our self: 'It is a love which, beyond rationality and logic, invites us to negate and rebel against ourselves in order to work towards a goal or for the sake of others. It is in this stage that a free man is born, and this is the most exalting level of becoming an Ensan' (Shariati, 1981: 62). Shariati concludes that 'although the West has made better use of scientific truth, Shi'i Islam is still in possession of the only ontological truth, and therefore remains in a superior position' (Mirsepassi, 2000: 124).

Using Shariati's ideas, it can be concluded that to whatever extent Habermas accommodates human needs and endows human beings and society with self-consciousness and power, he also limits humans through his materialism. Materialism 'recognizes man to be composed of material essence. With this definition it imprisons man within the evolutionary frame limited to being matter. If this is the case, it is impossible for him to evolve beyond the capacity of the matter's dimensions itself' (Shariati, 1981: 52). When Materialism eliminates God from the world, it has to fit human beings within material nature and, as a result, it sacrifices humanity. Indeed, if Habermas strips human beings of their God, they will no longer remain human. In other words, if Habermas uses materialism as a foundation for human beings, he incarcerates each of them in the prison of his or her own self, because a human being can only escape from this prison through religion.

7. Bourgeoisie, Scientism and Machinism

To be modern is to find ourselves in an environment that promises us adventure, power, joy, growth, transformation of ourselves and the world –and, at the same time, that threatens to destroy everything we have, everything we know, everything we are. Modern environments and experiences cut across all boundaries of geography and ethnicity, of class and nationality, of religion and ideology: in this sense, modernity can be said to unite all mankind. But it is a paradoxical unity, a unity of disunity: it pours us all into a maelstrom of perpetual disintegration and renewal, of struggle and contradiction, of ambiguity and anguish. To be modern is to be part of a universe in which, as Marx said, "all that is solid melts into air" (Berman, 1982: 15).

Shariati identifies modernity with the rise of the bourgeoisie and the phenomena he labels 'scientism' and 'machinism'. For him, the bourgeoisie are an emergent middle class leading an urban life centred on the money economy, commerce, and industry. This class demolished the feudal system and established itself in history by changing the simple divisions between peasant and landlord, aristocracy and serf. In his analysis of the bourgeoisie, Shariati argues that modern civilisation is the spiritual manifestation of the bourgeoisie, expressing the principles of transformation and improvement.

What the bourgeoisie rejected was the religious culture of the Middle Ages; a corrupt spirituality, since man's loftiest heritage was in the hands of the fossilized clergy in the service of feudalism. By shattering the culture and morality of the Middle Ages, the new bourgeoisie bestowed a great service upon the growth of freedom of intellect, civilization and science, and pushed aside feudalism and the clergy. In the process it also buried the most valuable foundations of mankind's spirit, culture and morals under the rubble of the Medieval period (Shariati, 1981: 25).

According to Shariati (1990: 100), both intellectual factors and the economic and social system caused the social changes in the Middle Ages and the Renaissance. In contrast to Marx's views regarding the origins of the modern ages, Weber conceived Protestantism as the greatest element in the emergence of capitalism and the technical progress of the West: 'According to Weber, the Reformation taught its followers to resolve religious anxiety by being successful at their work. The pursuit of worldly success, he believed, inadvertently created a congenial "ethic" for the development of methodical capitalist enterprise' (Ozment, 1991: 218). Shariati (1990: 101-105) argues that this was a period in which the Christian intellectuals of Europe protested against the religious attitudes and superstitions of the Catholic Church and its intercession between God and people. Catholicism promoted a religious ethic that endorsed a rejection of the world, but Protestantism endorsed a 'worldly asceticism'.

This worldly asceticism did not give direct support to the emergent money economy. However, in offering a religious endorsement of individuals' worldly activity, it promoted the ethic of hard work, thrift, and capital accumulation, which in turn provided the foundations of modern capitalism. As Weber notes, wherever Protestantism thrives, the bourgeoisie, industry, and material civilisation develop too: Mclellan (1987: 165-166) adds that: 'As Karl Lowith has put it, the spirit of capitalism exists for Weber only in so far as there is a general tendency towards a rational conduct of life, borne along by the bourgeois stratum of society, which establishes an elective affinity between the capitalist economy on one side and the Protestant ethic on the other'. In contrast, in relation to industrialisation and capitalism, Catholic societies were relatively ill-equipped for engaging constructively with economic changes. As Shariati (1981: 105) says:

Max Weber discussed the relationship between capitalism and the Protestant ethic. He argued that those predominantly Catholic countries such as Spain, France, and Italy were less progressive than England, Germany, and the United States which were predominantly Protestant. Namely, Weber maintained that there was a direct relationship between [the] Protestant ethic and capitalism.

Shariati points out that the essential element that characterised the stagnation of thought, civilisation, and culture in Middle Ages Europe was the Aristotelian mode of analogical reasoning. This analogical reasoning was rejected by Protestantism. According to Shariati (1990: 78-79), the church mounted Christianity on Aristotelian philosophical bases and then adopted an assemblage of both Aristotelian and Christian convictions. This sort of Christianity was not one of Palestinian description, but rather a Greek Aristotelian philosophy with a

Christian appearance. Accordingly, what emerged from this mixture of Aristotelian philosophy and the principles of Christianity was a 'Scholastic' theology that governed all other scientific disciplines. It was this Scholastic Greek philosophy that was adopted for defending religion and religious creeds, and Shariati considers this to have brought about a stagnation in both Christianity and human beings' thought, because Greek philosophy was not capable of discovering the correct method of reasoning. However, the correct cognitive method for the discovery of truth is more important than philosophy, science or the possession of mere talent. As Shariati (1979: 59) puts it:

Aristotle was without doubt a greater genius than Francis Bacon, and Plato a greater genius than Roger Bacon. But what enabled the two Bacons to become factors in the advancement of science, despite their inferiority in genius to men like Plato, while those geniuses caused the millennial stagnation of medieval Europe? In other words, why should a genius cause stagnation in the world, and an average man bring about scientific progress and popular awakening? Because the latter has discovered the correct method of reasoning, by means of which even a mediocre intellect can discover the truth, while the great genius, if he does not know the correct method of looking at things and reflecting on problems, will be unable to make use of his genius.

Shariati (1990: 106-116) interprets Protestantism as the 'Islamisation of Christianity', in the sense that he believes it accepts the Islamic worldview, but remains a form of Christianity. His argument is that Christian intellectuals drew upon the Western experience of Islamic societies, with the effect that they began to protest against the fossilised religion that governed over them. Shariati (1990: 143-147) holds that the West adopted a number of things from the East through the

Crusades. Firstly, it developed a tendency towards taking on the universalist and materialist life that existed in Islamic societies during this period. The main reason behind this was that the Middle Age period displayed an extreme other-worldliness, focused on the resurrection and the life of the world to come. However, this other-worldliness was changed into a social and political life when it made contact with Islamic societies, because Islam is a social, political, and worldly religion. Secondly, its contact with the East led to an instability in the correlation between church and people. There is no formal organisation called 'the church' in Islam. Rather, there is religious freedom and individual Ijtihad. According to Shariati, there is no church that constrains the beliefs of individuals In Islam. Third, there is political centralisation in Islamic society. Europe adopted this political centrality and destroyed the decentralised feudal system. By doing so it created freedom, religious plurality, and free religious scholarship. Evidence of the causes of these changes in the West can be seen by the fact that when the Crusades decamped, a mass of the Western population moved to the East, mixed in Eastern societies, and borrowed the 10th and 11th century social systems from the East. It used these to fight feudalism, the church and Popism, the sale of indulgences, and the despotism of clerics. Indeed, the Crusades terminated with 'the influence of Islam upon the transformation of the West, the emergence of the Renaissance and the collapse of feudalism, the end of the Middle Ages, the victory of science and freedom in Europe and the emergence of the new civilization' (Shariati, 1986: 130). According to Shariati, modern Western civilisation was not established by negating or denying religion. It was a reformation that changed religious attitudes and justifications in society. In other words:

In the Crusades, the Islamization of Christianity created Protestantism. Christianity, which throughout centuries was the cause of retardation, was transformed into a builder and energizer to Europe. Unlike what we have been told, it was not the negation of religion which created modern Western civilization but the transformation of a corrupt and ascetic religion into a critical, protesting, and mundane Christianity. That is, Protestantism was the creator of modern Western civilization, rather than materialism or anti-religious sentiments which did not exist in the Renaissance (Shariati, 1981: 41).

This view has been challenged by Ozment, however, who argues that Luther – the founder of the Reformation – 'viewed existing political institutions as established by God (Rom, 13: 1). Luther is said to have instilled in his followers an uncritical approach to government by teaching "religious obedience and humble submission." Troeltsch believed that Luther sanctioned and even glorified unconditional obedience to reigning political authority' (Ozment, 1991: 119). In other words, 'the only ethical result was negative; worldly duties were no longer subordinated to ascetic ones; obedience to authority and the acceptance of things as they were, were preached' (Weber, 1948: 86).

Shariati considers scientism to be the second feature of modernity. He holds that scientism claims that the only authentic knowledge in science is based on experience, observation, and comparisons in relation to nature. Therefore, physics, chemistry, astronomy, and sociology are sciences, but philosophy and religion, which are not verifiable through experiment and comparison, cannot be numbered as sciences. In other words, religion and philosophy cannot be apprehended by the scientific method. Scientism reached its peak during the 18th and 19th centuries, and mounted vigorous attacks on philosophy, religion, and even literature. In analysing the doctrine of scientism, Shariati (1990: 226) suggests that it consists of the following doctrines: 1-All ideas and meditations must be based on scientific laws and analyses; 2- Religion, God, the soul and many spiritualities are false, or do not exist, because they are beyond the scope of science; 3- Many instincts, ethical customs, and social relations are superstitions, as there is no scientific basis for them; 4- One must reject everything that is old and embrace everything that is novel; 5- One should apply the logical method to all concepts. Accordingly, science came to displace God for the first time, and undertook the role of directing human life – a mission that had, until then, been guided under the auspices of religion. Put differently,

What were the watchwords of this upsurge? Human freedom from the bonds of the all-compelling will of heaven, release of the intellect from the dominance of religious belief, release of science from scholastic dogma, a turning from heaven to earth to build the paradise that religion had promised for the hereafter, right here on earth! What exciting slogans! Freedom of the intellect; science to be our guide; paradise on the spot! But what hands were to build this paradise on earth? Those of colonized nations, exploited human beings, with the assistance of scientific technology (Shariati, 1980: 39).

However, all the passion, credibility, faith, hope, and optimism that the people and scholars of the 16th to the 19th century had for science and its mission, achievements, and power in the future were reduced to pessimism: 'Science was freed from subservience to religion only to become subservient to power and at the disposal of the powerful. It was transformed into short-sighted, rigid scientism' (Shariati, 1980: 39). When science aims to grant absolute power to humans, it loses its sanctity, because sanctity is generated by conduction and guidance rather than by authority. When science puts aside the notion of truth-seeking, and stops giving meaning to human life, it reconciles itself with money and power:

In order to create power, the scientist needed money and this tendency landed the scientist in the lap of the capitalist and bourgeoisie ... Further, a researcher has no role at all in what he does. He is told what to conduct, discover, and make, just like Mussolini's philosophers. When today's intellectual wakes up late and sinks so low, he will notice a few stars shining above who are grappling with: 1) science which, in its slavish form, is ruling the world; 2) humanism which has imprisoned man in its material framework; 3) scientism, meaning the neutrality of science and its transformation into a tool in the hands of the powers-that-be; 4) lack of responsibility on the part of the science in guiding man and giving him awareness; and 5) rationalism as the only criterion for understanding the truth of the universe (Shariati, 1981: 79).

Therefore, it can be claimed that human beings have become more capable of dominating nature, but preside over themselves less than ever. That is, human beings are less able to control their desires. Because of this, Shariati states that he is not only against scientism, but also all intellectuals who believe in mankind's dignity, freedom and perfection. Scientism is a tool in the hands of the ruling class, and contributes to petrification and irresponsibility. According to Shariati, science has contributed to the expansion of capitalism and hegemony, rather than creating a better modern world for humans. As Weber (1948: 143) puts it:

Under these internal presuppositions, what is the meaning of science as a vocation, now after all these former illusions, the 'way to true being,' the 'way to true art,' the 'way to true nature,' the 'way to true God,' the 'way to true happiness,' have been dispelled? Tolstoi has given the simplest answer, with the words: 'Science is meaningless because it gives no answer to our question, the only question important for us: "What shall we do and how shall we live?"' That science does not give an answer to this is indisputable.

However, unlike Weber, Shariati (2011: 222) argues that science has alienated mankind because it is concerned with how to live but not why to live, and its objective is to provide power rather than to create beauty. Its mission is to discover rules to allow humans to acquire more in life, rather than discovering the truth of the universe and human beings. In an interview that I conducted with Aavani on Monday 17th of January 2011, he claimed that modernity separates science from theology, and that this detachment is the greatest danger to humanity as it leads to nihilism. In modern science, all things are counted quantitatively and science is used to dominate nature. Thus, the comprehension of truth is turned into a meaningless concept. Western modernity is mistaken, because it wants to impose its objectives and thought on the entire world, and to cast aside other civilisations, which it considers backward. It also tries to negate and challenge Eastern tradition, even though it is a tradition that carries a rational approach to knowing Almighty God and a practical manner to reach to God.

Finally, the association between scientism and capitalism created 'machinism': 'the machine that was to have been humanity's tool for ruling nature and escaping enslavement to work was transformed into machinism that itself enslaved man' (Shariati, 1980: 39). Shariati considers machinism to be a system that came into being in the West and devoured humankind, machine, science, life, philosophy, literature, art, spirit and sympathy. Hence, the machine is not a marketable commodity, but the foundation for the modern social formation of machinism: 'Machinism is a sociological phenomenon. It is a particular social order, not a marketable, consumable, or technical product or commodity' (Shariati, 1990: 315). Machinism is the result of an unwholesome union between the bourgeoisie and scientism, and this new social system extended itself into different spheres of Western life. Machinism was created by the emergence of private ownership, and it is principally a superstructure of private ownership.

Shariati (1987: 224) contends that with the emergence of machinism, commercial capitalism was replaced by the Industrial Revolution, and class divisions were sharpened even further. The magical production power of the machine added to both the accumulation of wealth and to the exploitation of the working force. The workers increasingly lost their human essence as they were turned into objects in the incredible production systems. Thus, machinism created a hollow life and a phoney mankind, and one specific character of machinism for Shariati is its negation of originality:

The machine must increase its production progressively each year. People's consumption, however, does not increase at the same rate as does production. Therefore, new fields of consumption must be provided ... Since the machine compulsively produces excess goods, it must step over all national boundaries and push goods into the world market ... When in the eighteenth century the capitalists gained control of machinery, as well as technology and science, man's destiny was determined. Every single human being on the face of the earth was to be coerced into becoming a consumer for the produced merchandise. European goods had to go to Africa and

Asia. Asians and Africans had to consume the surplus European products (Shariati, 1978: 11).

Thus, to be attracted to European commodities, non-Western peoples had to be modernised and westernised. The aim of this was to create a single interest – global imperialism – involving political, military, economic and cultural colonisation. Machinism also produced and developed technocracy and bureaucracy, which have resulted in anxiety, alienation, distress, and abhorrent fascism. Shariati (1990, 345-346) holds that fascism is a socio-political, philosophical, psychological, and economic system, as well as a racial dictatorship, and is generated by a technocratic class of society. Fascism was not only the result of Hitler's and Mussolini's orders in Germany and Italy, but also a gargantuan growth in a technocratic class. That is why Gurvitch claims that Europe was advancing to individual freedom and democracy during the 17th and 18th centuries, but is moving towards a chronic form of fascism today, albeit one that is hidden behind the facade of democracy and liberalism. In an interview that I conducted with Whitehead on Sunday 26th of June 2011, he claimed that the solution to abating this movement is to begin educating people about the fact that current wars are not about the differences between Christianity and Islam, Catholicism and Protestantism, or Sunnism and Shi'ism, but about the desires of powerful countries to make profit from the resources of third world countries in order to maintain their way of life. The solution, as Marx told us many years ago, is that we must dismantle the social system that solely promotes the capitalist ideology, and bring other values into our political system. We think we fight for various freedoms, democracy, and human rights, but this is just a smokescreen to cover up the relentless search for money and power.

Machinism inevitably leads to technocracy and bureaucracy, and these in turn lead to fascism, because a technocratic class lacks both roots and ideology. Although it attempts to create an ideology, it ends up in racism and false pride. Shariati adds that machinism makes this exploitation more extensive and disastrous than it was previously. Hence, it provides human beings with futile lives that do not rely on ethical values. In my interview on Monday 8th February 2010, Pedram said that Shariati shows a range of sensitivity to Western machinism and liberal democracy. According to Shariati, liberal democracy relies substantially on ideas that are grown out of feeling rather than born of rationalisation. He decisively argues that fantasised factors impress more than those of logic in producing ideas.

Shariati (1990: 357-358) believes that we must recognise and challenge machinism in order to save science from scientism, nature from materialism, machine from machinism, and humanity from all of these harms. Thus, Islamic intellectuals must resist imitating Europe. In fact, an intellectual can neither accept inherited and petrified forms of tradition, nor adopt imposed packages of ideologies that are souvenirs from the West during these centuries, because an intellectual is himself able to think, make choices, and create. Current experience shows that the consumption of Western products does not rid Eastern people of any pain. Instead of traditional historical poles, and those of Western-exported imitation, the intellectual must choose a third alternative. According to Boroujerdi (1996: 111-112), Shariati insisted that:

Intellectuals had to distinguish themselves from their European counterparts, who could generally be recognized by their belief in the following set of ideas: irreligiosity, nationalism, scientism, materialism, cosmopolitanism, and antitraditionalism ... [And] Shariati contended that internationalism, humanism, and the ideal of universality are great lies promoted by the West, which aspires to negate the cultural character of oriental societies.

8. Knowledge, Religion and Art

The wrong turn was taken when Kant's split between science, morals, and art was accepted (Rorty, 1985: 167).

In criticising modernity, Shariati (2007: 110-111), like Habermas, argues that the separation of knowledge, religion, and art was the catastrophe of modernity, because it caused these three spheres of human life to take different courses from one another. Influenced by the spirit of the new Western bourgeoisie, knowledge discharged itself from the responsibility of discovering truth and saving mankind and turned into a tool for capitalism, technology, and consumption. Shariati argues that since the 17th century, the more that intellectuals have become familiar within the foundations of scientific epistemology, the further they have run from religion, and the more they have distanced themselves from the common people as a result.

For Shariati, religion has also become detached from knowledge and science, and frozen into petrified forms of dogmatism comprising old, futile, unconscious, nonsensical and static traditions. It has rejected the evolutionary logic of human societies and life and, thus abandoning the responsibility of leadership for the people. It has become incarcerated in its dusty temples, contenting itself with stagnant layers of society. Finally, religion has come to be at the service of money and power. In other words,

As you see in the struggles in the 19th century, he [the member of the proletariat] supports materialism because religion was totally at the service of and dedicated to the gods of gold and power. Generally, gold, power and fraud were all prefabricated. As we see, the biggest share of capitalism in the West belongs to the Roman Church. The biggest investments in the world belong to them. Thus, it was not at the service of the people. This is why he revolts against religion and this kind of class system (Shariati, 2009d: 267).

However, 'Western regimes, Shariati contends, have eliminated the revolutionary potential in their countries by letting the workers "buy into" the bourgeois lifestyle at the expense of the Third World' (Mirsepassi, 2000: 120). In fact, capitalism becomes rational. That is, the disappearance of the differences in consumption has the purpose of safeguarding the differences in production, ownership and classes:

All the consumer goods exported from Europe to our countries during the last 20 or 30 years often had a 300%, 400% to 600% price increase. On the other hand, the raw material which they receive from us, Africa, Asia, and many Latin America countries, contrary to the demand and supply rules which state price increases in every 30 or 40 years, some of these raw material curves had small slopes and some none. The price of most of the exported raw materials from the backward countries to Europe had declined compared to 30 years ago. It has often been halved. Contrary to the last analysis of the most highly ranked, intellectual, progressive, and revolutionary socialists, which says that it is the capitalism rationality which has destroyed the revolution and has made the proletariat class become a bourgeois, I believe that the only thing we can pay them with in order to guarantee their exports, is our poverty (Shariati, 2009d: 275-276).

Shariati (1974: 17, 7) holds that art brings consciousness to the unconscious soul of the human being because art, awakening the sense of the abstract, allows us to come to know God. Therefore, art is a religion, a transcendent and sacred truth, a saviour of humanity. However, art has been turned away from this faith in modernity. Thus, 'the world has gone so far in the direction of worldliness that it almost seems as if another Jesus were needed' (Shariati, 1979: 79).

In his final message, Shariati (1990: 258, 358) says that we are standing on the brink of developing a new civilisation, the founders of which are not European, but intellectuals that have appeared from within Asian, African, and Latin American countries. Their main purpose is to save human beings from the 'malice' of colonisation, machinism, bourgeoisie, capitalism, and exploitation. Speaking of Islamic societies, he suggests that educated intellectuals have a truly religious school of thought, and that he strongly believes that removing the worship of God from a society will lead to its certain fall. Therefore, he urges the people of Eastern countries not to imitate Europe, but to create a new path, using their minds to reach a new destination, a novel idea of society, and a novel human being.

In conclusion, Shariati, like Habermas, condemns the separation of science, knowledge, ethics, religion, and art from each other. Habermas (1987: 329) emphasises that 'capitalist modernization has always appeared with the stain of dissolving traditional life-forms without salvaging their communicative substance'. Capitalist modernisation destroys these forms of life rather than changing them in such a way that three forms of knowledge of – cognitive-instrumental, moral-practical and expressive – could be combined. Moreover, both Habermas and Shariati believe that we must guide religion away from the systems of superstitions and dogmatisms represented by the 'formal' religions that now exist in the world. They try to secure freedom, equality, and justice from the system of capitalism, because it is evident that where money and power are valued above all else, both freedom and equality are illusions. Justice cannot be realised unless a society keeps away from bourgeoisie, scientism, machinism, exploitation, and class polarisation. Indeed, both Shariati and Habermas claim that the system of modernity creates an intellectual and creedal foundation compatible with the economical, social, and political structure of a society to justify the status quo. However, there are also significant differences between Habermas and Shariati, as I shall now show.

5.2. Religion and Public Life: The Views of Habermas and Shariati Compared

Shariati, like Habermas, displays an interest in Western scientific and technological achievements. However, he believes that the West has experienced an unbalanced form of social and cultural development, and that its progress in science and technology has been accompanied by a substantial decline and degeneration in ethics and freedom. Shariati believes that it is possible to create a society based on both religion and communicative rationality. According to him, religion is neither a rival nor a successor to reason. Properly understood, religion does not antagonise or vie with reason, but in fact supplements it, and thus religious persons ought to understand both the mission of religion and the importance of reason and use them appropriately. Shariati tries to separate religion from tradition, and claims that Divine religions are true, but that tradition contains mixtures of truth and falsity. Although Habermas and Shariati criticise modernity and tradition, they use both to rebuild their own system of thought. Whereas Shariati embeds his ideas within a religious system, Habermas develops his views within a secular one. Habermas has also demanded that all secular and religious people participate in running society through tolerance and communicative action: the pious are permitted to introduce their religious values in a customary language and turn them into laws if they reach a mutual understanding. Nevertheless, both Shariati and Habermas have a positive opinion about the future of human beings.

This portion of the chapter will assess the value and limitations of Habermas's work on religion in the light of Shariati's thought in relation to three interrelated themes: reason and religion, modernity and tradition, and public life and religion.

5.2.1. Reason and Religion

As an advocate of Iranian religious revolution, Shariati wanted to reconcile the experience of the reformation with Iranian traditional life, and to give Islam a dynamic quality so that it could triumph in modern times. Mirsepassi (2000: 116-117) notes that 'although Shariati sees modernity as characterized by warring ideologies, he will also raise the Islamic ideology from a mere intellectual option to the ontological necessity for mankind'.

Shariati did not engage with Habermas's thought directly. Nevertheless, a shared commitment to a radical critique of society and culture is evident in both their discourses. For instance, Shariati essentially constructed the critical approach in Iran, and has deeply influenced many Iranian religious reformists' views. Relying on his critical approach, Habermas assesses the views of many scholars, such as Marx, Weber, and earlier generations of the Frankfurt School. Shariati also utilises a critical methodology for challenging tradition and historical religion. Habermas criticises modernity, modern states, and their crises, while Shariati questions not only modernity, but also *Gharbzadegi* (Westernisation). However, these two scholars adopt fundamentally different approaches to modernity and tradition. Shariati's critical approach relies on *tauhid* and Islamic ideology, whereas Habermas believes in a self-building rationality. Habermas's critiques have attracted opposition from Western neo-Marxists, liberal democrats and the clergy, whilst Shariati's thought has attracted opposition from Marxists, secularists, and traditionalists in the East.

Habermas's greatest influence has come from the views of the Frankfurt School scholars, Marx, and Weber. He deals with a tension between modernity and religion, or reason and faith. Although he has referred to himself as a Marxist:

He [Habermas] made a point rather early on to critique Marxism in general and to define himself in a distinctive and different manner. He declared that the economic causal explanations of classical Marxism were definitely too narrow and too rigid and thus unsatisfactory a century and a half after they had been announced. He criticized Marx for his disinterest in freedom as a social issue and in the human dimension in general (Nemoianu, 2006: 33).

Marx considers religion to be a social institution. He states that 'religion is the sigh of the oppressed creature, the heart of a heartless world, just as it is the spirit of spiritless conditions. It is the opium of the people' (Elster, 1986: 182). According to Marx, religion is thus a reflection of human misery that gives illusory comfort and dissuades people from struggling for social equality. The Frankfurt School scholars initially adopted Marx's views about the role of religion in the public sphere, but later became impressed by Weber's arguments that religion plays an important role in social evolution. As a result of the French sociologist Gurvitch's influence on him, Shariati adopted a number of aspects of Marx and Weber's theories, such as the concept of revolutionary consciousness from Marx, and that of religious reformation from Weber. He explicitly puts Descartes' maxim: 'cogito ergo sum' aside, substituting it for Camus' dictum: 'I protest, and then I am': 'What Camus says is that contemporary man is alienated from everything. This alienated man feels closeness and familiarity more than ever and he needs to feel familiarity, yet his family and the world are more than ever alienated from him' (Shariati, 1974: 15).

5.2.2. Modernity and Tradition

Habermas and Shariati propose numerous criticisms of modernity with the hope of pushing human beings towards a deliverance from their current condition. Unlike the founders of the Frankfurt School, who lost hope in saving human beings from the bounds of technological and instrumental rationality, conceiving of modernity as an iron cage that has placed human beings in captivity, Habermas theorised that the lifeworld allows human beings to form a self-building sphere of communicative action beyond the power of capitalism. Thus, what Habermas means by communicative action is a proper type of social action and reaction within which participants expect one another to coordinate their different purposes and actions through a consensus that is produced by communication and mutual understanding (Habermas, 1990a: 89). For Habermas, this presents a notable model for democratic structures in society, particularly with regard to the notions of 'deliberative democracy' and 'emancipation'. However, Ricoeur (1981: 97) challenges Habermas's ideas on the grounds that:

The interest in emancipation would be quite empty and abstract if it were not situated on the same plane as the historical-hermeneutic sciences, that is, on the plane of communicative action. But if that is so, can a critique of distortions be separated from the communicative experience itself, from the place where it begins, where it is real and where it is exemplary? The task of the hermeneutics of tradition is to remind the critique of ideology that man can project his emancipation and anticipate an unlimited and unconstrained communication only on the basis of the creative reinterpretation of cultural heritage. If we had no experience of communication, however restricted and mutilated it was, how could we wish it to prevail for all men and at all institutional levels of the social nexus?

Separating lifeworld from system, Habermas tries to enable this self-building sphere to develop through the theory of communicative action. First, he is highly critical of what modernity has become, particularly with regard to what he calls the goal-directed rationality of the social 'system'. 'System', in his thought, refers to the instrumental rationality that produces economic and bureaucratic spheres within which social relations are controlled through money and power alone, since these become the key determinants of social action. Habermas holds that:

The public sphere, simultaneously prestructured and dominated by the mass media, developed into an arena infiltrated by power in which, by means of topic selection and topical contributions, a battle is fought not only over influence but over the control of communication flows that affect behavior while their strategic intentions are kept hidden as much as possible (Calhoun, 1992: 437).

Second, however, and in contrast to the goal-directed rationality of the social 'system', Habermas identifies the 'lifeworld' as the arena in which the modern project can reach its completion even though it is increasingly threatened or colonised by the system. Put differently, Habermas (like Weber) holds that there are two species of rationality in modernity: positive and negative rationality. However, through the course of time, positive rationality is affected by negative rationality and loses its importance. Negative rationality is the sovereignty of bureaucracy and technocracy that leaves human in an iron cage. Weber complains:

I cannot stand it when problems of world-moving importance, of the greatest intellectual and spiritual bearing, in a certain sense the highest problems that can move a human breast are transformed here into questions of technical-economic "productivity" and are made into the topic of discussion of a *technical* discipline, such as economics is (Marcuse, 1968: 202)

The difference between Habermas and Weber's conceptions of rationality, however, lies in the fact that Weber's positive rationality is in the sphere of system, while Habermas considers positive rationality to lie in the sphere of culture and lifeworld. According to Weber, positive rationality emancipated society from the dominance of some archaic influences at the beginning of the Enlightenment, such as those of metaphysics and religious superstitions. However, he holds that it was gradually replaced by negative rationality, with human beings themselves providing their means of self-alienation, in so far as they allowed negative rationality to pervade and govern society. Similarly, according to Habermas, because of the location of communicative action within the lifeworld, its colonisation by the system prevents the realisation of a full, free and meaningful life for people, and undermines the structure of mutual understanding (which constitutes the foundation of democracy). Indeed, negative rationality brings two discontents of the expansion of instrumental rationality and the loss of the firm grounding of traditional society. According to Vahdat (2002: 226), discontent of the first subtype can be broadly characterised as what Weber calls "loss of freedom," manifested in the impersonal, formal, and mass social settings and organisations to which Weber applies the metaphor of the "iron cage". In their attempts to achieve subjectivity, the free agents of modernity have increasingly objectified nature, and through rationalisation, bureaucratization, and reification, they have expanded instrumental rationality. In so doing, they have lost the very freedom they sought to attain. Discontent of the second subtype has to do with what Weber calls "loss of meaning" and what Hegel refers to as "vacuity". In Hegel's analysis, separating ethics from its superhuman source, as Kant and his followers do, renders it "vacuous". For Weber, disenchantment with and disbelief in a transcendental and substantive source of culture have resulted in the rejection of all particular beliefs and a resultant sense of meaning-lessness (cited in Habermas, 1981a: 44-47). It seems that meaning has to come to us from outside; left to ourselves, we are incapable of satisfying our own existential needs. By contrast, Habermas implicitly suggests throughout the two volumes of *the Theory of Communicative Action* that we are indeed capable of satisfying our own existential needs for meaning.

It is in the light of this that Habermas seeks to reconstruct the project of modernity, releasing it from the control of instrumental rationality and extending the jurisdiction of communicative action and the lifeworld. It is this desire to reconstruct modernity through the proper recognition of the nature and importance of the lifeworld that, in his later thought at least, allows Habermas to recognise the importance of religion, even within advanced modern societies. Moreover, even in his earlier studies, Habermas recognised that although modernity had brought some forms of development in the economic, political and cultural areas, it had left a vacuum in human identity and direction by removing the chains of tradition and the metaphysical element from the person. In fact, unlike Shariati, Habermas sees a secondary dynamism in modernity, and defends its feature of universal deliverance. However, it is impossible for European modernity to provide a universal structure for the entire world, as it is unable to overcome its inner contradictions to provide such an approach. In other words, Habermas's attempt to draw a unique prescription for the whole world is misguided, because he does not adequately accommodate for different cultures, civilisations, and pluralism. Habermas's ideas wrongly put Western civilisation at the centre of the universe and others in the margin.

Separating different dimensions of modernity, Shariati provides radical criticisms of modernity that approach, to some extent, the work of Nietzsche, Heidegger, Foucault, Derrida, and Lyotard. In an interview that I conducted with Manoochehri on Monday 8th of February 2010, he described Shariati as a modern thinker because of his attempts to introduce Islam as an emancipatory ideology but not a 'modernist' one. Shariati does not try to adapt the Koran to the modern mind, but rather calls for an encounter between the two. Neither is he a traditionalist. His reliance on early Islamic experience is not based on his traditionalism as he refers to this experience as the real historical manifestation of a worldview that is not only antithetical to oppression, but also provides the basis for a theoretical development for the practical negation of oppression. His unceasingly questioning mind, however, led him to both learn from and be critical of contemporary Western thought. Manoochehri also notes that significant studies on how to compare Iranian scholars' ideas with those of Western thinkers have not yet been widely undertaken in Iran, and he expressed the view that providing a new discussion on the role of religion in public life through engaging with both Habermas's and Shariati's perspectives could bring considerable results.

It appears that the different approaches that Habermas and Shariati adopt can be understood in terms of their specific experiences of modernity and their socio-political conditions. Habermas's criticism of modernity is influenced by particular features of German society, especially the problem of Nazism. He tries to analyse the conditions that resulted in the emergence of Nazism and to provide a set of conditions that will avoid any similar re-occurrence. Therefore, Habermas considers modernity as a universal structure or universalistic philosophy. However:

French critics of Habermas ready to abandon liberal politics in order to avoid universalistic philosophy, and Habermas trying to hang on to universalistic philosophy, with all its problems, in order to support liberal politics ... These critics doubt that studies of communicative competence can do what transcendental philosophy failed to do in the way of providing "universalistic" criteria (Rorty, 1985: 162, 164).

Habermas seeks to build this universal structure through interaction in order to realise communicative action: 'It is governed by binding *consensual norms*, which define reciprocal expectations about behavior and which must be understood and recognized by at least two acting subjects. Social norms are enforced through sanctions. Their meaning is objectified in ordinary language communication' (Habermas, 1971: 92). For this reason, Habermas sees self-consciousness as freedom in the appearance of universal structures. He seeks a universal institution to safeguard the human rights of all people in the world based on Western rationality. For instance, Habermas (1984: 44) holds that 'we are implicitly connecting a claim to *universality* with our *Occidental understanding of the world*. In determining the significance of this claim, it would be well to draw a comparison with the mythical understanding of the world'. Therefore, the analysis above is incomplete and one-sided. Furthermore, 'Habermas reconstructs historical materialism around *one* universal value: his own. But there are other universal values too. He overdetermines his theory in order to make us accept his own value as the exclusive or at least the highest one ... But those who are ready to create progress are confronted with different philosophies' (Heller, 1982: 41). In other words, Habermas tries to destabilise the notion of subjectivism and to make a new truth and consensus based on an emancipation that is embedded in the heart of interaction or communicative action.

Interaction, on the other hand, which Habermas equates with 'communicative action', 'is governed by binding *consensual norms*, which define reciprocal expectations about behavior and which must be understood and recognized by at least two acting subjects' ... I would say that he himself makes a triple reduction within the notion of interaction itself: first, it is wrong to treat interaction as equivalent, or reducible, to action:

second, it is wrong to treat action as equivalent, or reducible, to communicative action; and third, it is an error to suppose that communicative action can be examined solely on the level of norms (Giddens, 1982: 152,158).

Indeed, Habermas's philosophy seeks for an intersubjectivity of mutual understanding of social symbols that allows people to have open discussion that is free from any type of coercion and constraints. However, it is not only evident that everyday social interaction does not fit this idealised model, but also that Habermas is unable to develop a universal ethics for human beings without using a superhuman or transcendental source.

Shariati values some aspects of modernity, such as science, technology, and the critical approach. However, unlike Habermas, he considers the specific situation of Iranian society before the revolution, which was situated within the triangle of a secularist domestic despotism, modern Western colonisation, and constricted tradition. He describes it as a sinister triangle of *Zar, Zoor,* and *Tazvir* – the powers of wealth, oppression, and hypocrisy. Furthermore, Shariati has repeatedly noted the bitter experiences that African, Asian, and Latin American countries have had with modernity. According to him, modernity not only fails to provide an emancipatory experience for poor countries, but also produces disastrous experiences for them. For non-Western countries, the project of modernity brings non-identity, alienation, and contempt, and it is not capable of recognising the rights of poor countries.

Shariati considers the bourgeoisie, scientism, and machinism as the outcomes of modernity. In reality, modernity is the same as an iron cage – leading to human being's self-alienation, and the negation of nobility and diversity. In other words, for Shariati, modernity and globalisation involve casting human beings into a single 'talented' mould, destroying all their versatility, and turning them into one-dimensional creatures, as Marcuse held. Marcuse 'sees technological rationality colonizing everyday life, robbing individuals of freedom and individuality by imposing technological imperatives, rules, and structures upon their thought and behavior' (Kellner, 1991: xiv). Following Marcuse, Shariati argues that world imperialism, cultural colonisation, and de-traditionalisation are born of machinism – that is, a vigorous penetration of Western consumption into new markets and nations. 'In Baxter's view the care for external goods should only lie on the shoulders of the "saint like a light cloak, which can be thrown aside at any moment". But fate decreed that the cloak should become an iron cage' (Weber, 1930: 181). Whilst Habermas seeks to solve the crises of modernity using its own elements, Shariati (and postmodernists) hold that it is impossible to solve the difficulties of modernity from within its own mechanism. Shariati's solution for saving Muslims from the crises of modernity is '*bazgasht beh khishtan*', or rediscovery of our Islamic roots. He asserts that:

As the dominant spirit of modernity, "worldliness" has enslaved humanity to modern technology, rather than making technology a servant to human need. Shariati describes this condition as "the idiocy of the contemporary philosophy of man, the result of purpose-free technology," where "the whole meaning of civilization has been robbed of any ideas." [Shariati adds to explain that] authenticity (means rediscovery of our Islamic roots) is a modern prescription for adopting modernity without sacrificing cultural or political autonomy (Mirsepassi, 2000, 122-23).

This solution represents a typical form of particularism, the opposite to Habermas's universal modernisation. Shariati

(1974: 4) holds that 'we must stand on our own two feet. We must nourish ourselves from our own original, cultural resources. We must return to ourselves. We must pull ourselves out of our state of stupefaction of having passively sunk into western cultural values and models. This is only the starting point'. Although, Shariati introduced his strategy to Muslim countries, his early death did not leave him enough time to generalise his ideas to produce a universal project for humanity. However, 'Ali Shariati has become an international Islamic personality whose ideas and writings are studied, debated and emulated far beyond the borders of Iran' (Esposito, 1986: ix). Projects aiming at human freedom, such as the Abrahamic religions dialogue, and the dialogues between civilisations that have been undertaken by great Iranian religious reformists and supported by scholars from Iran and other world communities (such as the UN), are considered to be projects that have been built by Shariati.

In an interview that I conducted with Ehsan Shariati (Ali Shariati's son) on Tuesday 23rd of February 2010, he explained that Ali Shariati criticises Western technocratic modernity in his socio-economic project, and draws on Nietzsche, observing a destructive nihilism in the process of modernity. In Shariati's view, ideology is a critical theory of the status quo, which separates religion from historical superstitions, returning it to its original foundations in the traditions of the Koran and the Prophet. On the other hand, Habermas is optimistic about modernity, considering it to be an unfinished project. Despite all the differences, Shariati and Habermas both share a conception of technology and science as ideology, both appeal to discourse in the public sphere, both differentiate between the critical and traditional theories, and both have the project of emancipation.

I believe that Shariati's projects of 'distinguishing the emancipatory religion from the historical one', 'returning to the Islamic roots', 'rejecting *Zar, Zoor,* and *Tazvir*', 'protecting mysticism, equality, and freedom', and 'emancipating from one's self's prison' have the potential to form a rival to Habermas's universal project, in Middle Eastern countries in particular. However, in other respects, such as 'negating the bourgeoisie, scientism, and machinism', and 'condemning the separation of science, morality and art from each other' Shariati's project can be considered as complementary to Habermas's critique of positivism in seeking the emancipation of human beings. Like Shariati, Habermas (1971: 112) holds that:

Technocratic consciousness reflects not the sundering of an ethical situation but the repression of "ethics" as such as a category of life. The common, positivist way of thinking renders inert the frame of reference of interaction in ordinary language, in which domination and ideology both arise under conditions of distorted communication and can be reflectively detected and broken down.

Shariati introduces a third approach to Iranian society – *tauhid* – which is distinct from the abrupt revolutionary and conservative approaches. Indeed, the third alternative is an effective synthesis between historical Islam and Western-style modernity. Put differently: 'it was an alternative to Western capitalism and Marxist socialism, to the Westernization of society and to the rejection of modernization. These Islamic ideologues proclaimed the need for Muslims to take hold of their heritage and carve out a future that was modern, but more firmly rooted in and guided by their own Islamic history and values' (Esposito, 1986: x-xi).

Habermas also proposes a third approach – communicative action for all layers of society – as a challenge to the radical thought of Marx's class conflict, and that of Western liberal democracy. As I mentioned in chapter 4, Habermas's work offers a creative and potentially important attempt to move beyond the secular assumptions that have characterised much modern study of religion, wherein religion comes to occupy a central role in the mediation of the costs and benefits of modernity. Broadly understood, Habermas's work on the exchange of views and the intersubjectivity of mutual understanding between secular and religious groups and orientations, as well as on dialogues between religions and civilisations in the modern world, reflects his commitment to the importance of communication, dialogue and the need to prevent violence and war. This has not always been fully grasped by those who have engaged with his work on religion, and the limited reception of his work perhaps reflects the often abstract and technical nature of much of his writing, though the failure to fully understand his views of religion may also reflect the fact that his views on it have changed significantly over time.

As I have discussed, Habermas held religion to be one of the sources of modernity's inner problems in his earlier work, but in his more recent work he views religion as a principal source of the good life. As he makes clear in his lecture on religiousness at Tehran University, Habermas (2002c: 18) now believes that religion has not disappeared from the arena of the public sphere, and that it has an enormous effect on political public opinion. He leaves no doubt that he now wishes to engage constructively with the fact that religion is returning to the public sphere, and the fact that it is and will continue to have very significant affects both on social and political attitudes. Indeed, both Habermas and Shariati choose a policy of avoiding violence and increasing public consciousness. They hold that people should freely choose their faith, because faith is never reluctantly adopted and cannot be easily imposed on people. Ethics and morality would be valued in their own right in such a society, because disregarding ethics is on a par with violating religion.

5.2.3. Public Life and Religion

The views of the Frankfurt School scholars on religion have had a drastic effect on Habermas's attitude to religion. For example, Habermas (2008: 110) suggests that 'the translation of the theological doctrine of creation in God's image into the idea of the equal and unconditional dignity of all human beings constitutes one such conserving translation ... Benjamin was among the thinkers who at times succeeded in making such translations'. In his 'Theses on the Philosophy of History', Benjamin considers religion to have contributed to historical materialism. He alleges that historical materialism cannot refuse to employ religious metaphysical concepts:

The story is told of an automaton constructed in such a way that it could play a winning game of chess, answering each move of an opponent with a countermove. A puppet in Turkish attire and with a hookah in its mouth sat before a chessboard placed on a large table. A system of mirrors created the illusion that this table was transparent from all sides. Actually, a little hunchback who was an expert chess player sat inside and guided the puppet's hand by means of strings. One can imagine a philosophical counterpart to this device. The puppet called "historical materialism" is to win all the time. It can easily be a match for anyone if it enlists the services of theology, which today, as we know, is wizened and has to keep out of sight (Benjamin, 1973: 255).

Both in *Kierkegaard* and in his complete work *Negative Dialectic*, Adorno repeatedly refers back to topics that are derived from metaphysics and theology. Habermas also adopts this approach to metaphysics. For example, in 'Religion in the Public Sphere', he discusses the special power of religion and religious ethics to solve the susceptible forms of social life, and makes use of the term 'post-secular'. Habermas holds that it is impossible to keep religion out of the public sphere.

In a clear and unmistakable manner Habermas condemns all those who keep trying to sentence the religious discourse in the public square to silence, to eliminate and liquidate it altogether. It is therefore understandable that the nexus of faith and reason becomes the basis for building bridges to thinkers such as Habermas, who remained uncommitted to a religious orientation while still seeking connections with the world of the religious (Nemoianu, 2006: 27, 32).

However, the approach to religion that Habermas adopts is taken to be obvious in a post-modern space where there are contradicting and heterogeneous elements, such as different cultures and religions. It is thought that Habermas is thus obliged to take this approach. In my view, this attitude leads to a misunderstanding of Habermas's vision, because explaining the place of religion is embedded in Habermas's profound deliberation, although it has arisen in relation to the atmosphere of current changes on religion. The changes in Habermas's thought, though no doubt pragmatic, are not opportunistic or unprincipled: on the contrary, his more recent view of the need to accord religion a proper place in public discourse and communication appropriately reflects the underlying logic of his broader theoretical position. In fact, his advocacy of religion must be considered within the context of his worldview. According to Habermas (2005c: 20):

It would not be rational to reject out of hand the conjecture that religions – as the only surviving element among the constitutive building-blocks of the Ancient cultures – manage to continue and maintain a recognized place within in the differentiated edifice of Modernity because their cognitive substance has not yet been totally exhausted. There are at any rate no good reasons for denying the possibility that religions still bear a valuable semantic potential for inspiring other people beyond the limits of the particular community of faith.

In Habermas's and Shariati's thought, there are four attitudes towards religion. First, there is religion as a historical-social institution. When it is construed as a historical-social institution, it does not have an immutable, stable, and decisive position. This religion becomes liable to perfection and transmutation, and our understanding of religion becomes changeable. In fact, Habermas considers religion to have a direct link with social life. According to Shariati, religion has a socio-historical evolution, but this evolution has resulted in two different tendencies: emancipatory and historical religion. The characteristic feature of the emancipatory religion is its critique of the status quo, and thus its reference to human beings' deliverance. On the other hand, historical religion simply justifies the status quo, separating and aliening human beings from their own will and turning them into importunate beggars. However, Shariati construes the socio-historical evolution as a movement not as an institution. In institutionalisation, religion is a social organisation and a bureaucracy. It becomes genetic and hereditary. It is a tradition which is not consciously chosen by the individual. This is the type of religion that Marx conceived of as the opium of the masses. However, while Marx considers religion as a superstructure, Habermas and Shariati conceive of it as a vital element of the lifeworld. In other words:

Modern man needs religion even more than past generations. For in the past ignorance, weakness, fear, and the material needs of man were mixed with religion. But now man is looking for an authentic religion, a religion which explains the world to him and gives meaning to life (Shariati, 1988: 20).

The second attitude towards religion is as an instrument of criticism. This criticism produces changes in both human beings' relations and their surrounding environments. This attitude is not incompatible with religions through history, because the history of all Abrahamic religions indicates that they have mainly opposed and criticised the status quo. Shariati has included this attitude to religion within the emancipatory form of religion:

The prophets stood before a religion which, throughout history, has legitimated the oppressive and inhuman situation of the life of ancient societies from the economic, ethical as well as intellectual point of view and the worship of arrogant rulers who rebelled against God's Commands, in a general sense and idolism, in a particular sense. It was these prophets who opposed the spread of multitheism (Shariati, 1988: 34).

The third attitude that Habermas and Shariati highlight is that of religion as a worldview. Habermas (2008: 111) holds that 'every religion is originally a *"worldview"* or *"comprehensive doctrine"* also in the sense that it claims the authority to structure a form of life *as a whole*'. In fact, Habermas not only counts religion as a part of lifeworld, but also regards it as a worldview. In this worldview, any vivid movement in the lifeworld is traced, interpreted, extracted, detected, and adjusted. Interestingly, he considers religion as an inseparable part of lifeworld. Therefore, Habermas (2005c: 9) concludes that:

A devout person pursues her daily rounds by drawing on belief. Put differently, true belief is not only a doctrine, believed content, but a source of energy that the person who has a faith tape performatively and thus nurtures his or her entire life ... It [this mode of believing] belongs to the religious convictions of a good many religious people in our society that they ought to base their decisions concerning fundamental issues of justice on their religious convictions. They do not view it as an option whether or not to do it. Their religiously grounded concept of justice tells them what is politically correct or incorrect.

Shariati also conceives of religion as a worldview, stating that human beings' lives and actions are based on their worldviews. The portrait of existence that persons have in their memory affects their beliefs, behaviour, and social-political relations. Hence, 'as men we are what our world-visions are. As Sartre says, "Everyone lives according to how he perceives the world." Accordingly, the difference among Omar Khayyam, Hafiz, Mawlavi, Sartre, Camus, and others lies in each individual's world-vision; that is, how each individual interprets existence' (Shariati, 1981: 12). However, Shariati draws a geometric morphology that has *tauhid* as its base and ideology as its superstructure. *Tauhid* means all of creation is one empire in the hands of one Power, and that all human beings are one Source, guided through one Will, oriented one way, made of one type, and have one God. The ideology that is derived from this worldview has been generated from a social movement that is an outcrop of the necessities felt by a society. Therefore, 'to begin with, the individual feels the condition of his social class, as well as his economic, political, and social milieu. Since he is conscious of his condition, he is dissatisfied, he is suffering, he longs for change and transformation. Thus, ideology comes into being' (Shariati, 1981: 89). Both Habermas and Shariati hold that religion and its dimensions form an integral part of a social evolution. This social evolution does not exclude religion from the public sphere, and also presents it as a critical discourse that provides a good background for opinions related to independence, validity, and legitimacy to grow.

Fourth, there is the attitude towards religion as a common language. Habermas and Shariati claim that religion gives human beings the basic tool of a common language. It is a language that is applied to the intersubjectivity of mutual understanding. That is, the language of religion must belong not only to the 'special people' but also to the 'commoners'. Unlike the languages of science, philosophy, art, and literature – which are exclusive – religious language is comprehensible to all people. In other words, religion is a commonly intelligible language that has produced or pioneered the process of rationalisation. Put differently:

The force of religious traditions to articulate moral intuitions with regard to communal forms of a dignified human life makes religious presentations on relevant political issues a serious candidate for possible truth contents that can then be translated from the vocabulary of a specific religious community into a generally accessible language (Habermas, 2005c: 11).

In two interviews that I conducted with Nozari on 11th and 18th January 2011, he explained how Habermas has specified two functions for religion: 1- its subduing and subjugating processes, and 2- its compromising and reconciling processes. Under this interpretation, religion is interposed with other tools in such a way that it aims to produce sociability – namely, to make people accustomed to social norms. In other words, religion creates desirable characteristics in individuals such that they embrace social norms. Hence, religion brings sociability, expanding and developing personalities, and building a culture through the processes of subduing and compromising. In fact:

They [religious communities] provide arguments for public debates on crucial morally loaded issues and fulfill tasks of political socialization by informing their members and encouraging them to participate in the political process ... Religious citizens can certainly acknowledge this "institutional translation proviso" without having to split their identity into public and private parts the moment they participate in public discourses. They should therefore also be allowed to express and justify their convictions in a religious language even when they cannot find secular "translations" for them (Habermas, 2008: 125, 130).

Furthermore, some of Shariati's ideas conform positively with Habermas's theories on deliberative democracy and the public sphere. For instance, Habermas (2005c: 6-7) says that:

The democratic procedure is able to generate such a secular legitimation by virtue of two components – first the equal political participation of all citizens, which guarantees that the addresses of the laws can also understand themselves as the authors of these laws; – and second the epistemic dimension of a deliberation that grounds the presumption of rationally acceptable outcomes ... It is precisely the conditions for the successful participation in this practice of democratic self-determination that define the ethics of citizenship: for all their ongoing dissent on questions of world views and religious doctrines, citizens are meant to respect one another as free and equal members of their political community – this is the core of civic solidarity.

Shariati (1988: 39-40) holds that Islam addresses the people, and its aim is the establishment of justice and democracy in the public sphere. Islam is born of awareness and the need for love, worship, and consciousness in the people, as well as through a unified criticism of oppression throughout history. In the Holy Koran, God and the people form one front and rank. In all verses of the Glorious Koran that deal with social, political and economic issues rather than philosophical and scientific ones, the term 'people' can be replaced with the term 'God', and *vice versa*. That is, colloquially, 'our Lord' is equivalent to 'people'. The first word of the Koran is Allah (God) and it ends with Nas (people). Thus, it is the people that are always addressed by Islam. Shariati alleges that:

Islam is the first school of social thought that recognizes the masses as the basis, the fundamental and conscious factor in determining history and society, not the elect as Nietzsche thought, not the aristocracy and nobility as Plato claimed, not the great personalities as Carlyle and Emerson believed, not those of pure blood as Alexis carrel imagined, not the priests or the intellectuals, but the masses (Mirsepassi, 2000: 126).

In short, Habermas's and Shariati's works offer a creative and potentially important attempt to move beyond the secular assumptions that characterised much modern study of religion. They understand that religion now has a particularly central role to play in their interactions, negotiations and potential outcomes. For this reason, they are important theorists for theologians to engage with constructively and critically.

Chapter 6: Conclusion

At the beginning of this book I noted that while many modern philosophers, social scientists and cultural analysts have implicitly or explicitly accepted assumptions about the increasing marginalisation of religion from the public arena, this is no longer a viable option in the light of the global return to prominence of religious commitments. It is with relevance to this idea that I have examined the work of Habermas, which involves both a sustained philosophical critique of the relevance of religion to modernity and, more recently, an attempt to reassess the role of religion in the public sphere on the basis that many of his earlier arguments have proved unsustainable. In exploring the nature of and changes in Habermas's thought on religion – which, I have suggested, are still developing – I have also drawn upon the writings of the Iranian sociologist and political activist Ali Shariati to help illuminate the value and the limitations of Habermas's work.

The introduction of an Iranian intellectual perspective on the encounter between tradition and modernity has, I suggest, not only been of particular value through broadening debates about religion and modernity beyond the Eurocentric focus on secularisation as a phenomenon of Christian history, but also because it necessarily locates these debates within a global context – one wherein the resurgence of Islam is of immense importance. Habermas's recent engagements with religious intellectuals in Iran reflect his own understanding of the importance of broadening our understanding of religion in public life in this way. Indeed, in order to engage constructively with the rapidly developing nature of the debates about religion, public life and modernity in Iran, I have not only sought to explore how Shariati can help clarify the strengths and weaknesses of Habermas's arguments, but I have also conducted numerous interviews with key thinkers in Iran.

I have emphasised throughout this book that in order to understand Habermas's ideas on religion it is necessary to understand broader fundamental elements of his thought. Methodologically, Habermas's starting point is the division of human knowledge into three types – natural, cultural and critical sciences – all of which he understands as being related to the three interests – technical interests in the empirical-analytic sciences; practical interests in the historical-hermeneutic sciences; and emancipation autonomy interests in the critical sciences. Therefore, these three interests provide positivistic, hermeneutic and critical approaches respectively, the applications of which are distinct in sociological studies.

The positivistic approach represents human beings' interests in technically supervising nature and society. However, the hermeneutics approach represents human beings' practical interests in the intersubjectivity of mutual understanding through the medium of language and the maintenance of a social consensus. On the other hand, the critical approach represents humanity's interest in fulfilling truth, freedom, justice and a liberating knowledge, which are achieved through criticising power and ideology. Habermas claims that this approach enables the removal of the limitations and deficiencies of experimental and social hermeneutic sciences.

At the same time, he verifies the achievements of the hermeneutic methodology. This theory has a central role in Habermas's current ideas on linguistics and communicative action, although in criticising hermeneutic theory, he holds that this theory only suits social and historical sciences, and can contain some ideological dimensions.

To support and promote the foundation of critical theory, Habermas utilises universal pragmatics, which seeks to discover rules for human relationships that are based on intersubjective mutual understanding. Indeed, whereas the individual subject is pivoted in the modernists' vision, and post modernists deny the centrality of the individual, Habermas accepts the 'collective subject', because he considers collections of people as a subject. He believes that the function of universal pragmatics is to distinguish and rebuild the universal presuppositions of communicative action. In the process of reaching an agreement, the criteria required to validate a discourse are truth, rightness, truthfulness and comprehensibility. Habermas postulates that if these four validity claims for a discourse are present in one speaker, an ideal speech situation will be realised. As the past has been shaped by confused verbal associations, this has prevented truth from being fully uncovered, and the ideal speech situation cannot be seen in capitalism because it is impossible to dominate instrumental rationality as thoroughly as expected.

Utilising the ideal speech situation and communicative action, Habermas provides explanations of lifeworld and system. He claims that social evolution is a process that involves the rationalisation of the lifeworld as well as the segregation of lifeworld and system. The structural components of the lifeworld are culture, society and person. These principal elements of the lifeworld provide common beliefs for reaching an intersubjectivity of mutual understanding through criticising validity claims and finally overcoming their disputes. System – which is influenced by economics and state, or money and power – attacks lifeworld, and restrains individuals and groups of people from running their collective lives independently. Once communicative action is abandoned, instrumental rationality will take control of social life, preventing the establishment of a democratic agreement and harming the structures of the mutual understanding of the lifeworld. Under these circumstances, human beings lose the meaning of their lives, as well as their freedom, and system distorts the lifeworld. To rescue the world from legitimation crises, Habermas proposes that a deliberative or discursive model of democracy is put in place within the public sphere, where rational objectives can be illustrated properly. Language is the only medium of free conversation in this deliberative democracy, and it enjoys a deliverance role that provides a particular performance for the public sphere. Peoples involvement in a rational discourse of free dialogue, from which pressure and constraint have been removed, provides the conditions under which a deliberative democracy is realised. It is precisely for this reason that Habermas produces the theory of communicative action, as it provides a theoretical foundation of discursive democracy.

Thus, the immense importance of the notion of the 'public sphere' in Habermas's thought reflects his focus on the question of how to emancipate human beings and their societies from instrumental rationality. According to Habermas, the public sphere allows for an open negotiation and discourse about the common positions between citizens with the aim of reaching agreements through the force of sound argument. The public sphere is an intermediary between the public area of the state and the civil society, in which critical discussion takes place: citizens are able to criticise the state's performance and force the governmental structure to recheck and adjust its actions, and thus the public sphere becomes an arena in which practical ethics appear and a society can determine its reasonable objectives and claims in order to rationalise both the state and statesmanship. A *global* public sphere comes into existence when universal public opinion gains importance, and it is under these circumstances that intra-religious dialogues between religions and the cultural and intellectual elites are made possible in Habermas's later writings.

While the public sphere has always been at the centre of Habermas's concerns, his understanding of the place of religion within it has varied. As I have argued, Habermas's thought regarding the role of religion in the public sphere can be investigated at two levels. At the first level, his thought was influenced by the Frankfurt School, and he considered religion to be a tool that human beings had created to address their epistemological and existential problems, though one that is ill-suited to this task in modernity. As a consequence, he believed that religion must be replaced by philosophy and communicative action in the process of the modernisation of society. However, at the second level, he has now reassessed the place of religion in modernity and has sought to emphasise the key role it plays in the public sphere. Here, he not only notes that religion is returning to the public arena of contemporary secular societies, but he also accepts that this return represents a social and political awakening, conveying meaning and spirit to both private and public life for many modern citizens. Thus, Habermas acknowledges the revival of the great religions in the heart of Western societies, and tries to find a way to develop a global or local society based on interactions between both secular and religious citizens.

The outcome of his deliberations in this area is the conclusion that a global consensus can only be secured through enabling free participation and mutual dialogue, thus freeing all citizens from any forms of coercion and domination. Habermas holds that modernity uses itself to oppose tradition and tries to pursue a pretext when it uses reason. Hence, it selects its norms from within. It was only under the pretext of the enlightenment that modernity could show tradition to be unworthy and overcome it. Although postmodernists discredited modernity in the 20th century by criticising the grounds of its pessimistic attitudes, Habermas considers modernity to be an 'unfinished project' that still has the potential to rescue human beings if it is completed correctly. At the same time, he admits that modernity has deviated from its course through the interference of the modernist form of rationality, which has resulted in the domination of capitalism over objective and cultural conditions, and a decline in human self-determination. These negative consequences have occurred via the media of power and money and Habermas's solution is to extend the public sphere and communicative action.

In his current thought, then, Habermas challenges secular thinking in the social sciences and considers the revival of the Islamic and Christian creeds to be bound up with a rejection of modernity and political liberalism. He now regards the idea that the Enlightenment has led to religion vanishing from the public sphere as a consequence of a process of rationalisation – as a myth. In fact, he adopts the notion of 'post-secularism' because the logic of secularism has become ineffective, and he defends religion's role in both the private and public sphere. In other words, he restores religion to the public sphere by adopting a discourse between tradition and modernity. He is guided in this approach by a development of his notions of communicative action: it is this that acts as a reference point for producing a communicative ethics in political and social relationships.

Habermas was invited to Iran in 2002 by the Centre of Dialogue between Civilisations (run by the Iranian religious reformist administration). During his one week visit, he met with Iranian scholars, intellectuals and students, and delivered three important speeches: 'The End of Discrimination, the Beginning of Tolerance' (at the Iranian Philosophical Society on 12th May 2002), 'Religiousness in a secular context' (at Tehran University on 14th May 2002), and 'Philosophy and Politics' (in his visit with Iranian Professors of philosophy, sociology and politics on 15th May 2002). In these speeches, he said that religious tolerance requires religious traditions to re-examine the relations between religious communities and liberal states, and argued that the roles of religion and the state should be satisfactorily separated in the public sphere. In emphasising the importance of this separation, however, he sought to stress its value in securing the continuing importance of religion, rather than signalling its marginalisation: religious tolerance can be guaranteed only when the right of religious freedom is legalised, not through the reckless path that the modernisation processes have taken, in which religiously-based solidarities have been undermined and not replaced by anything else. Under such an approach, the legal protection of religious freedom would therefore serve to protect religiously-based solidarities.

In the West, intellectual life has been shaped decisively by modernism and the commitment to reason through the legacy of the Enlightenment. In fact, much of the modern European intellectual worldview has been founded on undermining the worldview of the Middle Ages with the aid of science, philosophy and art. However, modern Enlightenment thought in Iran has been faced with difficulties historically through the lack of a connection with popular movements, sentiments and groups. More recently, however, the engagement with Enlightenment thought amongst Iranian intellectuals, together with the emergence of broad-ranging national debates about religion and public life, has enabled a critical and constructive series of interactions between traditions, the social conditions of Iran, and Western modernity. As I have suggested, amongst Iranian intellectuals there have three prevailing approaches towards modernity: 1- Westoxication, 2- Traditionalism, and 3- Reformism. The first approach, also termed 'Westernisation', saw secular intellectuals wrongly emphasising only the positive aspects of Western civilisation. And as a result, they did not gain the support of the majority of Iranian people, and their schools of thought were not adopted by Iranian society. Traditionalists, in contrast, saw the oppressive aspects of Western civilisation and the union between Western Imperialism and domestic reactionary governments. Reformism, however, which came to dominate Iranian society, strongly values tradition, but seeks to maintain and reproduce it within the modern world, rationally defending religion.

It is in the light of these developments that I have sought to explore aspects of Habermas's work in dialogue with that of Shariati, who has been one of the most influential Iranian religious intellectuals of recent decades. Shariati exhibited a creative, modern, and yet thoroughly traditional engagement with religious thought, and his discourse is unique in Iran for being welcomed by both intellectuals and popular religious groups and institutions. His various works still inspire Iranian religious intellectuals and other Islamic nations after three decades. For this reason, and given Iranian intellectuals' (both religious and secular) attraction towards Habermas's philosophical and social ideas, (in particular his way of challenging tradition and modernity), this book has compared Habermas's thought with that of Shariati's.

I have argued that both Habermas and Shariati have a critical approach, but whereas Shariati's methodology does not rely on the self-building mind and considers *tauhid* as the origin of reality, Habermas holds that reality is obtained in the public sphere. Of course, both Habermas and Shariati have been influenced by Marx and Weber in their adoption of their critical approaches. However, unlike Weber, who considered modernity to be an 'iron cage', Habermas believes that there is a secondary dynamism within modernity, although he also criticises its current form very strongly. Habermas defends the universal emancipatory aspect of modernity, but Shariati stands in the postmodernists' camp by radically criticising modernity. Habermas's and Shariati's different ideas of modernity seem to be a reaction to their personal experience of modernity in two widely differing environments: Habermas, coming from a European intellectual tradition, seeks to amend modernity and enhance its emancipatory potential; Shariati, influenced by the modern history of Iran, considers the central concepts and problems of modernity to be insurmountable. Where Habermas defends global modernisation on the basis of a self-building rationality, Shariati accords a more fundamental role to the determining power of religion in society.

Like Habermas, Shariati holds that it is impossible to achieve democracy together with political and intellectual freedom under the domination of capitalism, individual ownership and class exploitation. In fact, democracy and capitalism cannot be united with each other, as although people may feel free under such a system, this feeling is necessarily illusory. Both Habermas and Shariati add that there is no need to trample down freedom of thinking, researching and choosing in the name of the most sacred principles. When a totalitarian government dominates, the idea that justice will be preserved is a perilous and delusive one; and when capitalism governs, no belief in equality, democracy and freedom will be void of credulity. However, while Habermas emphasises only equality and freedom, Shariati also places importance in 'mysticism and superior knowledge'. He believes that human beings possess needs in all these areas, and that these needs produce the search for justice, the demand for freedom, and the love of God. From his point of view, these three natural dimensions oppose the historical triangle of *Zar* (the power of wealth), *Zoor* (physical force), and *Tazvir* (religious hypocrisy), which are all features of historical religion. Moreover, Shariati holds that the only religion that uniformly and intelligently relies on the three dimensions of mysticism, equality and freedom is Islam.

While Habermas takes a negative view towards ideology, holding that it consists of ideas that veil arbitrary and illegitimate power, Shariati alleges that ideology and faith (rather than philosophy, science, industry, and literature) provide the foundations of civilisation and society. The spirit of civilisation is formed by human beings that are endowed with the same social objectives. Furthermore, social movements have ideological foundations, with ideology being a creed developed by a thinker towards an external reality and an analysis of this creed under the belief that a variety of abnormalities that should be modified for the better are contained within this external reality. Unlike Habermas, Shariati holds that there are two types of religion: the first takes the form of ideology mentioned above, the second the form of a social tradition or cultural religion that consists of an assembly of hereditary creeds, inculcated sensations, and imitated customs and rites that lead to a collapsed and reactionary creed. Unlike Habermas, Shariati proposes a 'return to ourselves' which implies discovering our identity and cultural-historical foundations, developing our self-awareness, and releasing ourselves from intellectual colonisation. Indeed, the purpose of the 'return to our Islamic roots' is to inhibit the influence of Western culture and its cultural exploitation.

Like Habermas, Shariati believes that instrumental rationality can comprehend only the external, objective facts, and prioritises them to achieve certain goals. Shariati says that this calculating rationality disables many human values and is unable to allow ideas and practices such as faith and worship in. However, there is another variety of rationality, which perceives realities and accepts them. This rationality is akin to the substantial element of religion. In Shariati's view, modern science is nothing but the outcome of instrumental rationality, which focuses on gaining money and power at the expense of truth.

Four types of understanding about religion can be found in the views of both Habermas and Shariati: first, religion is a historical-social institution, which forms an integral part of the lifeworld; second, religion is a critical instrument to challenge the status quo; third, religion is a worldview that extracts and adjusts any activity in the lifeworld; and fourth, religion is a common language that can be understood by all. Habermas, nonetheless, identifies two special functions of religion: its subduing and subjugating processes, and its compromising and reconciling processes. However, Shariati views the historical evolution of religion as resulting in the appearance of two different forms of practice: the religion of *tauhid*, and what he calls 'historical religion'. He considers only *tauhid* as an emancipating religion since it alone is a critical instrument for challenging the status quo. In other words, Habermas's ways of thinking about the nature and existence of religion and its applications in the public sphere over the past decades are, for Shariati, grounded in an optimistic view of religion as a whole. His departure from Marxist dogmatism, with its highly negative view of all religion, is a welcome and significant aspect of his work, but it also risks encouraging a simplistically positive view of the role of religious institutions over time. An objection that can be raised to this attitude towards religion, in the light of Shariati's work, is that it neglects the separation between emancipating religion and historical or cultural religion. These two forms of religion have been opposed to each other throughout human history, and neglecting this distinction precludes the idea that it is *historical* religion that has been the 'opium for the masses' over time, but that the emancipatory dimensions of religion have provided a productive and liberating force within different layers of societies, enabling them to acquire their social rights and freedoms.

I have suggested that there are different factors that explain why Habermas has changed his view on the role of religion in public life. Some of these are to do with changes in the world that he did not foresee or expect, but others are to do with the inherent nature and potential of his social philosophy. In other words, a developed understanding of Habermas's views about religion might usefully reflect upon the fact that, in contrast to historical materialism or Weberian notions of progressive rationalisation (with their necessarily negative assessments of religion in the modern world), Habermas's thought is centred on a theory of communicative action. That is, whilst his views of religion have certainly changed in recent years, his current ones reflect a development of his focus on communicative action from a discourse between secular actors to a discussion between post-secular and religious actors with different religious outlooks. In this regard, Habermas's recent ideas on the role of religion in the public sphere have made a positive contribution to a broader assessment of the importance and value of religion, helping to challenge, and perhaps modify, secular philosophers' more negative views towards it. Indeed, in my view, Habermas is helping to transform our understanding of the conflict between religion and rationality in modernity, taking religion seriously as a vital and proactive element of communicative action and the lifeworld. Although Habermas's ideas regarding the emancipation of human beings are often regarded as being idealistic, his focus upon communicative action and the forms of deliberative democracy in which it can be expressed nonetheless offer a basis for a positive engagement with various religious and secular communities today, not least with regard to seeking peace, security and human solidarity in a global context marked by diversity, change and potential conflicts.

In summary, then, this book has shown the value and significance of Habermas's achievements with regard to a number of different aspects of his work. First, his work is of value because of its broad, interdisciplinary scope, wherein he is able to draw upon and familiarise his readers with concepts and debates across a range of different scientific fields. It is also of note, however, that his theories are essentially self-critical, and thereby open to revision and development – something particularly evident in the evolution of his thoughts on religion. Philosophically, he seeks to link both theory and practice and the subjective and objective world in order to help human beings to understand the depth of their social nature, critiquing the subject-object philosophy by emphasising the internal relationship between knowledge and the lifeworld. He has also specified the nature and position of his theory of 'knowledge constitutive interests' in detail, in terms of technical interests in the empirical-analytic sciences, practical interests in the historical-hermeneutic sciences, and emancipation autonomy interests in the critical sciences. Having provided thorough criticisms of positivism, Habermas shows how positivism supposes technical interests to be obvious and pervasive by integrating rationality with instrumental rationality, and how this results in the negation of practical and emancipation autonomy interests and implies that practical reason is impossible. For Habermas, it is unacceptable for all scientific, ethical, political and cultural issues in a society to be defined and evaluated as technical problems. Consequently, it is wrong for scientists to attempt to settle these issues from outside the scope of democratic decision-making. It is in such a manner that science and technology are changed into an instrument for eliminating the crisis of legitimacy in capitalism and justifying the status quo.

In terms of his vision of modernity, while Habermas criticises visions of modernity in which the culture-value domains of science, ethics and art are separated from each other, he nonetheless goes beyond Weber's pessimistic approach to modernity to develop a more positive account in which rationalisation is seen as providing a forum for learning instead of as an iron cage. Indeed, having separated system from lifeworld, Habermas deals with the pathology of modernity, arguing that everything necessarily refers back to our lifeworld because all social and economic structures are integrated with action and consciousness in the lifeworld, which is utilised by everyone that is involved in communicative action. Lifeworld acts as a background consensus in everyday life, and a storehouse of knowledge that is handed down from generation to generation. Habermas tries to impede the transgression of instrumental rationality into this sphere of lifeworld, and it is in proposing the theory of communicative action that Habermas provides the possibility of democracy and democratic discussion. He aims to overcome the individualism inherent within the theory of liberal democracy, as well as the violence and war to which it can give rise. In fact, communicative action represents a position in which all disputes and conflicts are solved in a rational way without internal or external coercion, and agreement is secured through the force of better argument. He holds that this communicative action evolves only in the lifeworld.

Habermas has sought to recognise the importance of religion in the public sphere. Unlike Marx, he does not hold that religion is merely a secondary feature of economic production, but argues that it is a basic part of the lifeworld rather than a superstructure. A positive side of Habermas's approach is that he considers religion to be a direct link to social life, and believes that these two things join together at different points. He counts religion as an inseparable, basic and internal part of lifeworld, and clearly declares that we cannot have lifeworld without its constitutive elements, of which religion is one of the most important. It is through this focus on religion's importance within the lifeworld that Habermas has sought to draw an image of a better society, grounded on peace, unity and human happiness.

Bibliography

Abazari, Y. (1998) *Sociological Reason*. Tehran: Tarh-e No.

Abrahamian, E. (1982) *Iran between Two Revolutions*. Princeton, N.J.: Princeton University Press.

Adams, N. (2006) *Habermas and Theology*. Cambridge: Cambridge University Press.

Adorno, T. W. and Horkheimer, M. (1997) *Dialectic of Enlightenment*. London: Verso.

Ahmed, A. and Donnan, H. (1994) *Islam, Globalization and Postmodernity*. London: Routledge.

Ahmed, S. I. (2006) *Iranian Politics: Intellectuals & Ulama*. Delhi, India: Vista International Publishing House.

Akhavi, S. (1980) *Religion and Politics in Contemporary Iran: Clergy-State Relations in the Pahlavi Period*. Albany: State University of New York Press.

Al-e Ahmad, J. (2005) 'The Outline of a Disease'. In *Religion and Politics in Modern Iran*. Edited by Lloyd Ridgeon. London; New York: I.B.Tauris.

Ali, A. Y. (1999) *The Meaning of the Holy Quran*. Beltsville, Maryland, USA: Amana.

Al-Shavi, T. M. (1995) *Al-Shura*. Cairo: Daro-Zahra.

Amin, S. H. (2002) *Adjudication and Judicial System in Iran*. Tehran: Cultural Researches.

Amirsadeghi, H. and Ferrier, R. W. (1977) *Twentieth-Century Iran*. London: Heinemann.

Ansari, A. M. (2003) *Modern Iran since 1921: The Pahlavis and after*. London; New York: Pearson Education.

Arbaugh, G. E. and Arbaugh G. B. (1968) *Kierkegaard's Authorship: A Guide to the Writings of Kierkegaard*. London: George Allen and Unwin.

Asad, T. (1993) *Genealogies of Religion: Discipline and Reasons of power in Christianity and Islam*. Baltimore: Johns Hopkins University Press.

Bahram, M. (2003) 'Advantages of Truthful Reasoning in Comparison with Others: The views of Mulla Sadra on the Existence of God'. Tehran: *Journal of Roshed* 52, pp. 38-41.

Bahram, M. (2011) 'A Comparative Study of Faith from Kierkegaard's and Rumi's Perspective'. London: *Transcendent Philosophy* 12, pp. 69-92.

Bahram, M. (2012) 'A Critical Analysis of Huntington's Doctrine of the Clash of Civilization'. London: *Just Peace Diplomacy* 6, pp. 1-20

Banton, M. (1966) *Anthropological Approaches to the Study of Religion.* London: Tavistock Publications.

Bashiriyeh, H. (2006) *An Introduction to Political Sociology of Iran.* Tehran: negahemoaser.

Bayat, M. (1991) *Iran's First Revolution: Shi'ism and the Constitutional Revolution of 1905-1909.* New York; Oxford: Oxford University Press.

Beck, U, Giddens, A and Lash, S. (1994) *Reflexive Modernization: Politics, Tradition and Aesthetics in the Modern Social Order.* Cambridge: Polity in Association with Blackwell.

Behroozlak, G. (2007) *Globalization and Political Islam in Iran.* Tehran: Islamic Research Centre.

Benjamin, W. (1973) *Illumination.* Edited with an Introduction by Hannah Arendt; Translated by Harry Zohn. London: Collins – Fontana Books.

Berger, P. L. (1967) *The Sacred Canopy: Elements of a Sociological Theory of Religion.* Garden City, N.Y: Doubleday.

Berger, P. L. (1969) *The Social Reality of Religion.* London: Faber.

Berger, P. L. and Luckmann, T. (1967) *The Social Construction of Reality: A Treatise in the Sociology of Knowledge.* Harmonds worth: Penguin.

Berman, M. (1982) *All That Is Solid Melts Into Air: The Experience of Modernity.* London: Verso.

Bernstein, J. M. (1995) *Recovering Ethical Life: Jurgen Habermas and the future of critical theory.* London: Routledge.

Bernstein, R. J. (1985) *Habermas and Modernity.* Cambridge: Polity.

Beyer, P. (1994) *Religion and Globalization.* London, U.K.; Thousand Oaks, CA: Sage Publications.

Blaxter, L. (1996) *How to Research.* Buckingham: Open University Press.

Boroujerdi, M. (1996) *Iranian Intellectuals and the West.* Syracuse: University Press.

Borradori, G. (2003) *Philosophy in a Time of Terror: Dialogues with Jurgen Habermas and Jacques Derrida.* Chicago and London: University of Chicago Press.

Braaten, J. (1991) *Habermas's Critical Theory of Society.* Albany, N.Y: State University of New York Press.

Browne, E. G. (1928) *A Literary History of Persia.* Vol. IV. Cambridge: The University Press.

Browning, D. S. and Fiorenza, F. S. (1992) *Habermas, Modernity, and Public Theology.* New York: Crossroad.

Bryman, A. (2001) *Social Research Methods.* Oxford: Oxford University Press.

Calhoun, C. (1992) *Habermas and the Public Sphere.* Cambridge, Mass: MIT Press.

Clark, T. (2002) *Martin Heidegger.* London: Routledge.

Cohen, C. (1973) *Democracy.* New York: The Free Press; London: Collier-Macmillan.

Cohen, J. (1995) 'Secondary Associations and Democratic Governance'. In *Associations and Democracy.* Edited by Joshua Cohen and Joel Rogers. London: Verso.

Connerton, P. (1976) *Critical Sociology: Selected Readings.* Harmondsworth: Penguin.

Connolly, W. E. (1989) *Political Theory & Modernity.* Oxford: Basil Blackwell.

Craib, I. (1992) *Modern Social Theory: From Parsons to Habermas.* New York; London: Harvester Wheatsheaf.

Cunningham, F. (2002) *Theories of Democracy: A Critical Introduction.* London: Routledge.

Davari, A. R. (1984) 'Lavazem va Natayej-e Enkar-e Gharb' (The Necessities and Consequences of Refuting the West). Tehran: *Keyhan-e Farhangi* 1 (30), pp. 16-25.

Davari, A. R. (2000) *The Enlightenment and Intellectuals.* Tehran: Salam Press.

Davis, C. (1994) *Religion and the Making of Society: Essays in Social Theory.* Cambridge: Cambridge University Press.

D'Entreves, M.P. and Benhabib, S. (1996) *Habermas and the Unfinished Project of Modernity: Critical Essays on the Philosophical Discourse of Modernity.* Cambridge: Polity Press.

Durkheim, E. (1976) *The Elementary Forms of the Religious Life.*
Translated by Joseph Ward Swain. London: Allen & Unwin.

Edgar, A. (2005) *The philosophy of Habermas.* Chesham: Acumen.

Edgar, A. (2006) *Habermas: The Key Concepts.* London; New York:
Routledge.

Ehteshami, A. (1995) *After Khomeini: The Iranian Second Republic.*
London: Routledge.

Ehteshami, H. (2006) *A Study on the Globalization of Democracy
and its effect on International Peace and Security.* Tehran: Negah.

Elster, J. (1986) *An Introduction to Karl Marx.* Cambridge:
Cambridge University.

Enns, P. (2007) 'Habermas, Reason, and the Problem of Religion:
the Role of Religion in the Public Sphere'. *Heythrop Journal,*
XLVIII, pp. 878-894.

Esposito, J. L. (1986) 'Foreword'. In *What Is To Be Done.* Written
by Ali Shariati. North Haledon, New Jersey: Islamic Publications
International.

Esposito, J. L. and Tamimi, A. (2000a) *Islam and Secularism in the
Middle East.* London: Hurst.

Esposito, J. L. and Voll, J. O. (2000b) 'Islam and the West: Muslim
Voices of Dialogue'. *Millennium* 29 (3), pp.613-639.

Finlayson, J. G. (2005) *Habermas: A very Short Introduction.*
Oxford: Oxford University Press.

Firestone, R. (1999) *Jihad: The Origin of Holy War in Islam.* New
York: Oxford University Press.

Fischer, M. M. J. (1980) *Iran: From Religious Dispute to Revolution.*
Cambridge, Mass: Harvard University Press.

Forward, M. (1997) *Muhammad: A Short Biography.* Oxford,
England, Rockport, MA: Oneworld Publications.

Foucault, M. (1988) *Politics, Philosophy, Culture: Interviews and
other Writings, 1977-1984.* New York and London: Routledge.

Gadamer, H. G. (1975) *Truth and Method.* London: Sheed and Ward.

Geertz, C. (1966) 'Religion as a Cultural System'. In
Anthropological Approaches to the Study of Religion. Edited by
Michael Banton. London: Tavistock Publications.

Geertz, C. (1971) *Islam Observed: Religious Development in Morocco and Indonesia*. Chicago; London: University of Chicago Press.

Geuss, R. (1981) *The Idea of a Critical Theory: Habermas and the Frankfurt School*. Cambridge: Cambridge University Press.

Ghamari-Tabrizi. B. (2008) *Islam and Dissent in Postrevolutionary Iran: Abdolkarim Soroush, Religious Politics and Democratic Reform*. London: Tauris.

Gheissari, A. (1998) *Iranian Intellectuals in the 20th Century*. Texas: University of Texas Press.

Gibaldi, J. (1998) *MLA Style Manual and Guide to Scholarly Publishing*. New York: Modern Language Association of America.

Giddens, A. (1982) 'Labour and Interaction'. In *Habermas: Critical Debates*. Edited by John B. Thompson and David Held. London: Macmillan.

Giddens, A. (1990) *The Consequences of Modernity*. Cambridge: Polity.

Goode, L. (2005) *Jurgen Habermas: Democracy and the Public Sphere*. London: Pluto Press.

Grossberg, L. (1996) 'Identity and Cultural Studies: Is That All There Is?'. In *Questions of Cultural Identity*. Edited by Stuart Hall and Paul du Gay. London: Sage.

Gutmann, A and Thompson, D. (1996) *Democracy and Disagreement*. Cambridge, Mass: Belknap Press of Harvard University Press.

Habermas, J. (1971) *Toward a Rational Society: Student Protest, Science, and Politics*. Translated by Jeremy J. Shapiro. London: Heinemann Educational.

Habermas, J. (1972) *Knowledge and Human Interest*. Translated by Jeremy J. Shapiro. London: Heinemann Educational.

Habermas, J. (1974a) 'On Social Identity'. *Telos* 19 (Spring), pp. 91-110.

Habermas, J. (1974b) *Theory and Practice*. Translated by John Viertel. London: Heinemann.

Habermas, J. (1976) *Legitimation Crisis*. Translated by Thomas McCarthy. London: Heinemann Educational.

Habermas, J. (1979) *Communication and the Evolution of Society.* Translated and with an Introduction by Thomas McCarthy. London: Heinemann.

Habermas, J. (1981a) 'Modernity versus Post- modernity'. *New German Critique* 22, pp. 3-14.

Habermas, J. (1981b) 'New Social Movements'. *Telos* 49 (Fall), pp. 33-37.

Habermas, J. (1984) *The Theory of Communicative Action I: Reason and the Rationalization of Society.* Translated by Thomas McCarthy. Cambridge: Polity.

Habermas, J. (1987) *The Theory of Communicative Action II: Reason and the Rationalization of Society.* Translated by Thomas McCarty. Cambridge: Polity.

Habermas, J. (1988) *On the Logic of the Social Sciences.* Translated by Shierry Weber Nicholsen and Jerry A. Stark. Oxford: Polity.

Habermas, J. (1989) *The Structural Transformation of the Public Sphere: An Inquiry Into A Category of Bourgeois Society.* Translated by Thomas Burger with the Assistance of Frederick Lawrence. Cambridge: Polity Press.

Habermas, J. (1990a) *Moral Consciousness and Communicative Action.* Translated by Christian Lenhardt and Shierry Weber Nicholsen; Introduction by Thomas McCarthy. Cambridge: Polity press.

Habermas, J. (1990b) *The Philosophical Discourse of Modernity: Twelve Lectures.* Translated by Frederick G. Lawrence. Cambridge, Mass: The MIT Press.

Habermas, J. (1992) *Postmetaphysical Thinking: Philosophical Essays.* Translated by William Mark Hohengarten. Cambridge: Polity Press.

Habermas, J. (1996) *Between Facts and Norms: Contributions to a Discourse Theory of Law and Democracy.* Translated by William Rehg. Oxford: Polity.

Habermas, J. (1998) *On the Pragmatics of Communication.* Edited by Maeve Cooke. Cambridge, Mass: Massachusetts Institute of Technology Press.

Habermas, J. (2001) *The Postnational Constellation: Political Essays*. Translated, Edited and with an Introduction by Max Pensky. London: Polity Press.

Habermas, J. (2002a) 'Philosophy and Politics'. Habermas's lecture in his visit with Iranian professors of philosophy, sociology and politics. Tehran: *Scientific and Cultural Monthly Magazine* 26 (May), pp. 10-11.

Habermas, J. (2002b) *Religion and Rationality: Essays on Reason, God, and modernity*. Edited and with an Introduction by Eduardo Mendieta. Cambridge, Mass.: MIT Press.

Habermas, J. (2002c) 'Religiousness in a Secular Context'. Habermas's Lecture at Tehran University. Tehran: *Scientific and Cultural Monthly Magazine* 26 (May), pp. 17-19.

Habermas, J. (2002d) 'The End of Discrimination; The Beginning of Tolerance'. Habermas's lecture at the Iranian Philosophical Society. Tehran: *Scientific and Cultural Monthly Magazine* 26 (May), pp. 12-16.

Habermas, J. (2002e) 'Weber and Rationality'. Habermas's lecture at The Civilisations Dialogues Centre. Tehran: *Scientific and Cultural Monthly Magazine* 26 (May), pp. 8-9.

Habermas, J. (2003a) *The Future of Human Nature*. Oxford: Polity.

Habermas, J. (2003b) *Truth and Justification*. Edited and with Translations by Barbara Fultner. Cambridge: Polity Press.

Habermas, J. (2004) *Time of Transitions*. Edited and translated by Ciaran Cronin and Max Pensky. Oxford: Polity.

Habermas, J. (2005a) 'A Post-Secularist Consensus: The Habermas-Ratzinger Exchange'.http://www.heythrop.ac.uk/theological-spiritual-reflection/a-post-secularist-consensus-29th/april-2005.htm/

Habermas, J. (2005b) 'Religion in the Public Sphere'. http://www.Holbergprisen. No/downloads/diverse/hp/hp-2005/2006. Lecture Presented at the Holberg Prize Seminar, 29 November, pp. 1-14.

Habermas, J. (2005c) 'Religion in the Public Sphere'. www.sandiego.edu/pdf/pdf-library/habermaslecture031105_c939cceb2ab087bdfc6df291ec0fc3fa.pdf, pp. 1-22.

Habermas, J. (2006a) 'Religion in the Public Sphere'. *European Journal of Philosophy* 25 (14), pp. 1-25.

Habermas, J. (2006b) *The Derrida-Habermas reader*. Edited by Lasse Thomassen. Edinburgh: Edinburgh University Press.

Habermas, J. (2008) *Between Naturalism and Religion*. Cambridge: Polity Press.

Haghdar, A. A. (1999) *The Cultural-Political Discourse of Khatami*. Tehran: Shafiee.

Hakimi, M. R. (2002) 'Principles of Jurisprudence'. Tehran: *Hamshahri Journal*. 6/5/2002, pp.9-35.

Hamid, A.W. (1989) *Islam: the Natural Way*. London: MELS.

Harrington, A. (2001) *Hermeneutic Dialogue and Science: A Critique of Gadamer and Habermas*. London; New York: Routledge.

Harrington, A. (2007) 'Habermas's Theological Turn?'. *Journal for the Theory of Social Behaviour* 37(1), pp. 45-61.

Heelas, P, Lash, S. and Morris, P. (1996) *Detraditionalization: Critical Reflections on Authority and Identity*. Oxford and Cambridge, Mass: Blackwell.

Hegel, G. W. F. (1952) *Hegel's Philosophy of right*. Translated with notes by T. M. Knox. Oxford: Clarendon Press.

Heidegger, M. (1962) *Being and Time*. Translated by John Macqarrie and Edward Robinson. Oxford: Blackwell.

Heidegger, M. (1977) *The Question Concerning Technology and Other Essays*. Translated and with an Introduction by William Lovitt. New York and London: Harper and Row.

Held, D. (1987) *Models of Democracy*. Cambridge: Polity in Association with Blackwell.

Held, D. (1990) *Introduction to Critical Theory: Horkheimer to Habermas*. London: Polity.

Held, D. and McGrew, A. G. (2002) *Globalization/Anti-globalization*. Malden, MA: Blackwell Publishers; Cambridge: Polity Press.

Heller, A. (1982) 'Habermas and Marxism'. In *Habermas: Critical Debates*. Edited by John B. Thompson and David Held. London: Macmillan, pp.21-41.

Hiro, D. (1985) *Iran under the Ayatollahs*. London: Routledge& Kegan Paul.

Holsti, O. R. (1969) *Content Analysis for the Social Science and Humanities.* Reading, Mass: Addison-Wesley Pub. Co.

Holub, R. C. (1991) *Jurgen Habermas: Critic in the Public Sphere.* London: Routledge.

Holub, R. C. (1994) 'Luhmann's progeny: Systems Theory and Literary Studies'. In *The Post-Wall Era.* New German Critique 61 (winter), pp. 143-159.

Hunke, S. (1975) *Allahs Sonne: Uber dem Abendland Unser Arabisches Erbe.* Translated by Murteza Rahbani. Tehran: Nashr-i-Islamic Culture.

Huntington, S. P. (1991) *The Third Wave: Democratization in the Late Twentieth Century.* Norman, London: University of Oklahoma Press.

Huntington, S. P. (1993) 'The Clash of Civilizations?'. *Foreign Affairs* 72 (3), pp. 22-49.

Huntington, S. P. (1996) *The Clash of Civilizations and the Remaking of World Order.* New York: Simon and Schuster.

Hussain, A. (1985) *Islamic Iran: Revolution and Counter-Revolution.* London: Pinter.

Jahanbegloo, R. (2004) *Iran between Tradition and Modernity.* Lanham, MD and Oxford: Lexington Books.

Kamali, M. (1998) *Revolutionary Iran: Civil Society and State in the Modernization Process.* Aldershot: Ashgate.

Kamrava, M. (1992) *The Political History of Modern Iran: From Tribalism to Theocracy.* Westport, Conn; London: Praeger.

Katouzian, H. and Shahidi, H. (2007) *Iran in the 21st Century: Politics, Economics & Conflict.* London and New York: Routledge.

Kachouian, H. (2007) *Globalisation Theories and Religion.* Tehran: Nashreney.

Keddie, N. R. (2006) *Modern Iran: Roots and Results of Revolution.* New Haven, Conn.; London: Yale University Press.

Kellner, D. (1991) 'Introduction to the Second Edition'. In *One-Dimensional Man: Studies in the Ideology of Advanced Industrial Society.* Written by Herbert Marcuse. London: Routledge.

Khatami, M. (2001) *Dialogue among Civilizations: A Paradigm for Peace.* Editors Theo Bekker and Joelien Pretorius. Pretoria: Unit for

Policy Studies, Centre for International Political Studies, University of Pretoria.

Khatami, S. M. (2007) 'Globalization, Globalizing, Globalizm and Globality'. Tehran: *Research, Political and Social Monthly, Ayyn* 7 (June), pp. 76-80.

Khomeini, R. (1981) *Islam and Revolution: Writings and Declarations*. Translated and Annotated by Hamid Algar. Berkeley: Mizan Press.

King, A. D. (1991) *Culture, Globalization and the Wold-System: contemporary Conditions for the Representation of Identity.* Basingstoke: Macmillan.

Kolb, D. (1986) *The Critique of Pure Modernity: Hegel, Heidegger and After*. Chicago and London: University of Chicago Press.

Lalonde, M. P. (1999) *Critical Theology and the Challenge of Jurgen Habermas: Toward a Critical Theory of Religious Insight*. New York: Peter Lang.

Lalonde, M. P. (2007) *From Critical Theology to a Critical Theory of Religious Insight*. New York: Peter Lang.

Lawrence, F. G. (1990) *The Philosophical Discourse of Modernity.* Cambridge Mass: The MIT Press.

Lewis, F. D. (2000) *Rumi: Past and Present, East and West; The Life, Teachings and Poetry of Jalal al-Din Rumi*. Oxford: Oneworld.

Lewis, P. (1992) 'Democracy in Modern Societies'. In *Political and Economic Forms of Modernity*. Edited by John Allen, Peter Braham and Paul Lewis. Cambridge: Polity Press in Association with the Open University.

Locke, J. (1972) *History of Political Philosophy*. Edited by Leo Strauss and Joseph Cropsey. Chicago: Rand McNally.

Lyon, D. (1999) *Postmodernity.* Buckingham: Open University Press.

Lyotard, J. F. (1984) *The Postmodern Condition: A Report on Knowledge*. Translation from the French by Geoff Bennington and Brian Massumi; Foreword by Fredric Jameson. Manchester: Manchester University Press.

Magee, B. (1987) *The Great Philosophers: An Introduction to Western Philosophy*. London: BBC Books.

Mandaville, P. (2007) 'Globalization and the Politics of Religious Knowledge: Pluralizing Authority in the Muslim World'. *Theory, Culture & Society* 24 (2), pp. 101-115.

Mansurnejad, M. (2002) *Theoretical Approaches to the Dialogue between Civilizations.* Tehran: Human and Social Sciences Institute.

Marcuse, H. (1968) *Negations: Essays in Critical Theory.* Translated by Jeremy J. Shapiro. London: Allen Lane, Penguin Press.

Marshall, G. (1982) *In Search of the Spirit of Capitalism: An essay on Max Weber's Protestant ethic thesis.* London: Hutchinson.

Marx, K. and Engels, F. (1957) *The Holy Family, or Critique of Critical Criticism: against Bruno Bauer and Company.* Moscow: Foreign Languages Publishing House.

Matustik, M. B. (2001) *Jurgen Habermas: A Philosophical-Political Profile.* Lanham, Md.: Rowman and Littlefield.

May, T. (2001) *Social Research: Issues Methods and Process.* Buckingham: Open University.

McCarthy, T. (1978) *The Critical Theory of Jurgen Habermas.* London: Hutchinson.

McCarthy, T. (1994) 'Kantian Constructivism and Reconstructivism: Rawls and Habermas in Dialogue'. *Ethics* 105 (October), pp. 44-63.

McFadyen, A. (1990) *The Call to Personhood: A Christian Theory of the Individual in Social Relationships.* Cambridge: Cambridge University Press.

McLellan, D. (1987) *Marxism and Religion: A Description and Assessment of the Marxist Critique of Christianity.* Basingstoke: Macmillan Press.

McLennan, G. (2007) 'Towards Postsecular Sociology?'. *Sociology* 41 (5), pp. 857-870.

Mellor, P. A and Shilling, C. (1997) *Re-Forming the Body: Religion, Community and Modernity.* London: Sage.

Mellor, P. A. (2004) *Religion, Realism and Social Theory: Making Sense of Society.* London: Sage.

Meszaros, I. (2005) *Marx's Theory of Alienation.* London: Merlin.

Mill, J. S. (1996) *An Essay on Liberty.* Translated by Javad Sheikh-al-Islam. Tehran: Scientific Cultural.

Mirsepassi, A. (2000) *Intellectual Discourse and the Politics of Modernization: Negotiating Modernity in Iran*. New York: Cambridge University Press.

Moor, B. (1991) *Social Roots of Dictatorship and Democracy*. Translated by Hossain Bashiriyeh. Tehran: University Publication.

Mortimer, E. (1982) *Faith and Power: The Politics of Islam*. New York: Vintage Books.

Mottahedeh, R. (2000) *The Mantle of the Prophet: Religion and Politics in Iran*. Oxford: Oneworld.

Mutahhari, M. (1985) *Jihad*. Tehran: Islamic Propagation Organization.

Najafi, M. (2006) *The Philosophy of Modernity in Iran*. Tehran: Amir-kabir.

Nasr, S. H. (1990) *Traditional Islam in the Modern World*. London and New York: Kegan Paul International. Distributed by Routledge, Chapman & Hall.

Nasr, S. H. (2004) *Islam and Difficulties of Contemporary Man*. Translated by Enshaallah Rahmati. Tehran: Sohrevardi.

Nasr, S. H. (2007) *The heart of Islam: enduring values for humanity*. Translated by Seyyed Mohammed Sadegh Kharazi. Tehran: Ghazal.

Nasri, A. (2007) *Facing Up to Modernity*. Tehran: Elm.

Nemoianu, V. (2006) 'The Church and the Secular Establishment: A Philosophical Dialog between Joseph Ratzinger and Jurgen Habermas'. *Logos: A Journal of Catholic Thought and Culture* 9 (2), pp. 16-42.

Netton, I. R. (2008) *Encyclopaedia of Islamic Civilisation and Religion*. London: Routledge.

Outhwaite, W. (1987) *New Philosophies of Social Science: Realism, Hermeneutics and Critical Theory*. Basingstoke: Macmillan.

Outhwaite, W. (1994) *Habermas: A Critical Introduction*. Cambridge: Polity Press.

Outhwaite, W. (1996) *The Habermas Reader*. Cambridge: Polity Press.

Ovanessian, O. (1991) *Introduction to Rumi with commentary and Annotations to the Mathnavi-i-Manavi*. Tehran: Nashr-i-Nay.

Ozment, S. E. (1991) *Protestants: The Birth of a Revolution*. New York; London: Doubleday.

Palmer, R. A. (2005) *Hermeneutics: Introduction Theory in Schleiermacher, Dilthey, Heidegger, and Gadamer.* Translated by M. S Hanaee Kashani. Tehran: Hermes.

Pals, D. L. (1996) *Seven Theories of Religion.* New York: Oxford University Press.

Parekh, B. (1982) *Marx's Theory of Ideology.* London: Croom Helm.

Peters, R. (1996) *Jihad in Classical and Modern Islam: A Reader.* Princeton: Markus Wiener.

Pulladi, K. (2006) *History of Political Thought in Iran and Islam.* Tehran: Markaz.

Pusey, M. (1987) *Jurgen Habermas.* Chichester [West Sussex]: E. Horwood; London and New York: Tavistock Publictions.

Rahmani, T. (2005) *Religious Intellectuals and Modern Reason.* Tehran: Ghalam.

Rahnema, A. (2005) *Pioneers of Islamic Revival.* London, New York: Zed Books.

Rahnema, A. and Nomani, F. (1990*) The Secular Miracle: Religion, Politics and Economic Policy in Iran.* London: Zed Books.

Rajaee, F. (2003) *Components of Modern Iranian Identity.* Tehran: Ney.

Rasmussen, D. M. (1990) *Reading Habermas.* Oxford: Blackwell.

Ricoeur, P. (1981) *Hermeneutics and the Human Sciences: Essays on Language, Action and Interpretation.* Cambridge: Cambridge University Press.

Robertson, R. (1970) *The Sociological Interpretation of Religion.* Oxford: Blackwell.

Robertson, R. (1971) 'Basic Problems of Definition'. In *Sociological Perspectives: Selected Reading.* Edited by Kenneth Thompson and Jeremy Tunstall. Harmondsworth: Penguin, in Association with the Open University Press.

Robertson, R. (1987) 'Globalization Theory and Civilizational Analysis'. *Comparative Civilizations Review* 17, pp. 20-30.

Robertson, R and Garrett, W. R. (1991) *Religion and Global Order: Religion and the Political Order* vol. IV. New York: Paragon House Publishers.

Robertson, R. (1992) *Globalization: Social Theory and Global Culture.* London: Sage.

Roderick, R. (1986) *Habermas and the Foundations of Critical Theory*. Basingstoke: Macmillan.

Rodinson, M. (1974) *Islam and Capitalism*. Translated by Brian Pearce. London: Allen Lane.

Rorty, R. (1985) 'Habermas and Lyotard on Post-Modernity'. In *Habermas and Modernity*. Edited with an Introduction by Richard J. Bernstein. Cambridge: Polity.

Rothberg, D. J. (1986) 'Rationality and Religion in Habermas; Recent Work: Some Remarks on the Relation between Critical Theory and the Phenomenology of Religion'. *Philosophy and Social Criticism* 11 (3), pp. 221-239.

Saey, A. (2007) *Democratization in Iran*. Tehran: Agah.

Schimmel, A. (1982) *As Through a Veil; Mystical Poetry in Islam*. New York: Columbia University Press.

Schimmel, A. (1992) *I Am Wind, You Are Fire*. Boston and London: Shambhala.

Schmidt, J. (1996) *What Is Enlightenment? Eighteenth-Century Answers and Twentieth-Century Questions*. Berkeley and London: University of California Press.

Schutz, A. and Luckmann, T. (1974) *The Structures of the Life-World*. Translated by Zaner, R. M. and Engelhardt, H. T. London: Heinemann.

Shadman, S. F. (1948) 'Taskhir-e Tamaddon-e Farangi' (The Conquest of Western Civilisation). In *Arayesh Va Pirayesh-e Zaban* (Beautification and Purification of Language). Tehran: Chapkhane-ye Iran.

Shadman, S. F. (1967) *Terazhedi-ye Farang* (The tragedy of the West). Tehran: Tahuri.

Shariati, A. (1974) *Art: Awaiting the Saviour*. Houston, Texas: Free Islamic Literatures.

Shariati, A. (1976) *Shi'i: Yek Hizb-i Tamam* (Shi'is: A Completer Party). Tehran: Enteshar.

Shariati, A. (1977) *Hajj*. English Translation by Somayyah & Yaser. Bedford, Ohio: Free Islamic Literatures Incorporated.

Shariati, A. (1978) *Tamaddun Va Tajaddud* (Civilisation and Modernisation). Tehran: Ershad Publications.

Shariati, A. (1979) *On the Sociology of Islam: Lectures.* Translated from the Persian by Hamid Algar. Berkeley: Mizan Press.

Shariati, A. (1980) *Marxism and Other Western Fallacies: as Islamic Critique.* Translated by R. Campbell. Berkeley: Mizan Press.

Shariati, A. (1981) *Man and Islam.* Translated from the Persian by Fatollah Marjani. Houston, Texas: FILINC.

Shariati, A. (1986) *What Is To Be Done: The Enlightened Thinkers and an Islamic Renaissance.* Edited and Annotated by Farhang Rajaee; Foreword by John L. Esposito. North Haledon, New Jersey: Islamic Publications International.

Shariati, A. (1987) *Without Marx and the Pope.* Tehran: Chappakhsh.

Shariati, A. (1988) *Religion VS Religion.* Translated from the Persian by Laleh Bakhtiar; Foreword by Andrew Burgess. Albuquerque: Abjad.

Shariati, A. (1989) *School of Thought and Action.* Translated from the Persian by Cyrus Bakhtiar; Introduction by Hasan Yusefi Ashkvari. Albuquerque: Abjad.

Shariati, A. (1990) *Characteristics of Modern Centuries.* Tehran: Chappakhsh.

Shariati, A. (1991) *Woman: Fatima Is Fatima.* Tehran: Chappakhsh.

Shariati, A. (1993) *Worldview and Ideology.* Tehran: Enteshar.

Shariati, A. (1996) *Islamshenasi* I (Islamology I). Tehran: Ghalam.

Shariati, A. (1998) *Alavid Shiaism and Safavid Shiaism.* Tehran: Chappakhsh.

Shariati, A. (2005) 'Civilisation and Modernisation' In *Religion and Politics in Modern Iran: A Reader.* Edited by Lloyd Ridgeon. London and New York: Tauris.

Shariati, A. (2006) *Return to the Self.* Tehran: Elham

Shariati, A. (2007) *Revolutionary Self-Reconstruction.* Ninth Edition. Tehran: Elham.

Shariati, A. (2008) *Ali.* Tehran: Amoun.

Shariati, A. (2009a) *History and Study of World Religions.* Tehran: Enteshar.

Shariati, A. (2009b) *Iqbal and Us.* Tehran: Elham.

Shariati, A. (2009c) *Islamshenasi* II (Islamology II). Tehran: Ghalam.

Shariati, A. (2009d) *Islamshenasi* III (Islamology III). Tehran: Elham.

Shariati, A. (2010) Social Class Analysis In Islam. Tehran: Ghalam.

Shariati, A. (2011) *Man without Self.* Ninth Edition. Tehran: Ghalam.

Shayegan, D. (1999) *Asia in Contrast to West.* Tehran: Amir Kabir.

Shilling, C. and Mellor, P. A. (2001) *The Sociological Ambition: Elementary Forms of Social and Moral Life.* London: Sage.

Siebert, R. J. (1985) *The Critical Theory of Religion, The Frankfurt School: From Universal Pragmatic to Political Theology.* Berlin and New York: Mouton.

Sitton, J. F. (2003) *Habermas and Contemporary Society.* New York: Palgrave Macmillan.

Sultani, A. A. (2005) *Power, Dialogue and Language.* Tehran: Ney.

Taylor, M. C. (1998) *Critical Terms for Religious Studies.* Chicago and London: University of Chicago Press.

Thompson, J. B. and Held, D. (1982) *Habermas: Critical Debates.* London: Macmillan.

Turner, B. S. (1974) *Weber and Islam: A Critical Study.* London: Routledge and Kegan Paul.

Turner, B. S. (2003) *Islam: Critical Concepts in Sociology.* Vol. IV. London: Routledge.

Turner, C. (2005) *Islam: The Basics.* London: Routledge.

Vahdat, F. (2002) *God and Juggernaut: Iran's Intellectual Encounter with Modernity.* Syracuse: Syracuse University Press.

Weber, M. (1930) *The Protestant Ethic and The Spirit of Capitalism.* Translated by Talcott Parsons. London: Allen & Unwin.

Weber, M. (1948) *From Max Weber: Essays in Sociology.* Translated, Edited and with an Introduction by H. H. Gerth and C.Wright Mills. London: Routledge and Kegan Paul.

Weber, M. (1964) *The Theory of Social and Economic Organization.* Translated by A. M. Henderson and Talcott Parsons; Edited with an Introduction by Talcott Parsons. New York: Free Press.

Weber, M. (1965) *The Sociology of Religion.* Translated by Ephraim Fischoff. London: Methuen.

White, G. (2008) *An Introduction to Modern European Philosophy.* Translated by Nahid Ahmadian. Abadan: Porsesh.

White, S. K. (1988) *The Recent work of Jurgen Habermas: Reason, Justice and Modernity.* Cambridge: Cambridge University Press.

Worsley, P. (1982) *Marx and Marxism*: Chichester: Ellis Horwood.

Index